PALACE

PALACE

MY LIFE IN THE
ROYAL FAMILY OF MONACO

BARON CHRISTIAN DE MASSY
AND CHARLES HIGHAM

New York ATHENEUM *1986*

AUTHORS' NOTE: *The names and backgrounds of certain characters in this book have been changed to protect their real identities.*

BT

Library of Congress Cataloging-in-Publication Data

Massy, Christian de, baron, ———
    Palace : my life in the royal family of Monaco.

    1. Massy, Christian de, baron, ———.
2. Grace, Princess of Monaco, 1929–   —Family.
3. Rainier III, Prince of Monaco, 1923–   —Family.
4. Monaco—Princes and princesses—Biography.
5. Grimaldi family.   I. Higham, Charles.   II. Title.
DC943.M37A3 1986   944'.949'00994 [B] 86–47674
ISBN 0–689–11636–5

Published simultaneously in Canada by Collier Macmillan Canada, Inc.
Composition by Heritage Printers, Inc., Charlotte, North Carolina
Manufactured by Haddon Craftsmen, Scranton, Pennsylvania
Illustrations printed by Philips Offset Company, Inc., Mamaroneck, New York
Designed by Harry Ford
First Edition

To the staffs of the Hôtel de Paris and Regine's

in Monte Carlo, with many thanks

for having put up with my antics.

The Princely decree of 1882 defining the status of the sovereign family stipulates that every member of the family submits himself to the authority of the reigning Prince, who will determine their duties and obligations, and his orders shall have the force of law.

The House of Monaco

Honoré V, prince de Monaco (1778-1841)

Charles III, prince de Monaco (1818-1856)
m.
Annette Ghislaine (1828-1864)

Albert I, prince de Monaco (1848-1922)

m.(1)	m.(2)
Lady Mary Victoria Douglas-Hamilton (1850-1922)	Marie Alice Heine (1858-1925)

Louis II, prince de Monaco (1870-1949)

with	m.
Marie Juliette Louvet (1867-1930)	Ghislaine Brullé (1900-)

Princesse Charlotte de Monaco (1898-1977)
m.
Comte Pierre de Polignac

Antoinette Louise Alberte Suzanne
Baroness de Massy (1920-)

m.(1)	m.(2)	m.(3)
Alexandre-Athanase (Aleco Noghes) (1916-)	Jean-Charles Rey (1914-)	John Gilpin (1930-1983)

Elisabeth Ann de Massy (1947-) m. Baron Bernard Alexandre Taubert-Natta (1941-) Jean-Léonard (1974-)	Christian Louis de Massy (1949-)	Christine Alix (1951-) m. Charles W. Knecht Keith Sebastien (1972-)

| | m.(1) Maria Marta Quintana (1951-) Laetitia (1971-) | m.(2) Anne Michelle Lutken (1959-) | |

Honoré III, prince de Monaco (1720-1795)

Honoré IV, prince de Monaco (1758-1819)

Florestan I, prince de Monaco (1785-1856)

Princesse Florestine de Monaco
(1833-1897)
m.
Guillaume I, duc d'Urach
(1810-1869)

Guillaume II, duc d'Urach
(1864-1928)

Charles-Gero III, duc d'Urach
(1899)

Rainier III, Louis Henri Maxence
Bertrand de Grimaldi (1923-   )
m.
Grace Patricia Kelly (1929-1982)

Caroline Louise Marguerite
(1957-   )

Albert Alexandre
Louis Pierre
(1958-   )

Stephanie Marie
Elisabeth
(1965-   )

m.(1)
Philippe Junot

m.(2)
Stefano Casiraghi

Andrea Albert
(1984-   )

ILLUSTRATIONS

xi

Illustrations

PALACE

P R O L O G U E

THE LAST TIME I spoke to my aunt, Princess Grace, was to ask her, as I often had, to intervene on my behalf to resolve a family problem. It was a warm September day, one day before I was to marry my twenty-two-year-old Scandinavian fiancée. Having decided only ten days before to get married, I had invited our guests by telephone from my Saint-Tropez hotel room. There had been no word from my family as to who would be present. When I tried to find out what their intentions were, I learned that my mother, Uncle Rainier's elder sister, Princess Antoinette, had called her brother from her vacation spot in Scotland, to make sure that nobody in the family attended the ceremony.

I knew my mother to be totally opposed to this marriage, and her instigations did not really surprise me. Similarly, over the years I had had so many differences with my uncle that I had not really expected him to be there either. All the same, I still would have appreciated their presence for my wife's sake. More important, I had hoped that my sisters, Elisabeth and Christine, and my cousins, Caroline, Albert, and Stephanie, with whom I had no differences, could attend. Just be-

3

fore phoning Grace, I had also learned that Elisabeth would surely not be coming as she had been hospitalized the night before for an intestinal hemorrhage.

Grace was at Roc Agel, her mountain farmhouse above Monaco. She was the only member of our bizarre family who had both compassion and consideration; and it was to these qualities that I now appealed as I asked her to intercede to allow my cousins to be present at the wedding.

Grace sounded strained. She said, "Your mother has been asking us endlessly to be sure that none of the family attends. I don't approve of Tiny (Mother's nickname) putting pressure on us like this, and I think it's all very sad. You have my personal blessings. But I can't authorize the children to go unless Rainier himself gives his approval. I'll talk to him. Just give me a little time. It's worth a try, at least."

Knowing Grace as well as I did, and the positive influence she had exerted on my life, I knew she would do her best for me. She was completely truthful and trustworthy, qualities some in our family did not possess. I waited all day for her call, never leaving the room for fear I would miss it. At last the phone rang. It was Grace, but her voice was filled with disappointment. She said, very sadly, "I'm so sorry, I've tried everything, but I can't move Rainier. He complained that after all the trouble you had given him in the past he was now being further bothered by Tiny and her calls from Scotland insisting that your wedding must be completely embargoed. When I pressed him, he finally said he had had enough of this mess and the subject was closed. Permanently. Please understand, I've done everything I possibly could for you. Tell your fiancée for me that tomorrow, I shall be there in spirit, and I will be praying for you both."

Grace went on, "I am driving down from Roc Agel to Monaco on Monday." She paused. "Christian, I am worried about your future. When someone is driven from a family like this,

4

he can end up in the worst situation. I don't want to see that happening to you. I'm very concerned. All of us in the family must meet and find a solution as soon as possible. Otherwise, I am very much afraid of what the final outcome will be. . . ."

I was moved by Grace's concern for my welfare and my future. It was very sad to think that my cousins would not be present. Yet a further disappointment was that neither of my sisters could come to the wedding, Elisabeth because of her convalescence, and Christine, who would have attended, because she was at the hospital taking care of her. I thanked Grace for all she had tried to do, and as I hung up the telephone, I turned in resignation to my fiancée. She could see from my face what the news was, and she was very disappointed. But at least she knew at first hand that my aunt had cared and wished us well.

Next day we were married. Of my entire family, only my half-brother, Lionel, was present. That weekend Grace had Elisabeth's and Christine's sons with her at Roc Agel. Elisabeth also was up at the farm after being released from the hospital the day before.

There was some talk of Grace taking Christine's son Sebastien with her on the Monday when she returned to the palace, but luckily the plan was changed. When she drove off that morning, she took Stephanie with her, and they began the difficult descent down the Middle Corniche, the winding road that descends to Monte Carlo, the same one she had been seen driving in her famous film *To Catch a Thief*. This was to be her last journey, and when she died as a result of it, every last hope I had of a family reconciliation died with her.

O N E

$\mathcal{G}$RACE'S DEATH left a gap not only in my life but in the very existence of the principality of Monaco itself. She had brought to our wealthy if politically insignificant state what can only be described as a quality matching her own name. It is doubtful if our family will ever be the same again now that she has been taken from us.

To millions of people, Monaco represents the place on earth that comes closest to paradise. The fairy-tale princedom by the sea, its very name conjures images of sunny beaches, of luxury, amusement, expensive jewels, high rollers, and the pleasures of the senses. Its gala dinners and fireworks displays, its nights glowing with the Mediterranean stars, the moon shining on the wealthiest men and women in the world, are overwhelming; it is the gods' playground, and to play there is to be the envy of everyone. Wander into the bar of the Hôtel de Paris in Monte Carlo any night at eight o'clock in the height of the summer season, and you will see all the jet set there: the Niarchoses, the Heinzes, the Bacardis, the Portanovas, Helene Rochas, Estée Lauder, Florence Gould, Regine, Kashoggi, and the Princess Marie Gabrielle of Savoy. Here you find the highest concentration of jewels per square yard of any place on earth: clients of Cartier, Boucheron, Harry Winston, Van Cleef & Arpels, Piaget, and Bulgari, their gems flashing brilliantly in the reflection of the baroque mirrors and the glittering glasses of Cristal champagne. Look around and you can see the king of sewing machines, the emperor of soft drinks, the duke of processed foods, and arms dealers, swindlers, and the inevitable courtesans and hangers-on. Look outside the hotel's revolving doors and you can see the Rollses, the Bentleys, the Mercedeses, the Ferraris, and the Jaguars, all carefully parked like sculptures in a garden.

Yet to the ordinary citizens of a country smaller than Central Park, the picture is very different. The recently built apartment complexes appear striking and impressive until one realizes that a large percentage of the citizens of the principality cannot afford to live in Monaco because of the rents. And the same citizens, who go to the one public beach, find that these same high rises block off most of the sun in the afternoon, while the exclusive Monte Carlo beach frequented by the wealthy and privileged enjoys its full quota of sunshine.

My uncle, Rainier Louis Henri Maxence Bertrand, His Serene Highness, the Prince of Monaco, the world's last absolute monarch, rules with an insecure despotism over 25,000 residents of whom only 4,500 are Monegasques. Not only does his tiny kingdom have the highest concentration of banks and expensive real estate in the world, the biggest yachts and the costliest cars to be found in one place, Monaco also has more policemen per square foot than anywhere else on earth. My uncle has eyes everywhere and makes all the decisions about everything. He presides like a latter-day Julius Caesar over a government of only four ministers: of state, finance and economic affairs, public works and social affairs, and the interior, respectively. The National Council, which constitutes what we choose to call a parliament, consists of eighteen "notables" who feel all too important in their tiny, expert, calculating existences, their maneuverings, their pretenses, their airs and graces, and their minimal responsibilities. Elected to office for five years at a time, they carry out unquestioningly His Serene Highness's desires.

Aside from its natural beauty, Monaco has an irresistible advantage for the rich. There is no income tax. The moment its wealthy residents can show that they are financially independent and will not be a burden on the principality, that they will spend six months a year there, they are free of any obligation. Small, with few natural resources, Monaco introduced the tax laws well before Rainier's time. The benefits formed an irresistible allure, ensuring much investment and the residence of many prominent figures.

My uncle directs a security force of three hundred policemen. Records are kept on every new arrival. Phones are tapped. Cameras move to and fro restlessly at any number of street corners. The police constitute an elite squad of commandolike strength. They are under orders to fire point-blank if a suspect takes flight. So intense is the local censorship that many a magazine or newspaper undergoes scrutiny by police security before it goes on sale. One word that displeases the sovereign, and the publication will immediately be banned. It is then an irony that no place on earth is more frequently featured in the world's newspapers and magazines, and the ruler of this Walter Mitty kingdom has lived to see his daughters exposed to some of the most relentless publicity of any human beings in the twentieth century.

Monaco's history is relieved chiefly by one great figure of international science, the oceanographer and explorer Albert I, and by a series of remarkable women, among whom was Grace's predecessor, the blonde Alice Heine of New Orleans, who brought much of the same glamour, elegance, and distinction to our country as Grace was to do many years later. The Grimaldis, my Genovese ancestors, were unrivaled practitioners of the art of dynastic survival; murdering, marrying, and fighting, first for Spain and then for France, they obtained the tiny country by an ingenious ruse involving impersonation. The Genovese François the Spiteful helped to capture Monaco from a rival Genovese group, the Spinolas, in 1297, by posing as a Franciscan friar seeking food and lodging for the night from the two soldiers at the castle gate. The gullible guards admitted him, only to discover the sting of the Grimaldi sword as the so-called monk dispatched them quickly and summoned his clan, who were hiding outside the walls.

The Grimaldis were sea traders, a polite name for pirates, who bludgeoned their way into power in the Mediterranean basin. Their history—like that of their more recent heirs—was marked by intrigues, double crosses, and backstabbings. When one Grimaldi died, leaving the kingdom to his elder son, a younger son stabbed the sibling to death, and he in turn was killed by his nephew. There is also the story of the rejected mistress of one of our princes, who put a curse on all of us from that day to this, stating that not one of us would enjoy a happy marital relationship. With the exception of Rainier and Grace, the curse proved entirely effective.

In 1604, Hercule Grimaldi, who had aggravated the rival state of Savoy, fell victim to a venomous Savoyard, who saw to it that on his evening walk he was stabbed to death and thrown into the sea. Immediately afterward, a crowd of Monegasques rifled the palace from cellar to attic. For generations the Grimaldi heirs looked on Monaco as a place they could use only for getting rich. They preferred to live in Paris, in luxury. They would spend only short periods of time in Monaco and were alienated from the Monegasque people.

The first monarch who tried to improve the condition of our principality was Charles III, who entrusted François Blanc and his family in 1861 to establish the Casino, which netted an immense fortune for us.

9

Among the finest of all the Grimaldis was Prince Albert, after whom my first cousin and Grace's son and heir to the throne is named, a great figure of oceanography whose genius earned the principality more prestige than at any other time and gave us our first constitution in 1911. In 1920 Albert received the American Academy of Science's Gold Medal. He called on the close friendship he had with the German emperor, William II, and the formal ties he had as prince with the president of the French Republic, to try to defuse Franco-German rivalry and conflict. His first wife was Lady Mary Victoria Douglas-Hamilton. Daughter of the tenth Duke of Hamilton of Scotland, and true to the traditions of our family, she was rebellious and headstrong. Following a violent argument, she fled her husband in the middle of the night, five months after their wedding, to Baden-Baden in Germany, where she allegedly became entangled with a Prussian military officer and conceived her son Louis, later Louis II of Monaco. Albert made investments in oil fields in Wyoming, which he enjoyed visiting, as well as hunting with Buffalo Bill in the Rockies, and established a tradition of strong American ties that was to prevail and flourish in Grace's era.

Albert's second wife, the beautiful American Alice Heine, whose father had made a fortune in the antebellum cotton boom, had already buried a rich husband, the Duc de Richelieu, who died at the early age of thirty-one. According to contemporary sources, she inherited $6 million from him. Her father was determined she would marry royalty, broke off each of her two affairs with Jewish doctors, and pushed her into marriage with Albert. She converted Monte Carlo into a center of ballet and opera renowned throughout Europe during the 1880s. But it was not a happy match. She hated sailing, which was Albert's chief joy, and refused to go aboard the yachts *Alice I* and *Alice II*, which he named for her. He accused her of having an affair with a Jewish composer, Isidor

Cohen, whom she had invited to come to Monaco to work as part of her musical entourage, and finally they were separated in 1890 and were divorced in 1902.

This unhappy relationship seemed entirely in keeping with so much else in our dynasty. Albert's son, Louis II, also inherited the constant father-son hatred that marked our family. Albert despised Louis. German-born, he didn't learn French until he was fourteen and bore no physical resemblance to his father. Albert was extremely tough in his treatment of him. He poured upon him all of the ill feeling he had for Lady Douglas-Hamilton, whom he never forgave for the humiliation she had caused him by fleeing in the middle of the night, nor for his doubts about his son's origins. At sixteen Louis entered Saint-Cyr, the French West Point. As soon as Louis was of a sufficient age, Albert booted him out into the Foreign Legion, the traditional refuge for black sheep, renegades and common criminals. His whole life became the Legion. The only photographs he would keep in his room in the palace were pictures of his military expeditions in North Africa. His only real joy in later life was the Foreign Legion parade on feast days. During World War I, he fought for the French and was commended again and again for *"audace, sang-froid, et vigueur"* under enemy fire. At the end of the war he was made Grand Officer of the Legion of Honor.

Louis followed the family policy of breaking all the rules. In the 1890s, while in Paris, he fell in love with Marie Juliette Louvet. She had been previously married to a photographer named Achille Delmaet and was, according to some belief, working in a nightclub in Montmartre. He brought her to Algeria with him, where he was serving in the Foreign Legion and where her parents ran a laundry. Their illegitimate child, Charlotte, was born in Constantine, Algeria, in 1898. It was not until 1919, when she was twenty-one, that Charlotte was officially adopted by her father and solemnly legitimized in order to secure the dynasty's progression into the next generation. The following year, still further to secure the succession, it was arranged that Count Pierre de Polignac, an impoverished member of that famous family of patrons of the arts, would marry Charlotte. He needed the money, and the family needed a new infusion of blue blood. By all accounts his whole life was Society. When Louis bestowed on him the title of prince, Polignac found himself placed firmly in the royal house. But from the beginning he and Louis intensely disliked each other—a mutuality of ill-feeling later to be echoed during my cousin Caroline's short-lived first marriage to Philippe Junot. Prussian, severe, with a bristling mustache, Louis had no time for this effete gentleman of leisure and resented the fact that he had been compelled to make him his direct heir for the sake of convenience. Louis was never very interested in Monaco politics. He preferred to live in Paris and hunt at the Château de Marchais, avoiding the many backstabbings and intrigues that went on in the principality.

Charlotte, my grandmother, emerged from the beginning as perhaps the most extraordinary female member of our entire clan. Strong-willed, domineering, eccentric, her powerful personality a total contrast with her tiny stature, she played a particularly strong role in the turmoils of the late 1920s, when a group of people opposed to Louis II attempted to throw him off the throne. Though stricken with influenza in 1929, and told by doctors she might not live a week, she turned up at the Hôtel Negresco in Nice, holding court with the revolutionaries and entreating them, with all of her persuasive charm and passionate intensity, to remain loyal to her father. They yielded, and she managed to secure the State for the future. After giving birth to my mother and Rainier, however, and considering her responsibility as a princess accomplished, having always detested the spouse chosen for her, complaining that "to make love, he needs to put a crown on his head," true to the Grimaldi tradition, she left him for a Doctor Del Masso. Charlotte's relationship with Del Masso proved very Grimaldian. When he tried to leave her, she took out a pistol and fired at him. She missed.

In the meantime, further riots occurred in the principality. When he was told of the arrival of a delegation of citizens to persuade him to reinstate the National Council, Louis said, "Give them live bullets instead of a constitution." A team of French journalists tried for two years to interview Louis on the conflicts within Monaco. At last he agreed to see them. The butler asked them to wait in the sitting room of the royal quarters. He told my great-grandfather that the journalists had arrived. Louis asked him to inquire what their questions were. The butler said they were about the Council's suspension. Much to his embarrassment, the poor man had to return to say to the reporters, "His Serene Highness says that his enjoyment of his lobster is too great to spoil it by discussing such irrelevant and stupid matters."

Both Antoinette and her younger brother, Rainier, faced scenes of violence from the beginning. On one occasion, when they arrived at the Monaco railway station with their grandfather, the crowd pressed in on them, threatening their safety, and shots were fired.

Once his daughter's divorce became final, Louis ordered his carabiniers to eject Polignac from the palace, allowing him to come to Monaco only on express sovereign permission. He went to live mostly in Nice and in Paris, his allowance carried to him by the minister of finance. This was a repetition of his father's ensuring Louis's exile in the Foreign Legion and foretold my own father's later removal from Monaco, although that was under far different circumstances.

In keeping with the Monaco tradition of a royal upbringing, my uncle and my mother were raised not by their divorced and absent parents, but by their nanny, Kathleen Wanstall. It was she who was to provide them with all of the kindness, emotional stability, and caring that they did not have from their father or mother. Cousin of Winston Churchill, possessed of a similar bulldog character, this Englishwoman in her forties virtually ran the palace. As Louis grew older, she directed the servants, supervised the housekeeping, and was herself the equivalent of a princess in terms of her power and influence as the person most in touch with Louis. This was strange, as she was staunchly Anglophilic and never bothered to learn much French.

In 1936 there was a serious incident. My mother, then twelve years old, disliked her father, and while briefly Polignac was accorded custody of her in Paris (Rainier was at school in England at the time), she had a violent quarrel with him. Antoinette vanished, hiding with her grandfather Louis at his home, which also served as the Paris legation of Monaco. Nanny Wanstall engineered the escape. Polignac charged that Louis had ordered Nanny to bring off what amounted to a kidnapping. Louis responded that under the statutes of the royal family, he had full authority over all its members. Thus it was not a kidnapping but an act of sovereignty. Louis sent Mother off to Monaco and canceled Pierre's guardianship on the spot. Polignac sued in France. But when a special commission went to talk to Mother, she confirmed that she had gone to Monaco of her own free will and the kidnapping charges had to be withdrawn.

Not only did Mother dislike her father, she also hated and feared her mother, Charlotte, later known as Mamou, who now lived in seclusion at the Château de Marchais near Paris. Antoinette was constantly competing for her mother's attention with Charlotte's overweight terriers, who followed her everywhere and who intimidated the footmen into always carrying around pieces of food to give them without Mamou noticing. In this way the footmen ensured the safety of their legs, as the dogs would otherwise bite their ankles whenever they felt like it. Mamou did not believe in limiting her dogs' "freedom of expression." On her first trip to New York, she was shocked and furious to discover that her dogs were not accepted in restaurants. She left the very next day after her arrival on the same boat back home.

Charlotte had little time for my mother. She told her she was stupid and unattractive, which was not true, as Mother was very pretty as a girl. Charlotte did not meet her grandchildren until the eldest, my sister Elisabeth, was eight years old. Such was the animosity between them. When Charlotte renounced her rights to the succession in 1933, in favor of my uncle, this effectively removed my mother from any chance of the throne. Given the insults and degradation she suffered from Mamou, she grew up under circumstances that most people would consider insecure, unhappy, and mercurial. She would shift radically from pro-German to pro-American to pro-British sentiments as easily as she would later fanatically adopt homeopathy, yoga, acupuncture, and vegetarian and other diets. She would go through these different phases and change doctors with equal determination, only to condemn them later and discover a "new medical breakthrough." She eventually founded the Monaco Congress of Fringe Medicine. Continually complaining, since my earliest memories, of suffering from migraine headaches, she never accepted traditional medicine as being an adequate solution and instead was convinced that the only "proper" remedy for this "complicated disorder" could come from obscure and mysterious sources, which, if not recognized by the medical profession, would immediately win her acceptance. She herself, in the Grimaldi tradition, took out her childhood frustrations and isolation in her treatment of others. When tutors or governesses were appointed, she found fault with them. She would later take up ballet, tennis (under the world champion Martin Plaa), and piano lessons, and then abandon them temperamentally, pronouncing the teachers incompetent, even though they were the finest available. She would eat enormous amounts of food for psychological reasons, bloat up, and then diet down to nothing with equal fanaticism. She could never do anything by halves, and, as one might expect, the way she was brought up would eventually have some bearing on the way she treated her children.

At the same time, she always sought to acquire the love of the Monegasques. During the war she formed the Committee for Aid and Assistance to Prisoners of War and comforted the local population with food and blankets during nighttime alerts, joining them in shelter in the tunnel going through the rock on which the palace stands. At the palace she acted as first lady from the time she reached her majority. When she met my father, Aleco Noghes, a handsome tennis champion, she embarked upon a liaison with him in direct defiance of her grandfather, who, by the late 1940s, had himself defied convention by marrying an actress thirty years his junior, Ghislaine Brullé. Annoying many, he made a will bequeathing the Princess Ghislaine his fortune, running into many millions, figures that nonetheless seem diminutive today by comparison with his grandson's Civil List of approximately $8 million a year. Rainier blocked the will and had it modified so that Ghislaine received only an annual income.

After being constantly shuttled between and fiercely contested by Polignac and Louis, Uncle Rainier was sent to a prep school near Hastings, England, when he was ten, and then to the Stowe Public School, where he was nicknamed "Fat Little Monaco." He then went to Le Rosey, the exclusive boy's school in Switzerland. There, he was intent on not showing anyone he needed affection; and, trusting no one, he made few friends. This mistrust showed itself in his extreme shyness. He was difficult and over-sensitive, characteristics arising out of a lonely, insecure, and unhappy childhood.

Portly even as a young man, he fancied himself an athlete, but in fact his build and personality contrasted unfavorably with that aspiration. Whereas Antoinette inherited the imposing Grimaldi will, Rainier harked back to some of our weaker ancestors. Surrounded by yes-men, loathe to engage in direct confrontations of any sort, he was awkward, preferring to convey his feelings through others. The fact that he lacked a true father was crucial. Since the Prince de Polignac had no paternal involvement with his children, Rainier lacked the role model that might have made him a more secure prince. Had he had a father and a mother in the true sense, he most likely would have been a very different person.

And so I come to the moment at which I entered this bizarre family. I was inheriting a legacy of father hating son, mother hating daughter, children hating parents, sisters hating brothers, a tradition in the blood of our family of constant conflict. It is scarcely surprising that my own life from childhood on would be marked by the family strain of rivalry and dissension. The Grimaldi tribe had evolved from pirates to sea merchants, conquistadors disguised as monks to absentee landlords, gambling promotor to illustrious scientist, renegade legionnaire to an insecure Don Quixote, and women who had always been eccentrically "special." What was to come now?

T W O

I WAS BORN amid the fireworks and rejoicing of the people of Monaco. The celebrations, however, were not meant for me, but for the Monaco National Feast Day, which was also January 17, 1949. My mother had been hoping for this fortunate coincidence of dates. Significantly, one of the first decisions my uncle would make upon succeeding Louis II on the throne would be to change the date of the national holiday. My indiscreet arrival was my first step toward becoming Rainier's royal pain in the ass.

I was registered in the archives of the royal family at the palace as being born a Grimaldi. My uncle was also to alter this by a royal ordinance, however, on November 15, 1951, removing my family name and instead giving my mother the eighteenth-century title the Baroness de Massy, in addition to her title as Princess, and changing the names of her children to the same title. Our home, the Villa les Glycines, was set back from a small road that joined the Lower Corniche to the Middle Corniche. The Upper, Middle, and Lower Corniches remain the three roads linking the towns of the Riviera, winding, often in hairpin bends, through some of the most beautiful scenery on earth.

Beaulieu, one of those towns, is small and is best known for the famous La Reserve Hotel, which has a two-star restaurant, a private beach, and a pier. Beaulieu is also an elegant resort, renowned for its casino and its long list of celebrity residents, which has included David Niven. The area in which I spent my earliest days is still known as The Small Africa because of its vegetation of palm trees. It is warmer than the rest of the Riviera because of the great cliffs that overhang it, cutting off the breezes that freshen so much of the Blue Coast.

I moved from the Villa les Glycines when I was just a few months old, too young to remember it clearly. But I have good recollections of our next home, which was closer to Monaco, the Villa les Galets, named for the large, flat gray stones that children skim across water. The house was entered on a dangerous blind corner of the Lower Corniche; the asphalt driveway plunged steeply down to the house, with a small, flowered lawn to the right, and to the left more green grass, shaded by a giant pine tree. The drive wound around the house to the servants' lodge at the right, and then continued behind the residence to our private beach, with its own pier. The back lawn was studded with palms and big, shady olive trees.

The house itself had been built in 1910 by Walter Williams, the first winner of the Monaco Grand Prix, our famous automobile race. It was an ocher-colored Italianate villa built in three stories and consisting of eleven rooms, not counting the kitchen or the servants' lodge. There were eight bedrooms, a sitting room, a dining room, and what is called in France a winter garden, a spacious room containing plants, with bay windows overlooking the terrace, which in turn overlooked the back lawn and the Mediterranean.

The master bedroom on the first (in America, second) floor and my father's room were surrounded by a balcony on all three sides. Both rooms had their own bathrooms. My sisters and I were housed on the floor above, in a pink-walled nursery suite. My room faced the sea, with my elder sister's room on my right and my younger sister's room, which she shared with Nanny Wanstall, on my left. The children's rooms were furnished in the contemporary Provençal style, simply and without ostentation.

The formal sitting room was furnished in Chippendale, upholstered in red and white silk. There were marble vases and ivory figurines everywhere. The dining room, with its rose tapestry walls, large, round mahogany table with Chippendale chairs, and grand curved-glass windows, overlooked the sea. We had a staff of ten, including Menotti, the Italian butler and valet to my father; Joseph, his assistant; Lino, the chef, and his assistant; two maids, a gardener, and Dominique, my father's yacht captain. But the most important member of the household was the sweet and kind Kathleen Wanstall, the ever-loyal nanny to my mother and my uncle Rainier, who had been present at their births and whom my mother had "inherited."

My first memory is of taking a small rowboat out from our pier when I was about four years old. Nanny always watched me carefully from her position on the pier or from her deck chair in the sand. But despite her surveillance I would constantly upset the boat, rocking it from side to side until it would capsize, pinning me underneath. My father rescued me from drowning on several occasions; it might be said that I have been rocking the boat ever since.

That early time was the only period of happiness I knew as a child, and it was soon to disappear. Photographs of those days tell me that I was full of joy. I am always smiling in the pictures. My father is seen holding me in his arms, while my sister Elisabeth, two years older than I, stands in a white dress beside him. Another photograph shows Elisabeth and me on the yacht. I am smiling again, always happy to be on the boat. In one picture I am wearing a miniature version of the official carabiniere, or guard's uniform, of the Monaco palace. I could not possibly have understood at that time the significance of the uniform, or that I was a member of a royal house.

My father was my favorite playmate. He seemed to be constantly cheerful and resourceful, always able to find something exciting and interesting for us children to do. Many were the adventures when my father would take Elisabeth and me, and later my younger sister, Christine, who was born in 1951, out on the yacht. My first memories of my mother were as a disciplinarian. She always insisted we children be brought back by Daddy no later than two o'clock for our afternoon nap. My father was always puzzled as to why she didn't see fit for us to take our naps on the boat. She also demanded that we must not speak French, but only converse in English. Like Nanny, she despised the French, and indeed Nanny would talk French only to the dogs. Mother always denied that she had any French blood, despite the facts that both her parents were French and that she herself was born in Paris. Instead, she claimed to be a Scot, in reference to her great-grandmother Lady Douglas-Hamilton.

My father had two other boats, a cabin cruiser and a speedboat, in addition to the yacht. One day we were aboard the cabin cruiser. I had been watching Dominique, the captain, very carefully, studying everything he did, and then I decided to hijack the vessel. While the others went swimming, I suddenly darted to the engine and started it up. Daddy, who was a strong swimmer, swam after me and came aboard just before the cruiser took off with its four-year-old master to parts unknown.

In addition to his boats, Daddy had five cars. I loved them all. My lifelong passion for automobiles began then. I remember best of all the blue XKE 120 convertible Jaguar in which he would take me speeding along the Little Corniche. I enjoyed every second as Daddy roared around the hairpin bends at what seemed a terrific speed on his way to Monaco, where he had his lawyers' offices. I had no idea, of course, what he did for a living, or that Monaco was ruled by Prince Rainier, who had recently succeeded his grandfather Louis II on the throne. All I was thinking of was my pleasure in the fast car and the excitement of the drives.

How different Mummy was! When we returned from these exciting trips, Mummy was critical, convinced that I had been in danger, never trusting my father, who was an excellent driver. In fact, Daddy never had an accident.

Neither Elisabeth nor I learned to read or write until we were six. Most children learn these skills at home before they begin school, but Mother decided that there was only one person in the world who could teach us, and that was Maria Montessori, creator of the famous Montessori Method. Once Mummy made up her mind, nothing would stand in her way. When she discovered that Madame Montessori was in India, she simply wrote to her to ask her if she would return to take up the task of educating us. At last Mummy received a reply that said that Madame Montessori had just died. Still undaunted, she learned from a midwife that there was an acolyte of the Montessori Method who could be helpful. She wrote to this man, who sent us a large package. When Mummy unwrapped it, there spilled forth an array of cubes, triangles, and squares, which no one could make head or tail of. Even Mummy had to give up after that, and she instructed Nanny that henceforth we were to be taught according to the British methods learned by Nanny at Britain's famous Norlands Institute.

While we were living at Beaulieu, my uncle Rainier moved next door, to a villa named Le Sphinx. During that period he was involved with a movie actress named Gisele Pascal, who lived there part of the time with him. I could not have known that this liaison, prompting memories of his grandfather's marriage just a few years before, was causing much adverse comment in Monaco, or that before long the National Council would succeed in breaking it, partly on the basis that Mademoiselle Pascal allegedly could not bear children. Although we did not see very much of the beautiful actress who occupied his feelings and thoughts, and whom my mother liked, we did receive visits from Uncle Rainier. I had no idea he was a prince, or what a prince was, but I do remember that we thought of him as a kind and cheerful man who would walk through the gate connecting our two gardens. He would play games with us on the lawn.

When I was about five, we moved to a much more elaborate mansion, the Villa Mereze, which was about two miles west on the Lower Corniche and was located at Eze Sur Mer. The private road to the house went up as steeply as the driveway at Les Galets went down. There we had the privacy of a secret world. The eight-hundred-yard road led to a gate with tall stone pillars on either side, and to a red Tarmac drive, which in turn led to the front door. The lawns were decorated with palm trees, poplars, flowering shrubs, and cacti, and ivy crawled up the walls. Like Les Galets, Mereze dated from the early part of the century and combined both Italianate and English finishes.

The entrance was beautiful. Five marble steps led to the marble terrace and a big cast-iron front door. The terrace ran the entire length of one side of the house, overlooking the sparkling sea. Through the door, one walked into an impressive lobby that led to the main marble hall. An immense dining room lay right ahead. It had been designed during the height of Art Deco, with stained-glass door panels, and its leather-lined walls showed various pastoral scenes and motifs in high relief. There was a massive oak dining table, oak cabinets with drawers filled with silverware and linen napkins and place settings, and porcelain displayed in cabinets.

There were two sitting rooms, the formal one to the left

and the informal to the right. We children were on the first floor in simply furnished rooms up one flight of the grand marble staircase, and we had our own kitchen. My bedroom overlooked the driveway, and my sisters' rooms overlooked the sea. In the larder Nanny crammed a wide variety of British foods, including Marmite, a black yeast spread, Bovril, a hot drink, Ovaltine, milk of magnesia, and Sanatogen. She also supervised our menu, insisting that it be traditionally English, consisting of such foods as cottage pie, shepherd's pie, steak and kidney pudding, and brown Windsor soup.

Our bathroom was very large; the big metal bathtub stood up importantly in the middle, with pipes that came out one side to the hot and cold water taps.

When we took our meals in the dining room, they were always ceremonial in style. In the tradition of French aristocratic families, Daddy and Mummy sat at opposite ends of the table, which was decorated with silver candelabra, while Menotti, who doubled as headwaiter, stood with his back to a cabinet on a raised platform, watching to see when we would finish each course. He wore a black double-breasted jacket (in summer a white one) and pepper-and-salt trousers, a stiff collar, and a black bow tie. Nanny was always seated with us at table. She was one of the family.

My sisters and I seemed to be set for a secure future against this privileged backdrop. However, this was not to be so.

My father, Aleco Noghes, was descended from the first Spanish commander of the Monaco garrison. Noghes is an old Spanish name and one of the ancient Monegasque families. My great-grandfather, Alexandre, was the founder of the Monte Carlo Automobile Club. Alexandre would become president of innumerable committees, earning him the nickname "President of Presidents." My father's father, Anthony, assumed the presidency of the Auto Club and created the first Grand Prix ever raced in a city, our world-famous Grand Prix de Monaco. Anthony also created the equally renowned Rally de Monte Carlo and invented the checkered flag. He became president of the Assembly while my father's uncle, Paul Noghes, became secretary of state.

Daddy was handsome and remains so today; in his younger years, with his mustache, he resembled Clark Gable. He was an all-round sportsman, always impeccably dressed, cheerful, and charming. Mother was also very attractive. She was petite, and if she had been a more willing pupil, she would have succeeded in being a perfectly good all-rounder in terms of her education. Instead, her impetuousness and impatience limited her, and only Nanny Wanstall remained a continuing influence. Residing as a child almost entirely in Monaco, involved from her teens in the interests of the Monegasques, Mummy was the family member most beloved by the people.

She became involved with my father, who had been previously married, in the mid 1940s, entering into a liaison with him before his divorce had become final. In total defiance of royal convention, she upset the palace by marrying him in a civil ceremony outside the Roman Catholic Church. It was typical of her that she would do exactly what she wanted, regardless of the consequences.

My mother worked very hard in her younger years to establish a circle in the principality that could be relied upon to support her in the future. Several of them had been members of her Committee for Aid and Assistance to Prisoners of War in World War II. Many of these became members of the National Council. They were totally subservient, brought up from childhood to venerate the sovereign family while at the same time joining in her schemes to throw her brother out of office at the first opportunity. My father greatly irritated these courtiers with his dashing air and his love of boats and fast cars. My father was not a hypocrite; he made no bones about his behavior.

Problems arose almost immediately between my father and Rainier. As absolute monarch, Uncle Rainier expected and was used to total deference from his subjects, however prominent they were. In turn, they flattered him constantly, asked for favors, and submitted themselves in total obedience to his wishes. This reinforced, if reinforcement was needed, his love of absolute power. My father had traveled extensively, had graduated second in his class at the University of Paris, and had been an international tennis star whose record to date in the sport has never been equaled in Monaco. Daddy had become a distinguished and successful lawyer, but he was also a ladies' man and a charmer—a fact that could not have escaped his brother-in-law's attention and could not have pleased him. Even before his marriage to Mummy my father had enjoyed an enviable life style that had already created considerable jealousy among the Monegasques.

Bit by bit Uncle Rainier undoubtedly came to realize that only the breakup of my parents' marriage, brought about by my mother if she had sufficient cause for anger and a quest for vengeance, would allow him to have my father dislodged from Monaco and my mother brought into line at the palace.

Already the marriage had cost her not only her brother's support but her influence over him in the palace. Because of my uncle's disapproval, he did not increase her Civil List allowance upon her marriage. In those days the Civil List did not come under government ordinance. The sovereign prince was the sole dispenser of the List at his own pleasure or whim. And now she herself feared she might be losing power over Daddy. Constant rumors linked my father to other women. Mummy had never forgotten her mother Charlotte's childhood insults to her about her looks, which probably left her in constant fear that her handsome husband would leave her for someone more beautiful.

Uncle Rainier's spiritual adviser, Father Francis Tucker, who referred to him as "My Lord Prince," was to become the instrument of Rainier's will in upsetting the marriage once and for all. Born in Wilmington, Delaware, in 1888, the sixty-two-year-old Father Tucker had arrived on the Riviera when I was one year old. He had been assigned to the palace at Uncle Rainier's prompting by the Vatican. Father Tucker banished nameplated pews in church, stopped opera singers performing at the Mass, rode a motor scooter, distributed chewing gum to the choirboys, and adopted a soccer team. He was confessor to the 106 members of the palace staff and exerted a Rasputin-like influence over my uncle, constantly scheming and gossiping. He concealed a devious personality behind a mask of red-faced, robust, Friar Tuck-like charm and good humor. Despite his age, he possessed tremendous energy, and his bustling busybody presence was to be discovered everywhere.

Father Tucker must have realized that only a direct implication of adultery could permanently wreck my parents' marriage. One Saturday he phoned my mother and asked her whether she knew of the whereabouts of a certain very pretty young woman whose parents were anxiously looking for her. Mummy replied that she barely knew the girl and was puzzled by the question: how could she possibly know her whereabouts? Tucker was insistent that she must know, and finally he closed in: he asked point-blank whether her husband was cruising on his yacht that weekend. She replied, "Yes, off Saint-Tropez." Father Tucker delivered the *coup de grace*. "Ah!" he said. "No doubt that is where we will find her!" With that he hung up. Feeling shocked and numb Mummy put the phone down. Clearly the entire purpose of Father Tucker's call was to imply that Daddy was conducting a liaison at sea. Mummy was mortified but after very careful consideration decided to do nothing for the time being. Although undoubtedly at that moment (or not too long afterward) she decided to bring her marriage to an end, and thus resecure her position at the palace, there was also the problem that if she struck immediately against Daddy, he could fight her over the custody of my sisters and me.

Mummy worked out an ingenious plan. She did not actually present it to Daddy until shortly after we had all moved to the Villa Mereze. She proposed to Daddy that they would go through the performance of a divorce, simply so that she might resume her power at the palace, thereby tricking her brother, Uncle Rainier, into allowing her once more a foothold at the highest levels of Monaco. Once the divorce was completed, with no contest from Daddy, he could, she promised, have complete access to us children at all times and even resume his marital rights, in effect visiting her as often as he wanted in a resumption of their earlier liaison.

Once she had secured her freedom and had succeeded in making Rainier accept her again at the palace, she believed, she could then use her great popularity with the people and with the various figures of the Council whom she could influence, and who were opposed to my father, to literally usurp the throne. Although her detailed plans for what would amount to an attempted coup d'état were not laid down until the following year, the evidence indicates that she was already plotting toward it at this stage.

While the divorce was going through, my father, decently accepting the arrangement and unaware of Mummy's intentions, went to live on his yacht at Villefranche, three miles away. Mummy had secured a letter from him stating his willingness to accede to the divorce. Thus it proceeded smoothly— the wheels oiled by Uncle Rainier's sovereign influence. After the final decree was issued, which took very little time at all,

Daddy naturally expected that Mummy would stand by her bargain. She did not. She insisted that Daddy not enter her home again and not make the slightest attempt to have access to her children. When he objected to this, Mummy told him that the conditions of access to them could be decided only under sovereign family law by Uncle Rainier himself. Daddy would have to wait for the royal decision before he could see them again. That was the end of it. In retrospect one wonders if Mummy ever really intended to make good on the promises she had made to Daddy.

He was too much of a gentleman to begin an argument with Mummy, particularly in front of the household staff. Shocked and depressed, he left for his yacht, realizing that of course, since Uncle Rainier's power was absolute, there was nothing he could do to remedy the situation. Daddy's position in Monaco was of course now untenable. He was the chief object of the royal displeasure, and it was only a question of time before his law offices were closed and his many important clients left him.

He sailed to Cannes and moored there, trying to decide what to do next. He felt that perhaps he should go to the United States and start up some business there: he did not know what. But it would be safer to go to America, where Rainier's long arm could not reach him.

One night he went out late into Cannes. He returned to his boat in the early morning hours. Dominique, his loyal captain, greeted him carrying a shotgun. Dominique nervously told Daddy that at about 1:00 A.M. he had heard a suspicious noise on the boat. When he went to investigate it, he saw three men invading Daddy's cabin. He pointed his gun at them, and as they turned around, he recognized them. All three were known to him as prominent citizens of Monaco. Despite their position, Dominique did not hesitate to chase the intruders off with the shotgun.

Whether or not Uncle Rainier was aware of this episode, it jolted Daddy. He was convinced that he must leave the country as soon as possible. He went to the port authority and the municipal police, to inform them that if anything happened to him, they should know it was not an accident. He immediately began to make arrangements to move to the U.S.A.

T H R E E

ADDY'S LEAVING changed my life completely. Now that he was gone, I had no one to look to for affection except our nanny. Mummy was busy all the time; she was deeply preoccupied with her plans for the coup d'état against Uncle Rainier, enlisting support among the people and in the National Council, where her most important ally was the imposing Jean-Charles Rey, president of the National Council Finance Commission as well as Uncle Rainier's chief critic and opponent. He was to play a Machiavellian role in her life in the future.

Mummy, while plotting away behind the scenes, was also president of the Red Cross, arranging gala charity events and parties; and while she was ignoring her own children, she took a keen interest in the local orphanage. Also, while she invested time and money in charities, she ran her own household on grimly "democratic" principles. This was not a matter so much of her personal taste as of an implicit critique of her snobbish father, Polignac, just as her leaving of us children to a nanny was apparently her way of dealing with her own rejection by her mother.

The woman who did love us as a mother was Nanny, who

watched us playing on the swings of the playground, fishing for goldfish in the pond, with its heavy green water lily pads, climbing trees, or chasing each other down the lawn. I learned to ride a bicycle and to climb in the mountains, and all the time Nanny would stay with us, watching us to see we did not get into any trouble. I remember her sitting by the swings, with her sweet face looking at me contentedly as I kicked a ball against the massive walls of the Villa Mereze.

We usually would have our lunch on the terrace, high above the sea; sometimes Mummy would drop in to see us, but only for a minute or two, as she was always in a hurry. She always set her watch forty-five minutes ahead because she was afraid of being late for appointments. She was always late anyway. Mummy was also fanatically meticulous about our appearance, and Nanny took pains to make sure we were spotless. We were terrified that she might find fault with us, and often she did.

Our only pet was a golden cocker spaniel named Twinkle. Mummy found Twinkle a nuisance, and against all of our protests, she kept him locked up in a closet for most of the day. After Daddy left, Twinkle was put in a doghouse in the playground and was never permitted inside the house. Mummy had never forgotten her mother Charlotte's five wire-haired terriers or forgiven them for stealing her mother's affection. "Dogs remind me of my childhood," she would say endlessly. Many years later, in her characteristic turn-about manner, Mother would exceed Charlotte's passion for dogs, becoming president of the Monaco Society for the Prevention of Cruelty to Animals as well as of the Canine Club. Recognized in Europe as an authority on dogs, today she owns twenty of these animals and cares for thirty cats.

Mummy would kiss me good night after I was tucked up in bed, on her way, dressed up in an evening gown and jewelry, to an important party or ball in Monaco. Her kisses were perfunctory, hurried, at least so far as I was concerned. Perhaps after her own unnatural childhood, she had no idea how to bring up a child or what a child needed.

By contrast, now that Daddy had gone Uncle Rainier became a friend to me and my sisters. We had seen little of him during the course of our parents' marriage; now, at Mereze, he would drive in from Monaco two or three times a week, playing ball with us, pushing us on the swings, chasing us around in games of cowboys and Indians. We were always happy to hear the sound of his automobile driving up the long driveway to the house, and we were sad to see him go.

We would go to the palace nearly every afternoon during the week, and for hours before we left, Mummy would fret about our appearance and deportment. She would harass Nanny to make sure our clothes were perfectly creased and brushed, our shoes were polished like mirrors, our hair was brushed, and our fingernails were trimmed and clean. Every day when we took off to the palace, she would repeat her monotonous litany of instruction, which made us feel so tense and uneasy that it reduced our pleasure in going there.

She constantly found fault with Daddy's staff, which had lost all protection from her wrath now that he had gone. She replaced them, one by one, but none of the new staff stayed very long, because they could neither meet her exacting standards nor tolerate her temper. Elisabeth, Christine, and I would hear Mummy scream in anger all over the house at some real or imagined deficiency of the staff. Much of this behavior arose from her extreme nervous strain; not only was she preparing her plot against my uncle at the very moments he was visiting our house or we were visiting the palace, but also she was unused to the responsibility and challenge of being the head of a household, and this strung her out and made her more domineering than ever.

Drilled by Mummy, groomed to a fault by Nanny under her

instruction, the three of us would make our way by car to Monaco. We would arrive at the palace and wait in a drawing room of the royal apartments to go to religious instruction. Father Tucker and his colleague Father Joe instructed us in learning the catechism, the order of the Mass, and the responses; I was trained eventually to serve at the Mass in the palace chapel.

Each Sunday we would attend Mass, sitting bolt upright, under Mummy's severe eye. As always, these services were preceded by a harrowing series of instructions and warnings on our correct deportment during the service. She would tell us precisely what to do at each moment, and more importantly and emphatically, what not to do. She never assumed we could remember for ourselves; she repeated her instructions time and again, Sunday after Sunday. Our welcome relief during these preparations was the appearance of Uncle Rainier, who would enter in the midst of the solemn tuition and break the atmosphere by laughing, joking, and making us feel relaxed. Mummy would pretend to be equally cheerful, but behind the fixed, forced smiles or laughter, her face was tense and her eyes were watchful in case we should make some gaffe.

We could escape her sometimes to play with the palace butlers, and we would plot to find out where our uncle was so that we could bump into him "accidentally" and he would take us on the journey we looked forward to most: the tour of his private zoo. A world authority on primates, editor of a major book on the subject published in 1978, Uncle Rainier loved his collection of lions, monkeys, gorillas, and tigers. He seemed to enjoy an incredible empathy with them, and they with him; every creature, including the elephant, would greet him with a chorus of joyful bellows, roars, and screams. He had a magic touch with them and could go into the cages at times when even the keepers could not. He seemed to soothe the creatures if they were restive or irritable. Unluckily, this deep understanding of animals did not extend to humans. During all of these visits, he had no inkling that Mummy was planning to depose him or, as her plans soon evolved, that she intended to put me, age six, on the throne in his place.

This was our life: dealing with Mummy's grueling emphasis on perfection, being drilled like marionettes, and enjoying our young and fun-loving uncle and our dear nanny. We had no friends of our own age. We never played with other children, as the fear of kidnapping was always present.

It was the summer of 1955, and Monaco was now facing a major crisis that would soon threaten Uncle Rainier's power, raising problems with France, and would pave the path for Mother's proposed revolution. I didn't learn the details until some twenty years later, when I discovered a collection of news clippings that dealt with it. No one in my family ever spoke about such embarrassing past events.

On the 27th of June, 1955, the National Council had learned that Arthur Crovetto, director of the Prince's Cabinet and government finance counselor, had deposited fifty-five percent of the State's reserves in the Banque des Pierres et des Metaux Precieux, a new, private bank owned by a Greek acquaintance of my uncle's, without notifying, as he should have, the various departments concerned. The bank was on the brink of failure. The National Council was asked to advance 250 million francs to save it. Crovetto made the request himself. He did not tell the Council that over the next nine days it would be asked to advance an additional 260 million francs in a desperate effort to save the immense funds deposited there.

Until then it had been normal practice to spread out government reserves among the thirteen existing Monegasque banks. The National Council agreed to bail out the bank on assurances from Uncle Rainier that a fact-finding parliamentary commission would seek out the parties guilty of speculating and taking unheard-of risks with the State's reserves and that they would be appropriately punished.

Before this could happen, the bank collapsed on August 2. This financial scandal was also a political one because of the deep involvement of some of the most important people in Uncle Rainier's personal Cabinet in the ruined financial institution. It was disclosed that the principal reason for the bank's collapse was its financing of a group called Images et Son (Images and Sound), in which the palace itself owned five thousand shares and which controlled through subsidiary companies the Monte Carlo TV station as well as another TV station, Tele-Saare, and radio stations in neighboring French territory.

Advertising in the form of commercials on television and radio was forbidden in France. The scheme had been devised to bolster these stations' broadcasting capacities so that they could beam commercials into much of the French territory. The French government, which incidentally owned the majority of the shares of Radio Monte Carlo, took a dim view, as did the French press, of this method of side-stepping the anti-commercial laws it had laid down, and it forcibly stopped the project. Consequently, the shares tumbled and the company lost its only raison d'être.

When the National Council named the people responsible for this fiasco, Uncle Rainier was asked to suspend from their government functions both Arthur Crovetto and one of his collaborators, Cesar Solamito. Uncle Rainier agreed and at the same time secured the resignation of his private Cabinet. But only two months later he reinstated Solamito and Crovetto. On September 7 the majority of the National Council resigned, strongly encouraged to do so by my mother's secret ally, Jean-Charles Rey, who was president of the Finance and Fact-

Finding Commission of the Council. Those compelled to re-sign sought to protest what they termed his arbitrary decision and noncompliance with their agreements. There followed a parliamentary crisis, a general scandal, and Mummy's conspiracy. In effect, the reason for Uncle Rainier's reinstating Solamito and Crovetto was apparently that they had warned him of Mummy's proposed coup d'état. The bank scandal had provided the breach into which she now proposed to rush. Her intention was to depose Uncle Rainier and name herself as regent on the basis of having a son she could put on the throne. Because Rey had managed to get the majority of the National Council to resign, she no doubt thought there was enough discontent with Uncle Rainier in the government and among the population to give her a chance of succeeding.

In the wake of the incredible news that his own sister wished to replace him with his nephew, Uncle Rainier acted prudently. Instead of banishing Mummy completely from Monaco, he suspended her from her public duties, after warning her of what the consequences would be if she proceeded with her crazy scheme. He then issued an official communiqué from the palace saying that nothing had changed. It was important for him politically to give the appearance of a common front, at least within his family, providing the impression that it was standing by him in this hour of need. In view of Mummy's popularity with the public, this was a very shrewd move on his part. Had he dislodged her, she might have had a chance of achieving her purpose. There is no question of her great popularity both then and later; indeed, whereas Uncle Rainier had spent most of his childhood and early youth being educated and raised abroad, Mummy had not left Monaco, not even during the war. For this she was considered by many Monegasques to be more completely one of them than her brother was, and this fact, no doubt, fanned the fire of her ambitions—with disastrous results where I would be concerned.

Daddy returned from the United States in the middle of the crisis. He had written to Jean-Charles Rey and my mother telling them that he was very concerned that I not suffer the consequences in the future for my mother's plan to put me on the throne. He did not want me to be victim of Rainier's enmity for the rest of my life. He wanted to intercede with my mother to stop her scheme. She denied to him that she was planning anything of the sort. Yet it seems clear she was. And her plot would indeed seriously affect my relationship with her and with Uncle Rainier, and their actions toward me.

Uncle Rainier had given Daddy the right to see my sisters and me for a mere twenty-four days a year, and Mummy still tried to make it uncomfortable for him.

Daddy had kept his cars in the south of France, and also his cabin cruiser. His visits to us were mostly by speedboat when we were at the beach. I remember the first time we saw him again was a wonderful surprise. We were in the playground during our recreation period when we became aware of a man standing, looking down at us from a terrace of the garden set above the one we were on. Children tend to forget very quickly, and he had been gone for a year; we weren't sure who he was, and Christine thought it might be a workman. It was my elder sister, Elisabeth, whom we all knew as Betsy, who said, "It's Daddy!" And then we all ran up to him and hugged him excitedly. His visit with us ended all too quickly.

Over the next few weeks, he would drive the speedboat in, looking very handsome in his sports clothes, and would spend about half an hour or an hour with us. Mummy was very irritable over even these short visits. To minimize Daddy's pleasure in being with us, Mummy insisted that a plain-clothes policeman be present with us at all times. I remember the poor man sitting under the hot Mediterranean sun in his coat and trousers, sweating miserably as he stared after us, never letting us out of his sight for a moment.

Daddy thought that dropping by to see us at the beach, where we were going anyway, would not be considered a whole day spent with him. Mummy's view was different. One afternoon Daddy arrived as usual on the speedboat to find us missing. He was surprised and called up the house, asking Mummy why we weren't present. She replied that the twenty-four visits were up, advising him that her interpretation of Uncle Rainier's arrangement was that each visit counted as a day.

Nanny was determined to give us one more moment with Daddy before he left us, heaven knew for how long. A meeting was arranged at the bottom of the road leading from the Lower Corniche to the driveway at Mereze. My father got out of his car, kissed us, and then took off, not daring to spend a second longer. Somehow Mummy found out, and she informed him that as a result of his unlawful visit he could only have twenty-three visits the next year.

But there was another breach of the arrangement. Daddy knew that Betsy was to have her first Communion, and he longed to see her in her white dress before the ceremony took place at the palace. He called Mummy to ask if she could relax her rule a fraction so that he could see Betsy, just for a moment, as first Communion was very important in a Catholic family. Mummy refused point-blank. Risking dismissal, Nanny smuggled Betsy up to the private road so that Daddy could see my pretty sister dressed for the big occasion and hold her in his arms for one last time. If this, too, had been discovered, I am certain Nanny would have been dismissed on the spot.

At last Daddy had to admit he was beaten. He finally sold his cruiser and left for America, where he remained for much of his life. We didn't see him again for eleven years. He would have loved to have visited us, but the presence of a policeman, the sheer expense of these trips alone, and Mummy's unforgiving attitude made the conditions impossible. Moreover, he had to start his life over again. His initial plan had been to obtain his valuable antiques and to use them to start up an antique dealing business somewhere in the States. Mummy bluntly refused to ship any of those still in our home, even though she didn't like them and stored many of his valuable things in the basement. Many years later she gave them to the gardener. Daddy never saw them again.

Naturally he tried to write to us as much as he could. Not just at birthdays and Christmases, but all the year round. The mail would be delivered at the kitchen entrance and placed according to time-worn tradition at the breakfast table. Before the maids brought the mail to the dining room, Nanny would sneak into the kitchen when Mummy wasn't looking to skim through the letters and see if any were addressed to us from Daddy. More often than not, however, Mummy would catch her at it, scream at her in anger, snatch the letters or post cards from her, and destroy or confiscate them immediately. Only one or two cards managed to slip through the mesh and were hidden by Nanny so that we could look at them again and again, like special treasures.

There was no defeating Nanny. Winston Churchill's cousin was determined to outwit Mummy. She found another loophole in Mummy's surveillance. Uncle Rainier had given Nanny a little house to live in near the palace, as a reward for her dedicated upbringing of him and Mummy as well as us. Every Tuesday Nanny would take the bus with us along the winding coast road to Monaco, and we were always eager to visit her private domain. The house was decorated with hundreds of pictures of the Grimaldi royal family, the family to which Nanny had devoted her whole life. It was there that Daddy's letters began to arrive; by some miracle Mummy never thought of having Nanny's mail intercepted at her house. In this way we were able to catch up with Daddy's adventures in the New World. He was in Phoenix, Arizona, teaching tennis as a pro at the Camelback Inn. Even though he was very fit, he was thirty-seven. To spend ten hours in the sun every day on the courts was very taxing. Moreover, he had seen his world fall to pieces: all the way from being one of the most successful lawyers in Monaco, his practice was closed, and it was too late to start a new career by taking a U.S. law degree.

So life went on. With Daddy gone a second time, there was no escaping Mummy's dominance. After the crisis, all of our visits to the palace stopped. Mother had been deprived of her official duties, and, of course, Uncle Rainier no longer came to see us. We children had no idea of what had happened. Even Nanny couldn't tell us what had gone wrong. All we knew was that we missed him, a second father figure snatched away from us.

Simultaneously, events were transpiring concerning Gisele Pascal, the attractive movie actress with whom Uncle Rainier was involved. Before Mademoiselle Pascal, my uncle had had no romantic interests. Shy and reserved, he had not been typical of the Grimaldis in this sense. The Royal Council was opposed to their becoming engaged. It was stated that Gisele could not have children, a fact contradicted the following year, when she gave birth to a daughter. Another source, much quoted at the time, said that she was disapproved of because she was not of royal blood, which, given our family's marital history, made little sense. Once again the redoubtable Father Tucker was said to have engineered the breakup of the relationship. A rift was caused when Uncle Rainier saw Gisele dancing with Gary Cooper at the Cannes Film Festival. The Prince said in his authorized biography it was like "a knife going through my heart."

At all events, whatever the reason, by November their relationship of five years was over, although he continued to wear the ring she had given him for many months after they had stopped seeing each other. And not too long afterward, Mademoiselle Pascal married someone else. Shortly afterward, Aristotle Onassis asked Greta Garbo's business manager, George Schlee, who had been a frequent guest with her aboard the Onassis yacht *Christina*, to find an appropriate American celebrity who could be Rainier's bride. Schlee's wife, Valentina, the well-known New York couturière, began looking for someone, as well as offering rent-free villas to society notables who could be persuaded to winter in Monte Carlo. Finally Schlee went to see Gardner Cowles, publisher of *Look*, who made the suggestion of Marilyn Monroe. Cowles arranged for Schlee to meet with Marilyn at Cowles's Connecticut estate. She was intrigued by the idea of marriage to a head of state and life as a princess. She asked Schlee and Cowles whether Rainier was rich or handsome. Surprisingly, she had never seen a picture of him and wasn't even sure where Monaco was. The idea of being a princess was irresistible to her, however, and she said she would be happy to meet him. Cowles asked her whether she thought that Uncle Rainier would like her enough to propose. She replied, according to Cowles, "Give me two days alone with him and of course he'll want to marry me." It turned out that she never got her chance.

At that same Cannes Film Festival, by an interesting twist of fate, Gary Cooper's co-star of several years before in *High Noon*, Grace Kelly, was also present. She had yielded to the suggestion of her press agent, Rupert Allan, to accept an invitation from the French government to be guest of honor. Apparently, at the same ball at which Prince Rainier saw Gisele dancing with Gary Cooper, Grace Kelly was also on the floor, dancing with the actor Jean-Pierre Aumont. During her visit she had to make a rushed visit to Monaco to appear at the palace for a meeting with my uncle as part of a scheduled cover story in *Paris Match* arranged by the magazine's film editor, Pierre Galante. This obligation displeased her because she had to squeeze it in between other appointments and just before a reception in Cannes. On her way to the principality, she was involved in a prophetic accident: the car in which she was traveling with Galante and an MGM publicity man was crashed into by a following car containing the *Paris Match* photographic team. Grace was annoyed when Uncle Rainier was not present on her arrival. She said to Galante that it was rude of him to keep her waiting; she melted only slightly when he at last arrived, flustered after a hectic drive from his villa at Cap Ferrat, where he had lingered too long as host of a luncheon. When he offered to take her around the palace, she declined, saying that she had already seen it. Instead Rainier took her on a tour of the gardens and the zoo, where, among others, there was a tiger given to him by Emperor Bao Dai of Indochina. She was very impressed by Rainier's ease with animals. My uncle was impressed by Grace's perfect English diction, her reserve, and her relaxed but regal manner. And she began to warm a little as he proved very attentive. When asked about their meeting, Grace said he was charming.

Father Tucker was well aware of Grace's huge popularity in the United States following her Academy Award and many successful films, including *To Catch a Thief* and *High Society*, and of her impeccable Catholic background. Father Tucker said later in an interview in *The Saturday Evening Post* that Uncle Rainier, after spending an evening with Grace, phoned him up asking what the good father thought of her. Tucker replied, "That's exactly the kind of young lady I'd like to see you married to."

With the parliamentary and bank crisis that year, and plans to marry him to this or that aristocratic young woman shelved, Uncle Rainier needed to bring off a major coup in order to achieve popularity and once and for all prove to the Monegasques that he was a good figure of a man as a monarch. Father Tucker was committed to finding him an appropriate bride and evidently decided that Grace met the prescription from the beginning.

Grace, however, was continuing to see Jean-Pierre Aumont. After Cannes she was seen everywhere in Paris with him. But when she returned to New York later that spring, she made it clear that she would not be marrying him. She was allegedly annoyed because pictures had been taken of her with him that some claimed Aumont had arranged in advance. These had appeared in *Paris Match* and later in *Life* magazine. The story that Aumont had organized the pictures came from the brother of her former flame, the columnist Igor Cassini. Moreover, the Kelly family was unhappy with the idea of Aumont as her husband. The fact that he was French and several years older, along with the unwanted publicity, upset them.

Attempts were made to interest her in the Main Line Philadelphian William Clothier, but Grace was not strongly attracted to him. Nor was she interested in Gordon White, a wealthy Englishman who had once dated Audrey Hepburn.

That summer Grace was offered the role of the princess in *The Swan*. Oddly enough, in view of her immediate future, this was about the heiress to the throne of a Ruritanian nation, who would save the family's finances by marrying a Prince Albert. The costumes, designed by Helen Rose, were beautiful, and Grace loved acting out a royal role. The film was shot in Asheville, North Carolina, in the late summer and early fall of 1955.

In December Rupert Allan called Grace to tell her that my uncle was planning a visit to America and wanted to meet Grace again. *Look* magazine wanted to photograph my uncle with Grace on the set of *The Swan* in Hollywood. However,

Grace was anxious to deflect any public idea that there might be a romance in the wind. She told Allan she had never heard a word from Rainier in all of those months since their meeting in Monaco.

Rainier was quite direct in his purpose in going to the United States. He even gave an interview to *Collier's* magazine stating that it was essential he marry; he gave as a reason not, of course, his predicament in the bank and parliamentary crisis, but the need to secure the succession. If he died without an heir, he told David Schoenbrun of *Collier's*, the Grimaldi family would no longer be in control of the principality. And he added that his life was lonely and empty, and that he sought a bride who was "natural and charitable and had a sincere, deep, Christian charity, a love for one's fellow human beings." He wanted, "a girl who is fair-haired and of light complexion, graceful and feminine." In other words, he was describing Grace from beginning to end of the interview.

He traveled to America with the corpulent cupid, Father Tucker. Tucker arranged a meeting between my uncle and Grace through friends of the Kellys, Mr. and Mrs. Russell Austin of Margate, New Jersey, who had met Rainier and Tucker that August in Monaco. On December 22, Charles Vidor, director of *The Swan*, at last finished the much-delayed production. On December 24, Christmas Eve, Grace flew to Philadelphia from New York. That same evening, through the intercession of the Russell Austins, she met with Rainier, who was traveling with them, at the Kellys' traditional party of the season. For some unknown reason Grace was nervous about the meeting and panicked, almost backing out at the last minute. After the Christmas party, Grace and Rainier drove to her sister Peggy's, where they played family games until four in the morning. Next day my uncle and Grace went off together on a drive through Bucks County, and during the excursion Rainier presented her with a gold ring studded with rubies and diamonds. Grace's father was furious; he was opposed to what was apparently the beginning of a romance. When he asked Grace if it was an engagement ring that Rainier had given her, she replied it was just a friendship ring, and he said, "Friendship hell!"

Rainier and Grace defied John B. Kelly's wrath and saw each other every day. On the 28th of December, Rainier drove Grace to New York to see her agent. On the twenty-ninth Grace phoned her mother to say she was in love and that Rainier wanted to marry her. Tucker was called to New York and then sent to Kelly with a formal proposal. Jack Kelly said, "Royalty doesn't mean a thing to us," and then questioned Tucker about Rainier's finances. Reassured, he and his wife gave their consent, and on New Year's Eve of 1955 the couple became formally engaged. The entire courtship had lasted five days. The official public announcement came six days after that.

Their romance had the advantage of perfect timing. Political problems back home continued to dog my uncle, and he must have realized how much he and his country stood to gain from the international publicity resulting from the match. It was an answer to both their needs: for Rainier it was the necessary first step toward solving the dynastic problem, and held out the promise for effecting the sort of family life he had lacked; for Grace it was finding a husband whose position and achievements matched her own. Her beliefs and the way she had been raised made marriage and motherhood the natural next step after the success she had had in her work. It was thought out but also very romantic.

"It was never a fairy-tale romance," said Grace's sister Peggy. "It was just a very nice agreement," said another sister, Lizanne. But beneath the advantages of their match, there was love and mutuality of feeling as well. Grace was a very passionate person; it was not surprising for her to fall in love very quickly.

Of course, the announcement of the engagement on January 5, 1956, can only have been a considerable shock to Mummy. Not only did it checkmate the power struggle between her and her brother in the long run but also she would be dislodged as first lady of Monaco in the short run. She would have no chance of retrieving her position, since such important female public roles as president of the Red Cross would automatically be transferred to the new Princess of Monaco. No doubt smug in his certainty that he had once and for all put his problems behind him—Mummy included—and probably in a forgiving mood, Uncle Rainier chose his wedding as a reason to become reconciled with Mother publicly and to allow her return to public occasions. The most important of these, of course, would be the wedding itself. My sisters, aged eight and four, would be in attendance as flower girls, while I, age six, was given the honor of carrying the bride's ring (my distant cousin Sebastian, Prince Von Furstenberg, would carry Uncle Rainier's ring).

Mummy was in a state of panic that we would stumble and humiliate her during the ceremony. For almost a month she personally drove us into Monaco so that we could practice walking up and down the many steps of the cathedral, drilling us relentlessly as we went through our paces for hours at a time. The exact placing of one foot in front of another was monitored by her. The timing of the climb, the expressions on our faces, the precise deportment and posture, our backs and necks held in a straight line, were directed by her with intensity. Just how we were to enter the cathedral and sit in the family seats was of great importance to her. The wedding would ease her out of her position as first lady, but she was determined that her children would reflect well on her.

Most of all Mummy was concerned that I might drop the wedding ring. I carried in my hands a velvet cushion with a ring placed exactly in the middle. I never dropped it once; I wouldn't have dared. I walked up and down, up and down, endlessly, afternoon after afternoon, repeating, repeating the movement. I could have done it blindfolded by the time I was through.

Then at last one morning, after yet another rehearsal ordeal, my sisters and I were told to go up to the eastern fortifications of the palace overlooking the harbor of Monaco to see Grace arrive. It was still early that day of April 12, 1956. The palace had been freshly painted pink in honor of the bride. We stood looking out into the overcast morning across the Bay of Hercules. We were excited when we saw Uncle Rainier's yacht, the *Deo Juvante* II, sail out from the harbor to join the American liner *Constitution*, with Grace on board. We could just make out with field glasses Grace's distant form in navy blue and white, and a huge white hat, stepping across the gangplank from one vessel to the other, holding her dog Oliver, and then disappearing inside the yacht. The sea was choppy, but the sun finally broke out with theatrical timing as the *Deo Juvante* II sailed toward us. There was a sound of cheering from the crowds gathered on the harbor side, and on the apartment balconies, and along the battlements and balconies of the palace itself. We watched in amazement as Aristotle Onassis's seaplane circled over Uncle Rainier's boat, dropping red and white carnations in a gesture of welcome. There was a din of vessels sounding sirens, and we saw the first boats spouting water in accompaniment to the yacht's voyage home.

We could make out the yacht docking, and Uncle Rainier driving Grace in his green Chrysler up the Rock to the palace. Grace was officially presented to us all at a reception before a private luncheon in the dining room; no press was permitted. It was a very tense occasion. Grace was accompanied by her parents, her sister Peggy and Peggy's daughters, Meg and Mary Lee, her hairdresser, Virginia Darcy, and her friends the Ralph Sitleys, Maree Frisby Pamp, Marie Magee, the actor Donald Buka, the Isaac Levys, and Judy and Jay Kanter, among many others, and the Grimaldis were gathered in full force to receive her. My grandfather, Uncle Rainier's father, the dandyish Prince Pierre de Polignac, and his long-estranged wife, my grandmother Mamou, the Princess Charlotte, were there; and Louis II's widow, the former actress Princess Ghislaine, was also present. Before we children separated from the adults to join Grace's nieces, Meg and Mary Lee, at a separate meal, we attended the reception. I don't think anyone felt comfortable.

The expression on my grandmother Mamou's face was something to see. It was clear from her frosty eyes and formal demeanor that she was absolutely furious at finding herself in the presence of the groom's father, the Prince de Polignac, whom she detested with a Grimaldi-like fierceness. She was also upset by the presence of Ghislaine, who, though many years her junior, was her stepmother. And Mamou and my mother had been estranged for so many years that Mummy's presence was also a problem for her. Mingled with all of these strains was the fact that she was compelled to receive an American movie star as her son's future bride. Despite her own origins—or perhaps because of them—and despite the widely alleged fact that she had replaced her lover, Dr. Del Masso, with a new one, Rene Girier, the well-known French jewel thief, who was now acting as her chauffeur, she was a snob from head to foot and thought that a movie star was unsuitable as her daughter-in-law. Also, she was predisposed not to like Grace, as Polignac had expressed support and sympathy for her from the very start. When Grace shook her hand, Mamou made no secret, through her expression, of her contempt for the new arrival. My grandmother's glances at Polignac were pure ice. And worse was to come. When Grace's mother was introduced to the fiery Mamou, Mrs. Kelly made a fatal mistake in Mamou's eyes. She slapped her vigorously on the shoulder and pumped her hand with a powerful grip, shouting heartily, "Hi! I'm Ma Kelly!" By now Charlotte's expression was indescribable.

My turn came afterward. Mummy had drilled me again and again to bow and click my heels together as I greeted the future Princess. As it happened, Grace was wonderful. Sensing my nervousness, she bent down and kissed me gently on my cheek, using the nickname that Uncle Rainier must have told her about. "You must be Buddy," she said. I felt the tension break. At that moment she was to me the most beautiful apparition I had ever seen.

My sisters and I went to lunch with Meg and Mary Lee, while the grown-ups went their way. Afterward the party broke up. Grace and the Kellys stayed in the north wing of the palace, while Uncle Rainier went to the Villa Iberia at Cap Ferrat to preserve the necessary decorum. We returned to Mereze.

The next few days were damp and drizzly, yet it was still an exciting time. Uncle Rainier came with Grace to visit Mereze on April 13; we were once again taken with her charm. She took time to talk to my sisters and me, asking us about ourselves and what we liked to do. When the couple descended our driveway on their way out to the Lower Corniche, a reporter pretended to be run over so that when the royal car stopped he could jump up and take a picture. Uncle Rainier was furious and banned all pictures for some time to come. The *paparazzi* still pursued them relentlessly. The press contingent outnumbered Monaco's police eight to one.

Grace wanted Mummy to be involved in the ceremony, but unfortunately, despite Grace's good intentions, she made a serious mistake. It was, of course, mandatory that Mummy be present as part of the royal wedding party. However, Grace made the error of asking Mummy to be a bridesmaid. She had bought her a yellow organdy dress with matching hat from Neiman-Marcus, like those of Grace's sisters. My mother's costume had been ordered from a *haute couture* salon in Paris. Madge Tivey-Faucon, known as Tiv, an Australian lady-in-waiting to Grace and Rainier's former secretary, had the disagreeable task of refusing Grace's invitation on Mummy's behalf and of explaining to Grace that according to protocol a female member of the royal family could not be a bridesmaid. Grace broke into tears, crying, "I was only trying to be nice. And I brought her dress all the way from America!"

Some time after, when I was older, Aunt Grace told me that the royal wedding day and the whole period that preceded it were among the worst ordeals she had ever known. At the various official and unofficial occasions, the lunches, the dinners, and the other family gatherings, she was miserably aware of the tension that existed in most of the family, and especially between Charlotte and Polignac, who even carried on vicious arguments right in front of her and Uncle Rainier. At one point she heard Polignac say, in a deliberate slight to Charlotte, and referring to her illegitimate birth, "At least my son married a *real* princess!" Grace had naturally dreamed that her new parents-in-law would be pleasant and compatible; the fact that her mother-in-law was less than welcoming to her and that Mamou despised her own husband was very painful to Grace, for whom family links were of primary importance. One of her first wishes was to make the difficult, quarreling Grimaldis a family as united as hers. She now understood that this was impossible.

As for Uncle Rainier, his distress was obvious. He had hoped that Grace, coming as she did from a Catholic Irish-American family with a tradition of family values, would have a chance to get used bit by bit to the eccentric, unhappy Grimaldi clan, instead of being plunged, as she was now, directly into a cauldron. And so, under this shadow, Grace's fairy-tale marriage at last took place.

F O U R

YEARS LATER Mamou told me of some of the incidents that preceded the royal wedding that April. Grace's father, Jack, insisted upon reading the marriage contract; his blood churned angrily when he read the sixth clause, defining the rights and duties of the future spouses. It stated that each would share the household expenses. This, he thought, would mean that Grace would be obligated to meet half the bill for over a hundred servants, not to mention the gigantic expense of the upkeep of the palace itself! He said, "Gracie cannot sign that!" Madge Tivey-Faucon was sent to him to explain that the clause was not to be taken literally. He received Madge in his undershorts. For two days everybody was in suspense until he let Grace sign the contract.

Mamou was critical of Jack Kelly about what she called "turning the palace into a post office." It gives some indication of her disapproval of the Kellys that she found it inappropriate that he went down to the main Monaco post office, bought a huge quantity of special commemorative wedding stamps, and proceeded to distribute them to his own guests for the wedding, who numbered nearly one hundred. Mamou was

53

always looking for an opportunity to find fault. She also commented negatively on the gesture used by some of the younger members of the Kelly entourage of turning wine glasses upside down to indicate that they didn't want wine, and on Peggy's drinking a glass of milk while eating a dozen *escargots*.

Mamou, and others at the palace, criticized the presence on the scene of Virginia Darcy, a Hollywood hairdresser and make-up artist who followed Grace everywhere, grooming her hair, applying extra touches of make-up, lipstick, rouge, and mascara, and massaging her ankles to make it easier for her to stand long hours at her dress fittings. In retrospect, it seems totally natural for a lady in Grace's position to be attended, but Mamou and certain of the palace's ladies-in-waiting were always eager to snipe at Grace if they could.

While Grace stayed at the palace with her parents, her other relatives and the scores of friends went to hotels. She was distressed because her hectic schedule over the next several days made it impossible for her to look after her clan as well as she would have liked. Some were even pushed out of the cathedral ceremony for lack of seats.

The endless succession of official luncheons, dinners, and receptions was exhausting for Grace and my uncle. The press was relentless throughout, and on the day of the wedding some even donned priests' cassocks to penetrate the cathedral; my uncle did not have a deputy to undertake the job of press agent for the occasion. On April 17 the Monegasques staged a royal serenade for the couple in front of the palace. There was a performance in native costume, and dancers of the London Festival Ballet, including John Gilpin, also appeared. The civil ceremony took place in the throne room at the palace on April 18. That night there was a gala at the opera house at which the couple watched Gilpin again, with Margot Fonteyn and Belinda Wright.

Now came the moment I had been rehearsed for and over which I was so tense. It was the wedding day, April 19, a Thursday, and the sun shone brilliantly from the early morning on. Mummy took my sisters and me down to the courtyard of the palace very early in the morning, because she was so nervous we might be late. I was chewing my fingernails, petrified that I would do something wrong. I knew Mummy's wrath would be terrible if I made one mistake.

While the cathedral filled up with the famous figures of the world, Aristotle and Tina Onassis, the Aga Khan and his wife, Ava Gardner, Gloria Swanson, and hundreds of others, including representatives of the governments of almost every nation, we were still waiting restlessly in the courtyard. At last Grace joined us, with her sister Peggy Davis as matron of honor, and six bridesmaids, including the actress Rita Gam, in their Neiman-Marcus outfits. My sisters joined them as flower girls, along with Meg and Mary Lee, all four dressed in white Swiss *broderie anglaise*, also from Neiman-Marcus, their shoes and socks bought from J. C. Penney. Grace looked stunning in her Helen Rose wedding dress, given to her by MGM. It was made of antique lace, and the cap and bodice were embroidered with seed pearls. She later donated it to the Philadelphia Museum.

As Grace saw me in the courtyard, she gave me a friendly pat and told me I looked perfect in my white pageboy livery. She knew how uncomfortable I felt wearing a white eighteenth-century ruffled shirt, white satin britches, buckled shoes, and white stockings. She told me I would do just fine, and that made me feel better.

Fortunately Nanny had sewn the ring to the satin cushion so that it would not fall off. Now came the wedding.

We preceded Grace and Uncle Rainier up the aisle of St. Nicholas. The ceremony, which began at 10:30 A.M., was conducted by Monsignor Gilles Barthe, Bishop of Monaco, assisted by Father Tucker as master of ceremonies and Father Cartin, the Kellys' parish priest from Philadelphia, as assistant. Father Tucker, next to the altar, gave whispered instructions to everyone to make sure they performed correctly.

As we walked down the aisle, my cousin Sebastian and I went to our places on the side of the altar. I was counting my paces one by one, but he had not been instructed by his parents, and he kept breaking stride, almost throwing me off my own. We found our seats, and while I sat still, Sebastian tossed his cushion up and down, the ring flying up with it. He threw the cushion so violently that it was clear that at any minute the ring would fall. Father Tucker noticed this and frowned. Uncle Rainier wore a black and gold tunic, blue trousers with a gold band, and a midnight-blue bicorne hat with white ostrich feathers. I watched intently as the couple stood before the altar, under the severe heat of blazing arc lights provided by the television crews.

Now the dreaded thing happened. Sebastian threw the cushion in the air, and my uncle's ring fell to the floor. Luckily Father Tucker retrieved it just in time. Some time later, when Nanny was visiting England, someone criticized the page who had so misbehaved with the ring. They had assumed it was me. She was very offended, saying, "That wasn't my boy. He would never be less than perfect."

Uncle Rainier had quite a struggle getting the ring I had carried onto Grace's finger. I remember that when Father Tucker took it from the cushion, he had to pull very hard to break Nanny's strong cotton thread.

As we all emerged from the palace into blinding sunshine, the royal couple preceded by an American, English, and French guard of honor, Grace paused a minute before entering the cream and black Rolls Royce and waved to the crowd. The applause and the cheers were deafening. Police had to fight to keep the *paparazzi* at a distance. Back at the palace, as Grace got out of the Rolls Royce and saw me and my sisters, she said, "I am very proud of you all. You performed wonderfully." Even Mummy was proud of us after that.

I got to keep my cushion as a souvenir, but over the years it has been lost. I attended the wedding luncheon, with all of the Kelly and Grimaldi families present, which stretched the palace kitchen to its limits. Uncle Rainier said later that the wedding was a mess. He especially hated the presence of cameras and microphones everywhere in the cathedral.

Behind the glamour and fanfare of the wedding, there were some scandalous goings on. Jewelry estimated to be worth fifty thousand dollars was missed from the hotel suite of Grace's friend, the Philadelphia publisher Matthew H. Mc-Closkey. The rumor at the palace was that the jewels, left in a red velvet case in a wardrobe of their suite at the Hôtel de Paris, had been stolen by Mamou's chauffeur and alleged lover, Rene Girier. This theft was made public, although the thieves were never apprehended. It was kept a secret, however, that Mrs. Kelly, Grace's mother, who was staying at the palace, also had her jewelry stolen. And again there was a whirlwind of rumor that Girier was responsible. Mamou angrily denied the charges, furiously defending him.

Still later there was to be another problem related to jewels, a hundred-thousand-dollar gift of gems given to Grace by the Monaco National Council. The Paris jeweler involved claimed that he had not been paid for the diamond and ruby necklace and matching accessories, and it was believed that he had paid a five-million franc commission to a Council member who was influential in making the selection. The National Council made a down payment of twelve million francs on the necklace, but when the jeweler asked for the balance, he was told that the bank had not been authorized to pay. The jeweler, Arnauld Clerc, said to *The New York Times*, "It is all involved in Monegasque politics. The whole Council approved the purchase and now a majority are trying to accuse two or three members of having engineered the sale and profited by it. This is not true." Finally Uncle Rainier managed to force payment of the bill. But not until after a considerable struggle.

My uncle and Grace left on the *Deo Juvante* II for their honeymoon. It was a rough trip. Grace came under heavy criticism when they attended a bullfight in Spain. Grace had asked Rainier to stop the annual practice of live pigeon shooting, scheduled for January. But the sport brought into Monaco a small, rich and influential group and helped to boost the slack winter season. People were furious that she would put an end to this. Palace gossip said that if she was so particular about such cruelty to animals, why did she go to a bullfight?

Interestingly enough, although the two new sisters-in-law had their reasons to be disposed to disliking each other—in Grace's case because Mummy was a divorcee and Grace had a strong objection to divorce, and, more seriously, because she had to know from Uncle Rainier the details of Mummy's activities—they got on well with each other. At least until Grace would later ask Mummy to quit her apartments at the palace to make room for a reception area.

Grace had a tremendous job running the palace household. The major-domo had been doing everything the same way for the last thirty years and, like most of the staff, was not readily disposed to change. When she asked him to reduce the intense light of the dining room chandelier bulbs by using lower wattages, he obeyed, only to reinstate the old bulbs the following day.

Each week, to widespread criticism among the staff, crates would arrive from the United States bearing Aunt Grace's name. They contained American jam, ham, capons, nylon stockings, dog biscuits, Metrecal diet supplements, and Kentucky bourbon, Uncle Rainier's favorite drink. She even imported a huge crate of toilet paper because she didn't like the toilet paper in the palace bathrooms. To the dismay of many, including her own lady-in-waiting, she filled the palace's vases with mixtures of plastic and real flowers—a gesture that seemed curious considering the fact that our country is filled with a profusion of every kind of blossom. She also added a loveseat with "I Love You" embroidered all over it.

Grace also brought in American cooking utensils, which upset the palace chef and his kitchen staff because they were using antique brass pots and pans. The top-to-bottom Americanization of the palace was the constant hubbub of Monaco. Although we never learned the details, it was clear that Grace wanted to revise arrangements that had been standard for many years. Also criticized was the appointment of an English housekeeper, Christine Plaistow. At the beginning the staff was irritated to have to take orders from an Englishwoman. The rooms had heavy, somber wallpaper and large, unattractive antique furniture. Grace never liked the Prince's rooms on the ground floor next to the palace garden. She immediately went about changing the whole scene by brightening up the color schemes, putting in more elegant period furniture, and hanging new drapes. She worked very hard on this. She also worked very hard on her French, determined to overcome criticisms that she was not proficient in her adopted language. One day Father Tucker was commenting about her accent to Rainier, who snapped at him, "She speaks better French than you do." Tucker replied, "My Lord Prince, I always knew that love is blind, but this is the first time I realized that it is deaf, too!"

Grace redesigned the maids' uniforms, ordering them to be made of poplin with white collars and frilly aprons. The colors were changed according to the seasons, with black silk uniforms in the British manner in the winter months.

Grace was dumfounded by all the criticism as it leaked through to her; she was also lonely and missed her old friends.

One of her consolations was Oliver, her dog, who spent much of his time biting away at priceless antique sofas.

After the marriage, my sisters and I visited with Mamou, whom we had never met until the wedding. She had a villa at Cap Ferrat. Her tension during her son's wedding now dissolved. She liked us, and we liked her, and we could even put up with the terriers that snapped and bit at our ankles. Mamou never let her differences with our mother interfere with her feelings for us. Even though Mummy brought a certain sense of strain to these afternoon teas at the villa, by insisting we didn't speak until we were spoken to, Mamou put us completely at ease. She was a remarkable woman, as we would discover on a more intimate basis in later years at her beautiful castle, the Château de Marchais near Paris.

I did not see very much of my new aunt in the weeks after the honeymoon, when she began her life as a princess. Grace realized she was pregnant soon after her return, and she suffered from morning sickness that confined her to her apartments for a very long time.

Among Grace's interests was astrology; she had always believed in it, and never more firmly than when her Los Angeles astrologer, Carroll Righter, informed her that she would marry a prince. She read her horoscope in the papers every morning, and whatever she read influenced her in her decisions for the day. She called Carroll Righter in Hollywood (Marlene Dietrich was among others who did the same) for advice based on the position of the stars, and this advice would influence her in her activities at the palace and in the principality at all times.

Grace was a Scorpio and always asked what sign someone was when she met them. If the sign was not compatible with her own, it could influence her feelings about that person.

When Madge Tivey-Faucon became her lady-in-waiting and Grace determined that Madge was a Virgo, she said, quite bluntly, "Virgo and Scorpio don't get on."

It is surprising that Grace believed in astrology, being a devout Roman Catholic. The Church condemned astrology, and Uncle Rainier was a skeptic. As head of state and church in Monaco, he couldn't possibly endorse it.

Uncle Rainier was a Gemini. Grace pointed out to him that it was a rule of astrology that Geminis would inevitably be dominated by Scorpios, who are authoritarian, often gifted with great success in the world, and capable of perfectionism as well as spontaneous kindnesses. Gemini, the sign of the twins, was notable for its unreliability and changeability, its cheerful loquacity and its shifts of mood. Gradually Uncle Rainier came to accept the fact that Scorpio dominated him; eventually he would refer to Grace among intimates as "the government." There is no question that from the moment of her marriage, she was the leading presence at the palace.

Early on in their marriage, she and Uncle Rainier began calling each other Daddy and Mummy, in exactly those English terms, a habit which, even though Grace was three times a mother, seemed ridiculous to Mamou. As I came to know Grace better, in the following year, I came to learn how ironical it was that Mummy had so grimly prepared me for the so-called "ordeal" of meeting her. She had told us that Grace was fussy and demanding and needed us to be perfect children at all times, when in fact Grace was always warm, thoughtful, and kind to us.

It was typical of Grace that she would be sensitive to Uncle Rainier's feelings, because her mother had told her that husbands often feel neglected and pushed back when their wives are pregnant; that all the attention goes to the unborn baby. Concerned about this, bearing her mother's words in mind,

Grace spent weeks knitting a woolen vest or waistcoat for him. More than any Hollywood script, her real life now called for her to summon up all her acting ability. When she gave interviews to magazines, she was the very picture of glowing happiness and satisfaction. Not a soul would ever imagine that the Monegasques were backbiting constantly about her. Having met only GIs and American tourists, the Monegasques had prejudices about what it meant to be both American and a movie star, and neither image exactly met the Monegasque idea of a consort. Some of the palace staff resented being employed by an American movie star, and she was totally ignored by Mamou. Moreover, Grace was consistently not well and suffered from insomnia.

Grace was often tense and uneasy about dealing with all of the problems in the palace. The constant stream of criticism from the staff and relatives drilled into her persistently; she couldn't ignore it. She attended as many public events as she possibly could and overcompensated for her personal unhappiness by eating large amounts of food. Because she was pregnant anyway, she had no figure to worry about, and she would indulge herself with spaghetti bolognese and other heavy pasta dishes with rich sauces.

In September 1956 she went to New York—no doubt in part relieved to go home because she suffered from homesickness—to arrange for her apartment furnishings to be sent to Monaco. She had not had time to attend to this shipment before, because the engagement took place only days after the proposal and the wedding soon after that; she had also been very busy during the engagement completing a last film, *High Society*. The final scenes for that movie, in which she co-starred with Frank Sinatra and Bing Crosby, were completed only days before her departure for Monaco for the wedding. During the visit to America, she and Uncle Rainier were received by President and Mrs. Eisenhower at the White House. Secret Service agents accompanied her everywhere. Back in Monaco in November, she converted an empty chamber in which the prince had formerly kept his lion cubs into a big nursery, a self-contained apartment with bedrooms for future children and a bathroom and small kitchen. With the aid of an artist from the Disney Studios, Grace worked on a fairy-tale décor, evoking the figures of legend that Disney had made immortal.

During the months that Grace was absent in the United States, we at Mereze acquired a governess, Madame Marcelle Alizard, who did not replace our beloved Nanny but supplemented her. She was a very good, kind, energetic woman, thin, with red hair, and in her forties at the time. Her husband suffered from poor health and was unable to support her financially, a situation that had forced her into teaching for a living. She lived in Beaulieu, taking care of her son and husband with dedication and affection.

Whereas Nanny, who despised the French, had concentrated on teaching us the rudiments of British history, Madame Alizard attended to our French education. She taught us French literature, history, and grammar. It soon became clear to our new governess that our life of complete isolation from other children was abnormal; that my sisters should play with girls of their own age and I as the only boy in the family should have friends of my own. She took it up with Mummy.

Fortunately Mummy respected Madame Alizard's opinion and listened to her as she listened to few others. Within a short time of their talk about the importance of my having companions, some turned up at Mereze. Of course, Mummy would be concerned with our family's position. I couldn't play with just *any* children. Mummy herself made the selection from the available male children of Monaco. She chose the sons of the mayor, the Boisson boys, the son of the family physician Imperty, and the sons of the president of the Tribunal. I saw them once or twice a week.

Even though I liked Madame Alizard well enough, I didn't have any enthusiasm for my studies. As boring to me as these studies were, even worse were the visits to the opera house to see opera and ballet performances. Our attendance was compulsory, as Mummy felt that a royal education should include its fill of culture. Before we left with Mummy in the car for the Saturday matinées, she would give us her customary litany on good behavior. Because the eyes of our subjects were upon us in the royal box, she used to say, we must never forget to behave impeccably. The audience would watch us as we took our seats and the overture began. Even during the performance, many eyes would turn toward us. Life under such a public microscope was not easy, and especially so for a boy like me, who wanted to be spontaneous and to have fun.

We would invariably arrive late, despite Mummy's obsession with punctuality, and the performance would have to be held up for our arrival. Then the whole audience would have to stand as we took our places. We were dressed up formally, even on the hottest weekend afternoons. My sisters would usually wear Scottish plaid dresses, deliberately reminiscent of Mummy's great-grandmother Lady Douglas-Hamilton and reflecting her own obsession with anything Scottish. I would normally wear a buttoned-up gray flannel suit, my shoes polished and my hair perfectly combed. I would take my place with my family in red seats that had very hard, straight backs. I would have to sit upright. I would pick up the program, staring in a spirit of despair at the seemingly endless acts and entr'actes before the longed-for main intermission. I would sit, numb with boredom, while the performance continued, and then, when (after a seeming eternity) the intermission took place, we would proceed in correct order, Mummy going

first, to the private salon behind the royal box, where afternoon tea was served from a large silver pot, along with sand-
wiches and cakes from Madame Pasquier's British Tea Room.
The number of cakes we were allowed to eat was limited by
Mummy to three. To eat more would, in her view, seem glut-
tonous in the eyes of others present. Luckily I was able to
persuade one of the palace footmen in attendance on the royal
box to sneak out some more cakes and hide them under my
chair in the box. I would eat them when no one was looking
during the rest of the performance.

Later I discovered another way to escape my boredom.
When Uncle Rainier and Aunt Grace returned from America,
I watched them carefully in the box and noted that Uncle
was as bored with opera and ballet as I was. Because of his
position, he took his seat with aplomb and stayed wide awake
through the overture. But the moment it was over, and the
dancing or singing began, he fell asleep, and I saw his head
sink down onto his chest. Grace would stare at him very hard,
noticing that his eyes had closed, and as soon as he began
snoring, she would look alarmed and prod him with her elbow.
He would wake up with a start and sometimes immediately
begin applauding loudly, not aware that the performance was
still going on.

In view of the fact that my uncle had found a way to escape
the tedium at least temporarily in sleep, I would follow suit
and, resting on the arm of the chair, let my eyes fall and my
head go down. I often got away with it. Mother, determined
to see everything on stage and be noticed seeing it, often didn't
notice me.

Madame Alizard continued to be a godsend. Not only did
she want us to have friends of our own age coming to visit, but
she also felt we should not confine our lives to the claustrophobic atmosphere of Mereze. She wanted us to have some ex-

perience of the world outside our home. Surprisingly, Mummy agreed to this suggestion.

My sisters and I would go into Monaco, and while Madame Alizard taught at the lycée, we would go our separate ways, my sisters to their ballet class and I to gym, where I would work out with a private instructor, Monsieur Barral. I found much more pleasure in sports than in study.

After gym class I would rendezvous with my family at my sisters' ballet class. One day I noticed an attractive redhead among the classmates and suggested to Mummy, who loved dancing and dancers, that I join the class. She was suspicious of the suggestion, wondering what was behind it, but consented. At the barre, I arranged to stand right behind the redhead, and whenever I stretched my leg, I succeeded in touching her attractive posterior with my toe. After two or three lessons, Mummy and the instructor correctly figured out that my interest in ballet went no further than the redhead's best feature, and I was immediately transferred to a fencing class.

It did not take long to realize that Mummy had not the slightest idea of what she should do with me as a growing boy. I shall always be grateful to Madame Alizard for pushing Mummy beyond the lessons in Monaco in gym and fencing to a commitment to boarding school. Once Mummy came around to the idea that I must leave home and go to a school, she settled upon the most exclusive educational institution for boys in the world. This was Le Rosey in Switzerland, which my uncle had also attended and which had numbered among its pupils the Shah of Iran. There was a very long waiting list for Le Rosey, running for many years, but she succeeded in putting me down for the autumn term of 1958, when I would be nine.

Madame Alizard wanted me to be away from my family so that I might have an appropriate training for the real world. Also, she, like my sisters and I, was unhappy when it became obvious that Mummy and Jean-Charles Rey were becoming more and more deeply involved and that he would be playing an increasingly dominant role in our household. At the time, Rey's role in Monaco was as head of the opposition to Uncle Rainier, and for Mummy to enter into a liaison with him was very provocative to my uncle. Madame Alizard never approved of him, and she was sure that his interest in Mummy was only to further his own ambitions. She also felt that his influence on my upbringing could be disastrous. She was already aware of how little joy there was in our household; how little attention and meaningful interaction we had with our mother. She hoped that at Le Rosey I would lose the increasingly negative attitude I was taking about life, which could only grow worse living with a man I deeply disliked.

I remember the first time I met Rey. I went into Mummy's bedroom for something and noticed his feet sticking out from underneath the window curtain, like the hidden figure in a French farce. He emerged after my entrance and tried to make a joke about his presence there, but even at my age I wasn't fooled. Deliberate, obvious, heavy not only in the physical sense, he was not a figure I could ever warm to. It was quite clear that the sooner I went to Le Rosey the better.

That winter Uncle Rainier and Aunt Grace were back in Monaco, waiting for the birth of the child. Ma Kelly arrived, along with Grace's gynecologist, Dr. Hervet, and in anticipation of the event, the library was turned into a delivery room. Grace refused anesthetics. Despite her and Uncle Rainier's longing for a son, they were delighted when Caroline Louise Marguerite, a healthy eight pounds, eleven ounces, was born on a rain-soaked January 23, 1957.

In honor of the birth, three prisoners in Monaco's jail were amnestied. Among them was a titled noblewoman, who had been sentenced to one year for having stolen three one-thousand-franc notes from her hairdresser's till.

Rainier made a sixteen-millimeter film taking in both Grace's bed and the cradle, and the film was rushed onto television within a few hours. A cannon discharge rang through the city when the birth was announced. Because of the drenching rain, the detonations of the guns were at irregular intervals, and many people had difficulty in counting that there were in fact twenty-one salutes. Had it been a boy, there would have been a hundred and one. Interestingly enough, Carroll Righter had predicted the child would be a girl.

The rain continued, heavier and heavier, during the day. Grace's father, informed of the birth by telephone, exclaimed, "Hell! I wanted a boy!" He had five daughters and one son.

Pictures of Grace in bed with her baby were under the strict control of Uncle Rainier. When we were allowed to visit her bedroom after a week and see her with Caroline in her arms, I brought with me a Kodak box Brownie camera and took shots of the radiant mother and child. As we left, overjoyed at the big occasion, the official palace photographer, George Lukompski, who also doubled as a bodyguard, asked me politely for my roll of film. By royal order it would have to be developed in the palace darkroom and not in a commercial photography shop. This precaution was taken in case a civilian film developer should sell copies of any of the pictures to the press.

I finally got my pictures back, on the understanding that they must remain in-house. Grace told me on another visit to her room that she loved my picture of her holding Caroline in her arms, saying that it was one of the best ever taken.

The baptism was, by Uncle Rainier's wish, not turned into a public event as the wedding had been. No photographers were permitted in the private chapel of the palace, and it was strictly a family affair, supervised by the omnipresent Father Tucker. I had to carry an enormous candle in a silver stick, almost as high as I was, and it was very heavy; as I held it by

Father Tucker, while he dipped Caroline in the font, I accidentally brushed the flame against Father's surplice and he
caught fire. The flames shot up, but a moment later somebody
put them out. It would have taken a great deal more to extin-
guish Mummy's temper.

FIVE

NCLE RAINIER KNEW that Alexander, the beloved son of Aristotle Onassis, was going to Le Rosey at the same time I was, and he saw to it that we got to know each other in advance. It says much for Uncle Rainier's consideration that, although he was in perennial conflict with Onassis, he still was able to see that young Alexander would make a good friend for me.

There had been an uneasy relationship between my uncle and Alexander's father in those years. Onassis had first been captivated by Monaco when he was a sixteen-year-old, impoverished youth who had gone steerage on a ship bound from Smyrna to Buenos Aires, where he began the extraordinary career that made him a multimillionaire. He never forgot the effect that the glittering lights of Monte Carlo had on him as the boat docked. In 1952, when I was three, he tried to buy the Sporting Club and use it as the headquarters for his immense shipping interests. Uncle Rainier, however, evidently nervous about Onassis's power and influence even at that stage, declined the offer. Frustrated and determined not to be put down, Onassis began buying substantially into the SBM, the controlling financial force of Monaco. By 1954 he had bought the

Sporting Club anyway, able to do so because the SBM in effect owned it.

He enjoyed mooring his yacht, the *Christina*, converted from a destroyer at a cost of $2.5 million, in Monaco Harbor. One widely spread story stated that the bar and stools were fashioned from whales' teeth. There he entertained international celebrities and helped to lure investments into our principality.

Under his increasing control the SBM began to show a profit. Lavish party after party glittered with famous people and caused international publicity. At first my uncle was pleased with this dynamic new addition to his realm. He was charmed by Onassis, and the two men became friends. But by 1955 there were already rifts in the relationship. For months the two men didn't speak. The reason was that Rainier had expected Onassis to bring about major new developments and land reclamations in Monaco, but he became more and more suspicious that Onassis was simply milking the principality for money. Their rift was temporarily repaired when Onassis celebrated the royal engagement by giving one million francs to the Monaco Red Cross, which my uncle had founded. Onassis's gift to Grace of a diamond and ruby bracelet and tiara was also symbolic.

After this rapprochement, I was invited to the *Christina* to meet Alexander. The boat was the largest private vessel in the world, handsomely furnished, with a mosaic-floored dance floor that could be hydraulically raised to reveal a swimming pool, bathroom fixtures of gold and silver, fireplaces of lapis lazuli, a screening room and even an operating room. I liked Alexander very much; he was frail, dark-skinned, friendly, and good-natured, and I couldn't help but feel a contrast between his life and mine. His parents never tried to suppress his natural high spirits; I was amazed by the way he would ask and get permission to do almost anything, and his father approved of everything with the warmest of smiles. He was the apple of his father's eye.

Nine-year-old Alexander decided one day to take me for a ride aboard one of the yacht's several auxiliary motor launches. One of them was an Albatross, among the fastest speedboats in use at the time. He asked the sailor in charge to get off, putting the poor man in a difficult position, since he was under orders to accompany us. The sailor said that we could not take the boat out on our own; Alexander waited until he bent over to loosen the mooring buoys and untie the rope, then pushed him overboard. To my surprise, Alexander's devoted father simply came to the rail and told the sailor to dry himself and to come aboard the launch as a passenger, while Alexander took the wheel. The sailor climbed aboard dripping wet and did his best to shake off the water, and with Alexander at the helm, we took off rapidly through the Bay of Hercules and then into the Mediterranean for a ten-mile spin.

This was only one of the adventures I enjoyed with my new friend. I was at once envious of his incredible degree of freedom, which sprang from parental love. He had a little electric car, kept aboard the yacht and carried ashore upon mooring, which I would have given almost anything to have owned myself. He would drive it through the roads of Monaco and Monte Carlo, from harbor to beach, through dense traffic. The police dared not stop him; astonished drivers would look up and see him driving by, weaving happily in and out of the traffic.

Mummy took a typically disapproving attitude toward these visits. Not only did she frown on my going off with Alexander on these trips, but she also criticized the opulence of Onassis's yacht, saying, in effect, that it was obscene to have bathtubs of lapis lazuli with taps of solid gold when there was so much hunger and misery in the world, and when so many children were starving.

With the spring of 1958 came the birth of Prince Albert Alexandre Louis Pierre. Now I would have a close male relation, albeit nine years separated us. Grace had gone from one child to the other, but nothing could reduce the rejoicing she and Uncle Rainier felt when they had a boy. The hundred-and-one-gun salute that rang out from the palace cannon was symbolic of the fact that at last Monaco had a male heir to the throne; this meant that the principality could not be swallowed up in France, and its citizenry would continue to enjoy their tax-free status for the indefinite future. This time the christening was held in the cathedral, and I didn't upset any candles. It was a grand and happy occasion, with all of Monaco alive with festivities. At Albert's public presentation, Grace also brought tiny Caroline, all in white, to the palace balcony, where we all stood, and it seemed that the entire population of Monaco had gathered in the square below to cheer the mother. As she had with Caroline, she breast-fed the new child, a decision that caused further derision of her among the palace women. Grace was also quite debilitated after the second birth; her resistance was worn down, and she suffered from constant sore throats and colds. Even so she appeared at as many public events as she could and took a special interest in the opening of a new wing of the Monaco hospital, a home for the aged, and an orphanage.

At the time of Albert's birth, Jean-Charles Rey had further established his power in Monaco, blatantly leading the opposition to Uncle Rainier in the National Council. He even headed up an independent party or group within the Council, which called, among other things, for women's suffrage. He also was urging the complete revamping of the royal rule into a constitutional monarchy, which would be subject to the Council's final judgments in the same sense that the British queen was subject to the Privy Council. Uncle Rainier still did not know of Mummy's deep involvement with Rey, or that, indeed, they were considering marrying. Uncle had forgiven her for her political machinations and had made it clear to the public that the family was a consolidated force; it would have been very risky to her to have him discover that she was once again defying his imperial authority. Of course, it could not have been lost on Rey that once married to Mummy, he would, as the Prince's brother-in-law, strengthen his power even further in the Council. He might also secure the support of those Council members who might possibly be wavering but who retained a loyalty to Mummy.

Rey was not yet actually living at Mereze. But his visits grew more and more frequent, and he was often present at lunch and dinner. As he grew more confident, he installed his own butler and chef; the maids, accustomed as they were to Mummy's own brand of odd behavior, could not get used to his imposing presence. I remember that when I was playing with the footman, Rey would appear in the kitchen or at the gardener's cottage snapping orders at the staff, screaming at them that they should not waste valuable time playing with me when they should instead be attending to their household duties. A look of fear would cross their faces whenever his car entered the grounds. They shared my contempt of Rey, and that gave us a common bond. A kind of complicity, a conspiratorial friendship already existed between us under Mummy's regime; now it increased because of Rey's presence in the house.

Jacky, a husband of one of the maids, who was not on the staff himself, used to take me for rides on his motorbike on the Lower Corniche; this was as exciting to me as the trips on the harbor or through the roads of Monaco with Alexander Onassis. My love of speed and fast driving was enhanced by the memories of those great days with Daddy on the same road. I would sometimes persuade Jacky to stop at an under-traveled stretch of the Corniche and let me drive the motorbike myself for one mile and back around the hairpin bends.

One day, when Jacky was driving me home on the bike, Rey

turned up early from his office and saw us from his car as he passed us on the private road to Mereze. When we got to the front door, he screamed angrily at Jacky for taking me out on the motorbike. All rides were forbidden from that moment on, Jacky wasn't to be seen around anymore, and later on, his wife left.

Another time, when Alexander came to the house, he suggested we should take the moped and have a ride on it along the private roadway. I was tempted, but I knew Mummy was having tea on the terrace and would hear the sound of our driving. I told him, feeling ashamed about it, that I didn't dare. It was clear from the look in his eyes that he couldn't really understand how different my life was from his.

It was with relief that I at last went to Le Rosey for the September term of 1958. Jean-Charles Rey symbolically indicated his new importance in my life by taking it upon himself to drive Mummy, Betsy, Christine, and me all the way to Switzerland in his Rolls Royce. The farther I got away from Mereze, the better I felt. At last we arrived at the school, which was housed in the thirteenth-century Château du Rosey, just outside Rolle, a sprawling little town on the shore of Lake Geneva (Lac Leman), about halfway between Lausanne and Geneva. Le Rosey was surrounded by countryside, rich with vineyards and notable for Chillon, the château of which Byron wrote. We drove up a small road from Rolle, northward, crossed a railroad bridge, and turned left through two tall pillars framing a gateway and up a long road lined with trees to the main courtyard. On the left, water spouted from an antique face into a stone bowl; on the right, a tree spread its branches over a circular wooden bench. The château loomed up ahead, with four other buildings and extensive sport facilities, including football fields, tennis courts, and a swimming pool. Le Rosey resembled a luxury hotel more than a private school. It was clear that the pupils there would get their parents' money's worth, which was just as well, since the fees were among the highest in the world.

We met the headmaster, Louis Johannot. To me he looked old, but in fact he was only in his late thirties at the time, and as tall and solid as Jean-Charles Rey. He was a major in the Swiss army and a town councillor of Rolle, and he was married to a cousin of the Swiss ambassador to Washington.

I felt better when I met the good-natured Mademoiselle Schaub, who jointly ran the school with Johannot; she was the contact between the school and the parents, in charge of both the two hundred-odd boys and the office and housekeeping staffs. Members of the Rockefeller and Hunt families, the two sons of Onassis's rival, shipping millionaire Stavros Niarchos, several members of the Kashoggi family, Michael Korda, and dozens of other famous names had been at Le Rosey or would be there later. Its students represented in miniature the future ruling families of the world.

I was happy also to have Alexander Onassis as my roommate. When at last Mummy and Rey departed, I found myself in a comfortable bedroom overlooking the basketball court. I liked the look of the school; it was another world. I had escaped. Now I could be a boy in a community not controlled by constant family warfare and conflicted emotions.

I spent the first night in the room alone. Next morning Alexander turned up, and we met in a classroom with all the other new boys to be told the rules and regulations. Our junior section for boys aged nine to twelve was under the supervision of a Swiss couple named Stickel. She taught us some subjects and ran the domestic side of the operation, including the cleaning of the rooms, laundry, dry cleaning, and the kitchen, and he was in charge of most of the education and sports. It was clear to me from the outset that although we would be disciplined if necessary, any punishments that occurred would be fair, not arbitrary. I had at last entered a community run on rational principles.

Given my happiness with all I had seen, I was therefore surprised and disappointed to find that Alexander was unhappy with Le Rosey. In our room he told me point-blank he would not be staying there very long. He had already had a quarrel with Louis Johannot. Johannot had raised his voice to him, and Alexander, with all of the aplomb of his nine years, had told the head teacher that he was not accustomed to being addressed in that manner. Johannot threatened to call Aristotle Onassis, to which Alexander replied that he would be ill-advised to do so if he didn't want to get an unforgettable tongue-lashing from his father. I was astonished by Alexander's total confidence in his father's unquestioned support of him. During the next days Alexander continued to find fault with everything, and he told me that he would soon ask his father to send a helicopter to pick him up and take him away. He didn't like the food and skipped meals, and the discipline was intolerable to him.

I asked Alexander where he would go if he left the best boys' school in the world. Alexander assured me that his father would find something and that, in any case, he, Alexander, refused to take orders from that "imbecile Johannot." After a further confrontation, Johannot called Onassis to say that Alexander had no respect for him or the rules and it was obvious that he would be unmanageable. Onassis asked Alexander to try to stand it for a few more days, and Alexander replied that he would, but only if Johannot apologized to him. Needless to say Johannot did not, and one night Alexander said to me, "The helicopter will come. I'm not going to let that arrogant fool have the pleasure of expelling me." I was very sad when it came time to say good-bye to him. I never saw him again. And I never saw anything of his sister, Christina, either, apart from brief glimpses on the yacht. He was to die many years later in a plane that he was piloting.

Meanwhile I got used to the school regimen. We were wakened at 7:15 by a loud bell, we had breakfast at 7:40, classes from 8:00 to 12:00, with a ten-minute break for bread and hot chocolate at 10:15, assembly or gymnastics between 12:00 and 12:30, luncheon at 12:40, and an afternoon divided into sports and classes, with supper at 7:15 and bed at 8:30. Wednesdays and Saturdays were half-holidays. Surprisingly, there was no school uniform, but we were forbidden to wear blue jeans or shirts outside our pants, and we were always expected to dress in a coat and tie for dinner. We were allowed one dollar a week for pocket money, which was paid to us when we produced proof that we had written to our parents; and there was an autumn term dance at Rolle with girls from nearby schools. French was the official language at school, but most of us spoke English as well, perhaps because so many of us had been virtually raised by English nannys. Sports at Le Rosey were well run. I grew to love soccer and rowing, and I was never homesick for a moment. In fact, I looked forward to the winter term, when the entire school would move to three chalets in Gstaad, the exclusive ski resort in the Bernese Oberland, where we would have months of skiing, skating, and ice hockey along with our regular classes.

The pleasant days of the autumn of 1958 rolled on. I was not yet the school rebel I was to become later.

When I returned reluctantly to Mereze for the fall vacation, I found that the differences between Mummy and Uncle Rainier, which had been resolved temporarily during the all-important period of the marriage to Grace, had become insurmountable. At last my uncle finally understood the extent and significance of the growing relationship between Mummy and Jean-Charles Rey. Always anxious to avoid direct confrontations or dramatic scenes, he did not call either one to denounce them. Rather, he acted indirectly: it was then that Princess Grace quietly asked Mummy to quit her rooms at the palace on the pretext that she was putting through the new reception area. Mummy left the palace and withdrew to Mereze.

My mother's schemes were again doing her in. She might have sustained her position or even regained some of her public offices, had she not had this liaison with Rey. It was certainly clear to me that each was using the other: she was using him in order to secure greater power in the Council, to make up for her loss of public position. She espoused a deep interest in democratic principles, including suffrage and equal pay for women in Monaco, central planks in Rey's political platform. He in turn undoubtedly thought that through an alliance with her, he could draw on her personal popularity to effectively oppose her brother in the wake of the unsuccessful coup d'état. Certainly his desire to establish constitutional reforms, by which Uncle Rainier would be more firmly subject to control by the National Council, would clearly have itself weakened Mummy's position as a member of the royal family. But the birth of Albert finally had lost her the chance of ever putting me on the throne, and therefore, at this stage, she had nothing particularly to lose by supporting Rey's plans for a new monarchical structure.

Under these circumstances it wasn't surprising for me to find Mummy even more tense and edgy than usual and Jean-Charles Rey, who, along with the rest of the Council, would shortly be suspended from his political office, more self-important around and about the house than ever. As Christmas approached, Mamou, who was living in Paris, told Mummy that we children were to write to her to tell her what gifts we wanted. Typically, Mummy was anxious that we

shouldn't ask for anything too expensive. It now suited her
to try to regain favor with Mamou. They had scarcely spoken
in many years, only abruptly recognizing each other at the
funeral of Louis II and the marriage of Grace and my uncle.
Now my mother had to swallow her pride, since she needed
all of the support she could gather at the highest levels.
Also, she believed that her position with Mamou would be
strengthened in the reflected glory of her children's impeccable behavior.

I was therefore affected by Mummy's complicated sense of
intrigue, and writing what should have been a simple letter
became a great trial. I had to summon up all the courage I
possessed to ask for the one thing in the world I wanted more
than anything else.

I had never forgotten my rides with Daddy in his car, nor
had I ever been able to forget the spins around the streets with
Alexander Onassis. I had dreamed about Alexander's electric
mini-car, and now I wanted one of my own. It was with un-
certainty that I sealed the envelope and mailed the letter
to Paris.

Christmas Day arrived, and with it, my dream. Out on the
driveway waiting for me that morning was a stunning sky-
blue car. It had a two-stroke 50 cc gasoline-burning engine,
and it could do thirty miles per hour. I was beside myself. I
have never written a more fervent thank-you note in my life.

Mereze had a well-rolled lawn next to the private road,
studded with a dozen large pine trees. I immediately worked
out a circuit, reproducing the course of an imaginary Grand
Prix race; I had never forgotten the few occasions when we
attended the Grand Prix, watching it from the eastern battlements of the palace or from the royal box, and now I would
have a one-man Grand Prix of my own. Neither of my sisters
was allowed near the sacred car; it was mine, mine alone, the
first thing that I had ever owned that I really cared about.

Even today, as I look back on the many beautiful cars I have owned, I have never had such a feeling of joy as I had when I first took the wheel of that small car.

I spent Christmas Day on the lawn. Inevitably Mummy was irritated by the noise and by my endless driving round and round, which violated her principle that unrestricted pleasure had to be bad for children. Thereafter she limited me to one hour's drive in the morning and one in the afternoon during that December vacation.

At the entrance to our private road there was a public garage and service station; I can still recall my despair when, as I was about to start upon my regular afternoon drive one day, I found the car not in its usual place but being attended to by Monsieur Aumignon, the garage owner. He was fixing the throttle, reducing the car's maximum speed by half. This was a blow to me. When I went to Mummy to plead my case, she replied coldly, "Mother knows best, and children shouldn't question their parents' wishes." As far as she was concerned, that was the end of it.

At least she didn't take the car away. For the whole of the next week after the artificial deceleration, I drove it to the maximum speed now possible, without taking my foot off the accelerator between corners.

The entire Christmas vacation was consumed by the car. Those two hours each day represented paradise—modified paradise, perhaps, but paradise just the same. During the periods when I was not permitted to drive, I would sit on the grass gazing at the car in adoration or checking out every single part over and over again. I would open the hood and check the wires, valves, and oil level. I would refuel the car with a gasoline can and wash it three times a day with a sponge and bucket borrowed from the maids, using the best soap available. Half an hour before lunch or tea or supper, I would rush into the house and wash up; then, as soon as the meal was over, I was back outside again, covered in grease.

Mummy always held it over my head that if I misbehaved in any way, or failed to eat all the food she chose for us, she would restrict my driving time. So great was my dread that she would deliver on her promise that I forced myself to eat the things I hated—kidneys, brains, and liver—and cursed myself for being a child. In fact, I would daydream that I was suddenly eighteen, having skipped a decade, and found myself in possession of my own automobile, which I had bought with my own money and which no one could take away from me. In my dreams I was also a racing car driver; the truth is I never wanted to be anything else.

While this tiny but important drama was going on over my car, a major one was surfacing in Monaco.

Rainier was furious with Mummy for involving herself once more in the intricate politics of his sovereign state. Not content with removing her from the palace, and my sisters and me with her—I would not see Grace again for three years—he suspended the Constitution on January 29, 1959. He disbanded the legislature, plunging our principality into a crisis. There were no riots or bloodshed, but Rey was in effect rendered politically useless by Uncle Rainier's dispositions. Dr. Joseph Simon, president of the National Council, attacked Uncle Rainier's action as "a veritable coup d'état," saying, among other things, that "The Prince does not have the right to do what he did, even though he claims the contrary." Rainier told the press that one of the reasons for his action was that the National Council had refused to approve his annual budget. Both Louis II and Albert had similarly suspended the Constitution to remind the public at home and abroad that the Grimaldis were rulers by hereditary divine right. The divine right of kings exists nowhere else in the world. This arrangement in Monaco rendered our family absolute administrators of power. They could virtually make up the law as they went along, and any attempt to block their headstrong decisions could result in heads figuratively rolling in every direction. In his proclamation to the press, my uncle added, "For a year, the National Council has hindered the administrative and political life of the country. This attitude is a blow at the Constitution and at the vital interests of the principality." He added, "A certain Council member has been intriguing ceaselessly for many years for the purpose of furthering his own ambitions." There was no question in my mind to whom he was referring.

On January 30 there was an important benefit gala for the British American Hospital of the Riviera, held at the Hôtel de Paris in Monte Carlo. The table normally occupied by the National Council was empty. Meanwhile Uncle Rainier separately worked out a reform program to allow women to vote in order to quell criticism by women's groups that his anti-feminism was responsible for the dismissal of the Council. Grace told the opposition to "trust her husband and everything would be all right." She told the press that six months of princely rule would settle down Monaco's problems. Uncle Rainier appointed Emile Pelletier, former French minister of the interior in the de Gaulle Cabinet, minister of state. Because of the peculiar relationship with France, a French diplomat was always chosen by the reigning prince to assume the role of minister of state. This appointment of Pelletier was supposed to palliate the differences with de Gaulle and was therefore not insignificant.

All during this crisis, of which I heard distant murmurings, I was at the winter school of Le Rosey at Gstaad in the Bernese Oberland. It was a dream location for the older boys, who enjoyed the companionship of girls from the neighboring finishing schools and who had seemingly unlimited money to spend on everything from Rolex watches to sportswear. But for those of us still under eleven years of age, Gstaad had other meanings. There I learned to skate in a rink that was surrounded by snow-capped peaks and fir forests. I learned to play ice hockey but had little aptitude for it. My chief problem was that because I had been reared in the warmth of the Riviera, my blood was thin and I suffered from the mountain cold. I enjoyed skiing, but I would often ski faster than I should have and wound up head first in a snowbank.

I celebrated my tenth birthday that January at Gstaad. Grace sent me a Parker pen and pencil set. I do recall that Mamou sent me extra pocket money, but the best gift of all was presented to me on my return home for Easter.

One of the members of the staff with whom I got on especially well was Marcel, the chef. The day after I returned, he gave me a small but heavy parcel. I opened it to find a tool kit in a leather case with a clip. When I thanked him for the gift, Marcel winked at me and beckoned me to follow him into the garden. We circumnavigated the lawn, carefully avoiding the windows in case Mummy should be watching. At last we made our way to my car. Marcel took the kit from me and removed from it a screwdriver, a wrench, and a pair of pliers. He glanced around nervously to make sure no one was spying. Then he quickly applied the tools under the hood. When he was finished, he turned to me and said, "Happy birthday!" Now I understood what he had done—and the great risk he had taken for me. He had fixed the car so that I would be able to drive it again at thirty miles an hour! I flung my arms around him. His words in French, *"Eh voilà!"* ("There you are!"), ring in my mind to this day.

S I X

IN 1959 MAMOU, my impressive grandmother, became an important presence in my life. I hadn't seen her since we had visited her at Cap Ferrat, three years before, but the gift of the little car had secured her place in my heart. I was therefore happy when Mummy told me that we would be spending a month that summer with Mamou. Mummy had not softened in her attitude toward her mother. They still strongly disliked each other and always would. However, Mummy was continuing in her campaign to try to woo Mamou as an ally during her exile from the palace. And of course Jean-Charles Rey wanted to be sure that he would obtain her approval as her future son-in-law.

Their aspirations were futile, but Mummy and Rey didn't realize that their presence was more of a trial than a pleasure to Mamou. We took off on our visit to her at the Château de Marchais at night. We went in the station wagon because Rey and Mummy felt that to go in the Rolls would be showing off and might upset Mamou, who disliked the *nouveau riche*.

We were told, as we drove north, that we must follow certain carefully prescribed rules. We must behave perfectly. This had always been fundamental in Mummy's rule book, and now it was more essential than ever. In her private war with Uncle Rainier, she saw a way to use us children to her advantage. We must show ourselves to be ideal children from the beginning, so that Mamou, with her skeptical attitude toward her son's marriage, would, Mother hoped, compare us favorably with Grace's children. Now respectively two years and one year old, Caroline and Albert would undoubtedly be raised on American principles of greater freedom and relaxedness. Once again we were subjected to pressure. We were forbidden to ask any questions relating to the awkward Grimaldi dissensions, of which we must have had an inkling even at our ages, about the reasons our father was not in Monaco, or about anything else we might be inclined to question concerning our family's clouded past. And, finally, we were to give the impression that we adored Mummy and her Best Friend. Mummy was extremely anxious through the trip, biting her cheek in a new sign of nervous tension. We might as well have been going to a military school instead of to one of the most magnificent castles in France, owned by an impressive and generous princess, our own grandmother and her mother.

We drove all through the night, a total of six hundred miles, to the farming area of the Aisne. The countryside consisted of fields of sugar beets and small homesteads with white wooden fences. The old stone buildings lay back from the road, and there were cows, sheep, and chickens. Finally we turned off the paved highway and drove down a dirt road, and suddenly the great castle came into view. Built near the shrine of Notre Dame de Liesse, where pilgrims had come to attend the site of a miracle, its colorful history running back four centuries, the castle had been visited by many kings of France. It was a favorite of Francis I, Charles IX, and the Ducs de Guise. Abandoned in different periods, sacked and pillaged and burned, the castle always rose again as one of the most imposing residences in the country, and the Barons de Marchais filled it with treasures of art. The famous Duchesse de Berry stayed there, and in 1856, Charles III, hereditary Prince of Monaco and Duke of Valentinois, bought it from Comte Delamarre. It was Charles III who restored the residence, and it was under the Monegasque dynasty that it flourished again. In its fertile plain, surrounded by a great park, this sumptuous residence is used today as a retreat by Uncle Rainier, who restored it after a damaging fire.

However prepared I was, I could not have foreseen just how striking the castle would be as we drove up to it that morning twenty-seven years ago. Although the drawbridge had been replaced with a stone bridge, the moat remained, encircling the entire domain with gray-green water. As we crossed the bridge, we drove through the imposing portcullis, or armored gateway, which was framed by two stone gatehouses; one housed the officers of the administration, the accountants of the domain, and the other the gatekeeper and his family. As Jean-Charles Rey honked the station wagon horn, the gate swung open, and my sisters and I pressed our faces to the windows. We drove another six hundred yards past banks of rose bushes and rolling green lawns. Two towers loomed up, the left tower containing Mamou's private apartments and the right the chapel.

As we got out of the car, Mamou emerged from the front door with the terriers I remembered from Cap Ferrat jumping about. Mamou was elegant and poised. Dressed in tweeds, with discreet touches of jewelry, petite but very striking in her person, she had about her an effortlessly relaxed air of authority.

Perhaps significantly, Mamou embraced us children first. In contrast to our warm welcome, she embraced Mummy perfunctorily, and then shook hands with Jean-Charles Rey. From the look on her face it was clear that she did not approve of him.

I was uneasy as I entered the castle. As usual Mummy had conjured up such a picture of authority and dreaded punishment for all mistakes that I was too scared to strike up a conversation. I also sensed that Mummy's determination to avoid a confrontation with her mother would have us all on edge for the next weeks.

But despite my unease, I was impressed as I walked up the great stone staircase to my room on the third floor of the big tower. On either side as I climbed were medieval tapestries. The view from my window was breathtaking: the long, rolling greensward and beyond it the groomed trees of the park.

Dinner that night had a ritual quality. Aperitifs were served by members of Mamou's unlikely staff of jailbirds. She had performed social work at the prison of Pontoise in Paris for many years, and it was her custom to employ ex-convicts in order to rehabilitate them. It was funny to think that I might be receiving a glass of lemonade or soda from a former burglar, hit man, or arsonist. Their faces betrayed nothing of their shady origins or prison terms. Tamed by Mamou into obedience and respectfulness, they could just as easily have been born into service.

The sitting room where the aperitifs were served, with its oversize furnishings, enormous wood-burning fireplace, and chandeliers, was as palatial as anything I'd ever seen. The dining room seated twenty-four; Mamou sat firmly at the head of the table. Because tradition called for two men framing her, she was compelled to place Jean-Charles Rey at her right and me on her left. The table was laden with salt and pepper salvers made of sterling silver and navy blue glass, priceless antique cruets, silverware, and glasses.

Despite the surface luxury, dinner that night was not comfortable. Mummy gave us hard, pointed stares, to make sure we didn't speak until we were spoken to, and Rey dominated the conversation with heavy-handed attempts at humor. Mamou listened with an appearance of patience and interest, yet she never raised a smile at his punch lines. She barely managed to conceal her distaste for him, which did not escape my child's eye. Nor Mummy's, alas. By the time we retired to the sitting room for coffee, Mummy was busy biting her cheek again. Mamou barely had finished her coffee when she stood up, no longer able to endure Rey's presence, and said, meaningfully, that we must all be exhausted from our long journey and would surely like to retire. This ill-disguised note of dismissal was not lost on Rey, and he looked unhappy as we all went upstairs to bed.

This awkward beginning had only been made worse by an incident that had taken place earlier. With a grand gesture, Rey had presented Mamou with a small parcel that contained a velvet box with an expensive item of jewelry inside it. It was a breach of etiquette for Rey to hand her this gift; it also appeared to be an obvious attempt to buy her friendship and support. She had accepted it with icy graciousness, seeing through him immediately. She had put the small package into her crocodile handbag, and by the way she did so, I could see that she didn't consider the gesture appropriate. She was not about to sell her approval to anyone. I applauded her silently.

To my surprise, the summer turned out to be wonderful. Mamou was a wonder. Far from the ogre Mummy painted, she was a jovial, kind, and thoughtful grandmama to us. Things were not forbidden by her; she maintained discipline, but not by force. Her attitude was that we were at Marchais on vacation and that even Antoinette's children deserve their share of fun. She bought us bicycles, encouraged us to explore the park and its puzzle of small pathways, and ordered the staff to repair the disused rowboat, which lay with its planks rotted at a small pier on the moat, so that we could go out in it. I explored the ancient waterway and the small lakes on the property. I grew to love nature, and Marchais had an abundance of it. We who had been brought up never to ask for anything were now being asked what we wanted. Mamou was tireless in her efforts to please us: she or her staff helped us to explore the entire castle, from cellar to attic; she gave us a Ping-Pong table, she set up a clay pigeon trapshoot for us, and she encouraged me to shoot duck, pheasant, and partridge with the huntsmen and the beaters.

I remember a typical example of her behavior toward us. At dinner one night, I wanted a second helping of dessert and looked at Mummy. She glared at me, silently telling me no. Mamou crossed her by saying that surely a growing boy should eat up, and why wasn't I taking another éclair? The expression on Mummy's face was unforgettable. I looked at her directly as I bit into another.

In short, Mamou had totally usurped Mummy's prerogatives. Moreover, Mamou broke through the wall of silence Mummy had cast about us. She completely eliminated the rule that we must be seen and not heard. Right in front of Mummy, she encouraged us to speak as much as we wanted. I remember, once the ban was raised, I blurted out my feelings of gratitude for the mini-car. I went on endlessly about the car, giving details of the curves of an imaginary one-man Grand Prix circuit I'd invented, and I'm sure Mamou thought I would never stop. I don't think she understood that when I finally had a chance to share my joy with the person who had made it possible, nothing on earth could stop me in my headlong flight of praise.

Mummy tried her best to be present all the time, afraid that Mamou would say too much to us, revealing perhaps the circumstances of my father's removal from Monaco, and of the family's less glorious history. Her excessive concern and strained behavior was shrugged off by Mamou, who ignored her and did her best to make us happy at all times. We returned to Marchais summer after summer. I always looked forward to the visits. Later my cousins Caroline, Albert, and Stephanie would also spend summers there.

It was at Marchais that, under Mamou's protection, I could indulge my love for cars. The chauffeur, Martinez, drove a vintage Ford shooting brake, an extended station wagon used for hunting, and I got him to let me drive it on the country roads through the farming district outside the castle. Mamou knew about this, but she would say with a smile to me, "Buddy, you really do eat, breathe, and sleep cars," and caution Martinez to confine my exploits at the wheel to the castle grounds. She didn't try to suppress the adventures she knew meant so much to me.

Somehow we managed at first to evade Mummy's all-seeing eye; but then, after two weeks of drives, many of them more extensive than Mamou would have wished, one afternoon we drove right past Mummy, who was out for her walk. When I got home, Mamou and she were talking heatedly about it. Mummy told Mamou that Martinez's permitting me to drive was reprehensible, but that he should not be blamed because I had a way of influencing servants wherever I was to do exactly what I wanted. Mamou countered, "What are you worried about? I saw Buddy driving two weeks ago, and he was doing pretty well for his age. What are you so upset about?" That silenced Mummy.

While the visits to Marchais were marred by the constant undercurrent of tension resulting from Mummy's determination to curry favor with the mother she loathed, I also discovered Le Rosey could cause me its share of problems. It was in 1961, three years after my enrollment, that I began to emerge as the school rebel. The formula was classic: my repression at home drove me to defy authority wherever I found it. I became a kind of juvenile anarchist, specializing in the manufacture of homemade bombs and fireworks designed to explode in the well-ordered, most expensive boys' school in the world. My adventuring with explosives often resulted in my losing Wednesday and Saturday afternoon privileges in the village of Rolle.

One night I decided to bring about a massive bombardment of the personal rooms of Mr. and Mrs. Waller, a British couple on the teaching staff. I set up a line of twenty-five rockets connected to a single fuse on the hedge opposite their windows. The fuse line was extremely long so that once I had lit it, I would still have plenty of time to vacate the spot, find a member of the teaching staff to chat with, and thus, at a great distance from the scene, establish an alibi. Everything went according to plan. I lit the fuse, walked away quickly, engaged a teacher in conversation, and waited for the inevitable series of bangs. I achieved more than I had imagined. It turned out that the Wallers were entertaining friends at an evening party, and the rockets blasted right into the sitting room, exploding among the guests. The first sizzled through Mrs. Waller's hair, almost scalding her in the process, and the guests scattered, terrified.

Next day at breakfast, Waller picked me up by my collar and screamed at me that I had nearly killed his wife and that I would be punished for the rest of the term. I invoked my carefully constructed alibi, but it didn't work. Waller went straight to my room and found the evidence he needed: yards of fuse wire. My alibi was blown.

Lunch came along. After dessert, according to tradition, headmaster Louis Johannot would tap his glass with a knife and make daily announcements. When he said that I was to come to his office, my heart sank into my shoes. I thought I had had it.

When I got to his office, I was astonished to see the imposing headmaster standing at his desk, stretching his hand out to shake mine. He offered me his congratulations. I wondered if this was some form of sarcasm. But as it turned out, what he had to tell me was as unwelcome as news of my worst imagined punishment would have been. He informed me that the day before, Mummy had married Jean-Charles Rey at the Monaco legation in The Hague. He told me that they would be on their way to the south of France the next day, and that they wanted me to meet them in Geneva for lunch.

The news depressed me. Now that boisterous and ambitious provincial politician was legally my stepfather. Nevertheless, I had no alternative but to make my way by train to Geneva to the restaurant where we were to meet. I sat there with my "parents" and Henri, Rey's son by his earlier marriage, a student in his twenties at the University of Geneva, trying to endure the meal and forcing myself to congratulate the couple. It was one of the most unpleasant experiences of my life.

By a peculiar irony of fate, this marriage, seemingly born not of love but of convenience, entered into against the sovereign family laws of Monaco, which specified that the reigning prince's permission must be given for family members to marry, did not finally spell the end of either Rey's or my mother's career at the palace. Under any other circumstances, for Uncle Rainier's sister to marry his chief opponent would have resulted in her permanent banishment or worse. But as it turned out, destiny played into the erring couple's hands. Yet another crisis with France was the cause of this curious turn of events.

President Charles de Gaulle had always thought of Monaco as a small, irritating thorn in his side. Although he personally liked Uncle Rainier, he did not like the fact that Monaco, in his view, was willfully acting against the economic hegemony of France. French companies had poured into Monaco, from the former French North African colonies as well as from

France. De Gaulle was also annoyed by the fact that French millionaires were escaping French taxes simply by establishing residence in our principality.

Uncle Rainier was angered that French companies were trying to control the still ailing Image and Sound; he issued an ordinance preventing any further sale of its stock on the Paris Stock Exchange. De Gaulle was furious: what did Rainier think he was doing, he thundered, stopping French financial investment while at the same time throwing a blanket of protection over wealthy French tax exiles?

The collision was political, not personal. By January of 1962, however, it had crescendoed. De Gaulle demanded that Uncle Rainier's ordinance be immediately rescinded. He invoked a 1918 treaty between France and Monaco that obligated the Monegasque sovereign to act in conformity with the political, military, naval, and economic interests of France. Uncle Rainier asserted that the treaty was no longer valid. The first major scene of the crisis occurred at night in Uncle Rainier's office in the palace. Emile Pelletier, the Monegasque minister of state, was also a representative of the French government and had been acting as a mediator between Monaco and Paris. Under pressure from Rainier, Pelletier had signed the controversial ordinance regarding Image and Sound. But now de Gaulle demanded that Pelletier resume his loyalty to France and withdraw it immediately. Rainier was beside himself. He accused Pelletier of betraying Monaco, of bowing to de Gaulle in the most cowardly manner. The insults flew to and fro. Finally Uncle Rainier demanded that Pelletier quit both the palace and the principality immediately. The press said that Uncle Rainier had actually shoved Pelletier, but this was officially denied by the palace.

Pelletier emerged flushed and angry. He publicly accused Uncle Rainier of stating that he regretted having served in the French army during World War II. Once again this was denied. But as a result, de Gaulle now began withdrawing France's investments from the principality. One French millionaire, who owed a great deal to de Gaulle, transferred $12 million from a Monaco bank to Switzerland. This may not have been an example of altruism or loyalty, but rather a conviction, shared by many others who also withdrew their money, that de Gaulle would literally fulfill his implied threats to end the independence of our sovereign state.

Then, right in the middle of the crisis, there was talk that Aristotle Onassis was also going to pull out his capital. There were threats that de Gaulle would cut off our electricity, telephones, and water, and that in reprisal Uncle Rainier would stop the French Blue Train from going through to Italy. The crisis was to continue for over a year. The effect on our immediate family was ironical. Uncle Rainier was compelled to reunite all the warring forces of Monaco, and he dared not continue to act without a parliament. He had to reconstitute the National Council, reinstate my stepfather to his powerful position within it, restore Mummy to her official social duties (though not to her rooms at the palace), and make a public show of reconciliation by inviting her to the palace as his guest.

The press had had a field day, headlining stories about Rainier's defiant sister marrying the enemy of the Prince.

It had to be a bitter pill for Uncle Rainier to have to accept publicly and deal officially with Jean-Charles Rey, and to have to put up with Rey, whose personality he found abrasive and uncongenial, in his own home. The luncheons, dinners, openings of the opera and ballet, charity balls, and all the other goings on of the principality must have become an endurance test for Rainier, who had never particularly enjoyed these events to start with. He had to see Rey's imposing face and figure at his own head table; listen to his loud, conceited monologues; watch him dancing with my mother; and share his food and his wine with this unwelcome brother-in-law.

The tension of all concerned at the palace was greater than ever.

Grace didn't like Rey any more than her husband did. In fact, the reacceptance of Rey was just another of the endurance tests that she had to undergo in her existence at the palace. She had been greatly saddened by the recent death of her father from cancer, and she was offended by the vulgarity of the fact that copies of his will were sold for seven dollars each by a book distributor. A bronze statue was erected in his memory in Philadelphia, showing him seated in a rowing boat with oars. Kelly had never been comfortable at the palace and had made remarks like "There are too many servants underfoot," which didn't exactly please Rainier; it was also true that he couldn't get used to his daughter being a princess, and being treated as such, while he did not get the same attention.

Rainier felt that he was an outsider among the Kellys and that Grace changed slightly when she was with them. Very sensitive to her family's reaction to her, she tried to become again "just one of the girls." Both Grace and Rainier had entered the marriage determined to make the necessary compromises, but Grace had to make more concessions than he. She had to go everywhere accompanied by a palace staff member and with Rainier's agreement. She missed being able to see her girl friends and going out casually with them.

Grace found relief in Roc Agel, a farmhouse nestled high in the mountain slopes above Monaco, which Uncle Rainier had bought in 1957. Grace spent much of the period of my mother's exile, a period during which we children could not meet her, remodeling the building, preserving its stone walls and terra cotta tiled roof. She rode horseback up there, cooked Chinese and Indian dishes, and set up barbecues. She put in a swimming pool to make the farm a more joyous escape for herself and her children.

96

Now that the awkward "reconciliation" had taken place between Uncle Rainier and Jean-Charles Rey, it was time for the royal couple to dine with us at Mereze. Preparations for the momentous evening occupied both Rey and Mummy to such an extent that they went to unheard-of lengths, even for them, to ensure that nothing went wrong. My stepfather seemed to forget that Mereze was a State-owned property and behaved as though it were his own home, bought and paid for by him. More accurately, my mother was allowed to live in the residence only by the principality's grace and favor. But this reality seemed to have escaped him.

As always, we children were drilled to be as perfect as puppets. Never before had the staff been so hard-driven as in the forty-eight hours preceding the crucial dinner. From morning to night Rey and Mummy put the cook, Marccl, the maids, and the entire household staff through a hellish ritual of serving table, opening doors—all the customs of deference to be accorded a royal couple. It was insulting to our experienced staff to be told precisely in which order to serve, beginning with Princess Grace, continuing with His Royal Highness, then Mummy, then Rey, and finally we children. It was obvious to me that the staff were angry, contemptuous, and fed up with Rey's and my mother's imperiousness.

Even Nanny got her share of drilling before the arrival of our guests. Her separation from my uncle for the three years following the crisis of 1959 had been very sad for her. Since she had never married or had children of her own, he was the nearest thing possible to a son to her. It must have been insulting to her, therefore, when Mummy said, over and over again, that there must be "no souvenirs," no recollections in Uncle Rainier's presence. In other words, no mention whatsoever of the past, or our family's bizarre history, or any of the subjects that Nanny's memory-letting would undoubtedly evoke.

At last the all-important evening arrived. Mummy was biting her cheek and Rey was a picture of tension, until both assumed waxen smiles as the royal car drew up at our front door. The butler performed the well-rehearsed action of opening the door. Immediately Uncle Rainier dissolved some of the tension by entering with a joyful expression. He succeeded in disguising his true feelings; even his Oscar-winning wife couldn't have matched the performance he gave that night. He shook hands with Rey, embraced my mother, and hugged us with all of the affection we had remembered from his visits to our garden long ago. As for Grace, I was struck once again by her beauty. She, too, acted with considerable skill on this difficult occasion. She took my mother's hand, and Rey's, without any definable expression crossing her face. However, there was real warmth and sweetness in her manner as she hugged us, dressed up as we were. I regretted all the more the three years in which I had not been able to see her.

Mummy went mechanically through her movements of reception and welcome. Rey did not cease bragging and striding about, excessively jovial and false. It was absurd watching him act out his pathetic "all's well" charade. Most of all I felt sorry for Nanny. When she embraced Uncle Rainier she could barely get out the words "My big boy, my big boy," and she started crying on his shoulder. I could see that he was genuinely touched, and Grace also looked at Nanny with sympathy and affection. It was clear that Mummy did not react in the same way, however. She told Nanny to go and attend her duties, and it was quite clear from her tone that Nanny was not to return. Mummy and Rey had decided earlier that Nanny was not to be permitted to participate at dinner, for fear she might say too much.

Dinner began with the serving of caviar. This was supposed to be a family dinner, devoid of pretense, and caviar was more normally an entrée for formal occasions. But everything that night was in the same tone. The finest wine was poured, and course after course appeared of the most elaborate cuisine that the hard-pressed Marcel could muster. Although Uncle Rainier had simple tastes and disliked ostentation, Rey was determined to offer the most opulent of receptions to his brother-in-law. It had little to do with deference or gestures of good will in the wake of this recent reconciliation. It was yet another sign of his ostentatious personality. I thought we would never get to the dessert.

The evening was rendered even more embarrassing by Rey's insistence upon sharing his usual repertoire of unfunny jokes. The look on Grace's face betrayed boredom and irritation. Uncle Rainier pretended to laugh and then told stories of his own, all of which were as subtly witty as my stepfather's were obvious and heavy. As for my sisters and me, we were of course under orders not to speak until spoken to. Fortunately Uncle Rainier had the sensitivity to understand that these orders had been issued and deliberately involved me in the conversation. Since he had been to Le Rosey himself over two decades earlier, he was eager to be brought up to date on the Swiss school. He asked me what my favorite sport was, and when I told him it was soccer, he said he had played midfield and asked, what position did I play? I told him fullback. He also wanted to learn all about the present order of the school, the teachers, the winters at Gstaad, and so forth. Grace joined in the questions, and for a while, I was the center of the conversation. Grace wanted to hear my sisters' news of their ballet classes and their private tutoring; they never went to school. Whereas the royal couple's conversations with Rey and Mummy seemed artificial, their affection for us was genuine.

When the couple departed close to midnight, Rey had a beatific smile on his face: the face of someone who had executed a plan to his complete satisfaction. Even Mummy couldn't find fault with her household that evening. In their minds, at least, they had scored a victory.

I, in turn, carried from it the beginning of a clearer understanding of the differences that lay between my mother and Grace. They had been extremely cool, although rigidly polite, in the brief moments in which they were engaged together in conversation at the table. Over the years that followed, I was able to piece together the reasons that that special form of polite coolness existed.

Grace was, of course, offended by Mummy's marrying my uncle's chief opponent, but there was more to it. She was aware of the contrast between the Monegasques' attitude to her and Mother's popularity, a popularity carefully secured from her earliest youth and sustained after her removal from public office by virtue of her undeniable skill in public relations. Even when she was no longer head of the Red Cross or on the board of various charitable institutions, Mother never ceased to visit as much as she could with shopkeepers, tradesmen, and wives of various businessmen and officials in order to maintain her popularity among the citizenry. Grace, in spite of the fact that she had borne an heir to the throne, had quickly learned that the cheers that greeted Albert's birth did not drown out all criticism. In a society like Monaco, she still suffered from the fact that she was an American. She had never learned to be a super saleswoman of her own charm, and to many she seemed not only foreign but distant, her natural shyness and near-sightedness mistaken for an indifference and coldness toward the populace of her adopted home. They thought she had a colonial attitude of Coca-Colonization, an issue with many in Europe at that time, and were afraid she would turn Monaco into an American province. They gave her no credit for the fact that she was doing her best to learn French, despite having no particular gift for languages, and that her children were being raised bilingually. Nor was she credited until much later for having brought Monaco to international attention, inflating the principality far beyond its actual importance in the eyes of the world. Their provincial gossiping contained a kernel of resentment that she looked more royal than her own husband. There was an unpleasant contrast between the Monegasque refusal to accept Grace and the Belgians' acceptance of the recently crowned Queen Fabiola—but then Fabiola was not an American but a Spaniard. It would be some time before Grace overcame the indifference of her people and was no longer referred to, with some condescension, as "the American Princess" but was finally called "our Princess."

Grace unwittingly added fuel to the criticism, from her acquisition of American furniture and her importing of it from New York to her hiring the American decorator George Stacey to redecorate her palace apartments. At Roc Agel she put in both imported American wallpaper and carpets; installed an American kitchen, done in aquamarine; and covered her toilet walls with stills from her pictures.

Her palace apartments—the drawing room, library, dining room, bedroom, wet bar, and kitchen—were also criticized. Especially the fact that not only were the rooms heavily carpeted, but everything, from the pastel sofas to the vases to the desk to the tables and the bathroom fixtures, was similar to what one might find in a New York flat. The servants cleaned and dusted the rooms and left them to report that not a thing was French-made in that private domain.

Grace's tightness with money became a subject of gossip. Because her father had risen from bricklayer to millionaire, she believed in the virtue of economy taught to her from infancy. Her earnings as a movie star remained untouched when she became Princess. Her gifts were not lavish. At one Christmas she gave members of the staff gift-wrapped boxes of soap. Those who received them were not grateful. Not only were the gifts without value; they implied, the servants said, that the staff didn't wash. On one occasion Grace brought her lady-in-waiting the present of a mauve feather duster, saying as she handed it over that she knew mauve was the woman's favorite color. Furthermore, it was palace gossip that Grace would rewrap the gifts she had been sent and turn them around, so that sometimes people would receive the very present they had given her. She never threw anything away, and sometimes people would receive a two-year-old box of chocolates that had suffered from deterioration. She wore the same maternity dresses for both Caroline and Albert and hated to either throw out or give away her clothes, wearing them over and over again until they were out of fashion. In the early years, whereas most ladies in her position ordered their dresses from the famous couturiers of Paris, she ordered hers by catalogue from department stores in New York.

In order to assure the people of Monaco that she really was one of them, Grace embarked on what came to be known in the press as "Operation Smile." This was a campaign in which she would democratically do her personal shopping in Monaco, stop to chat with passersby, hold conversations with shopkeepers, and have afternoon tea at Madame Pasquier's Tea Room. She also visited the Cellarios, a modest family with the largest number of children in the principality. Unfortunately, it was misinterpreted as a public relations device intended to match Mummy's similar perambulations around our tiny state. It always seemed that whatever Grace tried to do awakened ill feelings in the people. All of this was far from the admiration and affection in which she was held in the United States.

There was more trouble in that spring of 1962. This concerned Grace's understandable nostalgia for the movie career she had given up in order to marry my uncle. In 1956, not long after her wedding, it was announced that she would appear with Gregory Peck in a comedy, *Designing Woman*, but this was untrue. In 1958 Father Tucker told *Look* magazine, "Grace go back to films? Nonsense. They couldn't offer her a role in Hollywood as good as the one she is playing now." The word "playing" pleased neither her nor my uncle. In 1958 Grace appeared in an hour-long documentary praising Monaco and showing picturesque views of the principality. Princess Caroline played herself in a story of a six-year-old British orphan who took a kitten to the palace as a gift for her. Uncle Rainier appeared in the movie and turned up in a skin-diving sequence shot underwater.

In 1962 Alfred Hitchcock was determined to have Grace play a kleptomaniacal woman suffering from frigidity in his melodrama *Marnie*, co-starring Sean Connery. The part called for Grace to appear in scenes in which she committed robberies. Rumors that she intended to make another picture still further enflamed her critics in Monaco. By a very serious mistake, the palace issued a statement on March 19 that Grace had agreed to appear in this controversial movie during her summer vacation. The communiqué stated, "Prince Rainier will most likely be present during part of the film-making, depending on his schedule." The press immediately published the statement and suggested that Grace was "bored and fed up" with life as Princess of Monaco. There was speculation on how much she would be paid. Rainier was appalled that the statement issued by the palace not only jumped the gun but also failed to mention the couple's decision that if she did go ahead, her fee would be donated to the Monaco orphanage.

The criticism was harsh, and Grace was upset and hurt by the backlash of public opinion. Uncle Rainier was compelled to hold a press conference to give the real reason for the cancellation of her casting: public criticism. Luckily, no contract to appear in *Marnie* had actually been signed. Finally, Grace herself was forced to announce that she would not continue with her plans. This was apparently one of the unhappiest days of her life.

Grace showed none of these signs of sadness in front of us. Following her visit with Uncle Rainier to our home, we once again were invited to visit with our aunt and uncle at the palace.

SEVEN

Now that I was thirteen, I really had a clear series of visual impressions of the palace. We would drive through the main gate to the Court of Honor, where between eight and ten ancient horse-drawn carriages permanently stood. We entered past the carabiniers, whose changing of the guard took place twice a day to the sound of trumpets. We were admitted by a footman through the Door of Honor, which was framed by a classical porch formed by two pilasters and surmounted by the coat of arms showing my Grimaldi ancestors taking the palace.

The four wings of the palace served separate functions. Seen from the south, the east wing housed the offices of the dignitaries and chief officers, the archives, and the public apartments of the royal family and the secretary of state. The west wing contained Grace and Uncle Rainier's private apartments. The north wing contained the chapel and the library, and the south wing included two large galleries known as La Galerie des Armes and La Galerie d'Hercule.

We walked through the public and private rooms. The stairway of the Court of Honor was decorated by seventeenth-century frescoes representing the twelve labors of Hercules and his gruesome death. There were friezes of the triumph of Bacchus and the divinities of the sea. The royal public apartments featured gold-leaf furniture and the vast Salon des Glaces. In the Red Salon there were paintings by Jan Breughel, including "The Cabaret by the River" and a grand scene of a battle in antique times, portraits of Cardinal Mazarin, Louis I of Monaco, and Cardinal Jerome Grimaldi. The York Chamber had a ceiling painting of the four seasons, centering upon Fame bearing Monaco's arms. This room, in which heads of state or royal visitors were housed, was decorated in the style of Louis XIV, with tabletops of mosaic marble. The Yellow Salon was also filled with portraits and landscape paintings. The Louis XV Chamber was furnished with chairs covered in Pompadour pink, while the Blue Salon glittered with chandeliers, rich wallpaper, and gilded furniture. The private apartments consisted of two large drawing rooms and a museum of Napoleonic artifacts. There was a library with thousands of volumes, where Princess Grace often spent hours researching the family history, in which she took a deep interest. The marble floors, the frescoes, the gilded mirrors, the luxurious Louis XIV and Louis XV furnishings were magnificent. Yet at the same time there was a certain oppressiveness about them, making me understand why Grace wanted to render her own rooms less formal, heavy, and opulent. Sometimes I would gaze with curiosity at the faces of my ancestors, the ingenious Grimaldis.

In the more natural setting of the palace garden, where a pool had been installed, my stepfather, my mother, my sisters, and I would go for afternoon swims on our first visits to the palace after the reconciliation. The pool was surrounded by tropical plants. The vivid blue of the water, the iridescent blaze of flowers, and the pink palace looming behind all created a paradisiacal surrounding.

My sisters and I would swim about in the water, and even

Mother couldn't assume an air of formality when dressed in a bathing suit. As for Grace, she was very cautious of the sun; her milky white skin freckled and burned if she was exposed for more than a few minutes, and she had to sit most of the time with a large floppy hat on, in big sunglasses, under an umbrella, watching us all having fun. Sometimes she would come to the water and breaststroke up and down for a while; then she would return to her place again, put on the sunglasses and the hat. It was interesting to contrast her extreme whiteness, which was part of her classic beauty, in a setting in which everyone else was brown. Uncle Rainier had naturally dark skin and tanned fast. He was already showing a protruding stomach but swam well and enjoyed playing with my sisters and me in the water.

On Sundays we went to Mass in the palace chapel. During the three years of exile, we had gone to the little church in Beaulieu, France, across from the La Reserve Hotel. I always felt uncomfortable when collection time came. Rey, who parked his Rolls Royce close to the church and deposited hundred-franc notes in the collection box, seemed to me to be drawing too much attention to himself. I felt that under God's eyes everyone was equal, and I was embarrassed, knowing that the locals would resent his ostentation.

At the palace chapel, we also took Communion. The order of protocol was that Uncle Rainier, Grace, Caroline, and Albert would sit in the front row, and Mother and Rey, my sisters, and I in the second. Mother always looked strained and uncomfortable because Communion was not allowed to those who had divorced and remarried outside the Church, and therefore she and Rey were skipped during the ceremony. It was upsetting to Mother to see her children receive Communion when she could not.

Father Tucker was conspicuously absent from these occasions. I asked why, but was not given a response. This was typical. I could hardly have been told the truth at the time, however, or for several years to come. It is rumored that he was no longer present because he had been discovered sexually molesting a young boy. If this is true, one can imagine Uncle Rainier's horror at learning that the palace chaplain, who had engineered his marriage and had played a crucial role on behalf of Cardinal Spellman and the Vatican, and who had been at the center of every palace intrigue, should be guilty of child molestation. The effect of this on Grace, who for years had taken Communion from Father Tucker and had regarded him as her spiritual adviser, would have been even more devastating. She was more morally correct and upright than all of us. Not a touch of scandal ever stained her name.

At all events, Uncle Rainier, determined to avoid a public scandal, arranged for Father Tucker to leave the principality and retire to the United States, where he subsequently died. Perhaps the ignominy behind his fall from power was punishment enough. Anywhere else he would have been tried and sent to prison. Such was not the policy of our sovereign state, where the palace worked overtime to hush up all scandal.

Grace never ceased to take an interest in us. Her questions were always full of genuine concern. Whenever she met Nanny—which Mother made sure was very infrequently—she was clearly respectful and loving, since she knew Nanny had played such a crucial role in the Grimaldi history. Her marriage with Uncle Rainier was solid and affectionate, and they had a deep complicity and understanding. Nothing showed this better than their teamwork. He took care of business and government, and she took care of culture and welfare. Not only did Grace play an important role in the social life of Monaco, as its glamorous PR woman but she also keenly felt a responsibility for the welfare of the Monegasques. As Rainier did not trust most of the people around him, Grace was a friend as well as wife and consort. They both learned to bowl so that they could do it together. He would accompany her shopping. Sometimes Uncle Rainier would bring Grace to the Hôtel de Paris, where they would dine at a quiet table for two on the terrace and dance by themselves. Grace was a caring, loving wife with an ability to guess her husband's thoughts, a sensitivity to her new home, and a strong desire to preserve Monaco's heritage. She believed in her country's traditions and history, and fought to prevent Monaco from "becoming another Saint-Tropez." All through those years, I watched Grace with fascination. Her sweetness of character and her goodness could only seem miraculous in the palace context.

That summer, as a public show of reconciliation, she made sure that Mother was once again invited to the Red Cross Gala, from which she had been noticeably absent for the last several years. Surprisingly, the crowd of well-wishers who gathered to greet the arriving guests as they pulled up in their limousines—the first containing the royal couple, the second the as yet uncrowned King Juan of Spain and his wife, and the third Mother and Rey—reserved their most enthusiastic greeting not for Grace but for Mother. Still waging her own private war, Mother was ecstatic. She had succeeded in proving that she still had a powerful hold over the people. Her carefully orchestrated campaigns of securing popular support were continuing to pay off.

There were to be no reconciliations between Le Rosey and me. Following the summer of Grace's troubles with *Marnie*, I embarked upon my fifth year at the Swiss school in September 1962. I was now the number one school rebel, again and again denied Wednesday and Saturday afternoons off, again and again held for extra detention after school hours. Although part of me appreciated the school and its fair and reasonable disciplines, it was my true spirit to be opposed to authority in any form. Drawn naturally to mavericks, I was automatically to become the best friend of the most unlikely of new arrivals in this exclusive school, Flavien Kasavubu, son of the president of the then Belgian Congo. Kasa, as I called him, was the first and only black pupil at Le Rosey. Some of the American students were against having him in their midst. I was shocked by their attitude and by their demonstrations of it. There was a democracy at school based on achievements in sports and a refusal to betray one's friends. Kasa was an excellent right wing at soccer; I could not accept that because of his color he became the odd man out. I was the black sheep; he was the black new boy; we had much in common.

Kasa covered his sense of difference with funny, antic behavior. I liked him. He had a good voice, enjoyed the same kind of rock music I did, and sang currently popular songs like a pro. We played soccer together, and he took part in my explosive stunts. We put fireworks into the desks of new teachers and awaited the inevitable bangs. Neither Kasa nor I enjoyed our studies, and these mischievous, anarchistic acts that interrupted class represented a way of breaking up the monotony.

We were continually breaking the rules. Late one night, around 10:30, long after lights out, we met in my room. Kasa had given five Swiss francs to an assistant cook in order to rent his moped to go to Rolle on a Friday night. The drop to the driveway from my window was approximately ten feet. I knotted a sheet together, tied it to the window catch, and made my way down. Kasa simply jumped down to the ground with the agility of a cat. The moped was quickly picked up, and we took off down the road to Rolle.

We were reported by some older boys, who saw us in the local café. As a result we had our semiweekly leaves suspended. That didn't stop us. We took off by train to Lausanne and Geneva to play pinball machines in parlors and to go to café bars to listen to music and flirt with girls. We were playing at being big boys. We even managed to charm a barmaid in one place into letting us drink. Once again we were re-ported.

This latest expedition was more serious than simply going to Rolle. Trips to Geneva and the like were considered totally out of bounds and could result in expulsion. Moreover, taking alcoholic beverages was just as serious an offense.

The afternoon after this last adventure, I was playing soccer with Kasa and the other boys when the sportsmaster stopped the game and told Kasa and me that we were to see the head-master at once. Dressed in our football shorts, we waited ner-vously in the anteroom of his office. I was called in first. Johan-not screamed at me, but after my experiences with Rey and my mother, his fury had little effect. He reminded me that I had been misbehaving for a long time, and now he was hold-ing me responsible for negatively influencing a newcomer. I replied that I couldn't force Kasa to do anything that he didn't want to do.

Now Johannot asked Kasa to come in. Still furious, but more controlled, he told Kasa that he had disappointed him and that he had embarrassed his father, the president of the Congo. Kasa told the headmaster that he had gone only be-cause I had asked him to, and he said that on every occasion I had assured him that we had permission from Johannot to go. I couldn't believe my ears: if we had had permission, then what was I doing knotting a sheet to get out of a window or, on the Geneva expeditions, walking through the fields to get to the station so as not to be seen on the road? I told Johan-not that what Kasa said was absolutely untrue. Johannot slapped me across the face and told me to shut up, that he didn't want to hear anything more from me. He told me I had no respect for the rules and regulations, and forbade me any free afternoons for the rest of the term. He said that if there was any more trouble, he would expel me.

As Kasa and I left Johannot's office, I was very disappointed. Kasa's betrayal of me was a shock. I looked at him. His head was bent, and he was looking at the floor, very embarrassed. My anger changed to sorrow. As a child also raised in the full glare of public scrutiny, I understood only too well the pressure he was under not to disappoint. But it was a long time before I spoke to Kasa again.

I returned to Mereze and to the inevitable criticisms from Mother and Jean-Charles Rey. Now that I was growing older, I could take their behavior more in my stride. And anyway, it was Christmas 1962, a time when even my mother and stepfather would have to assume an air of seasonal good cheer.

Christmas Eve meant going without dinner in order to take Communion at midnight Mass. My mother instructed me to dress in a black tuxedo, and accompanied by my sisters, who were beautifully dressed, I was driven to the palace by my parents. The Mass was solemn and lasted about an hour.

We left the chapel and proceeded to the large salon that was situated over the Door of Honor, where we were to exchange gifts. Uncle Rainier and Aunt Grace stood by the enormous Christmas tree in the corner of the drawing room. The presents were heaped up in piles and wrapped with fancy ribbons.

We then proceeded to the dining room overlooking the public square. The big dining room table could seat thirty-six people. If there were more, Grace would have small tables seating eight. The palace's distinctive gold and white china dinner service was laid out at each place, along with the polished antique sterling silver collection. The white damask tablecloths with the family's coat of arms were hand-embroidered and made in the palace linen room. Each table was attended by footmen in full livery. Prepared by the palace chef, this late-night supper customarily consisted of dishes such as cold salmon, blinis, turkey, cheese, salad, and various desserts. Because I was a member of the royal family and was now at an age at which I was expected to take a part in official receptions, I was to entertain the dignitaries and their wives at my table. My sisters, Betsy and Christine, sat at neighboring tables, chattering away to their own quota of guests.

Fortunately Grace had separated me from Mother and Rey, who, to their chagrin, were seated at a table where they couldn't keep an eye on me. I had taken my first step to adulthood; I had Grace to thank for it and for this subtle, skillfully managed dividing up of the family.

It was well into the small hours when we retired to the drawing room. Coffee was served from magnificent silver pots. During supper, and more particularly in the sittting room afterward, I noticed not for the first time the medieval character of our court intrigue. The various dignitaries, some of whom would go to extraordinary lengths to secure invitations to the palace, would maneuver themselves to get close to Uncle Rainier or Grace, to tell them amusing stories, flatter them, and curry favor with them. I understood now that it really was a mixed blessing for Uncle Rainier to be the last absolute monarch in Europe. It was pathetic to watch one sycophant after another circle around him and Grace like bees seeking honey, trying to make themselves important, interesting, and pleasing enough in the hope that eventually the couple would bestow favors upon them. I thought: my uncle and aunt can never trust any of these people, can never be sure who their friends are. And indeed, they knew that many of them, while smiling and clasping Grace's hand, would be the first to snipe about her at home. It must also have been difficult for Grace, having grown up in America, to feel comfortable having people bow and curtsy to her with forced deference. It was sad to think that even at a Christmas party at the palace there were very few true friends there. For the most part the guests were consumed with self-interest, trying to secure their own futures for another twelve months.

On these and subsequent semiofficial occasions, I realized that professional and private success in Monaco was linked to the degree of approval one had at the palace. Much as I loved Grace, I had to admit that she also was capable of being used. For example, a lady friend of hers, often seen at court, saw her incompetent husband, a former Nazi officer, who had already caused two administrative fiascos, given an important position and even Monegasque citizenship. Those who succeeded in getting Uncle Rainier's ear could find that they were enhanced professionally and sometimes promoted to higher posts. Most people are susceptible to flattery, and Uncle Rainier was no exception. Indeed, it always seemed to me that if someone was not unabashedly sycophantic, he would be suspect of them, so used was he to the constant breathing of meaningless flattery.

Belonging as we did to the sovereign family, Mother, Rey, my sisters, and I had to stay behind in the drawing room of the palace until every last guest had left. For the first time I became aware of how rigidly we were bound by the rules of protocol.

Once again I was able to observe Uncle Rainier's humanness, with which I had so identified as a young boy. I recall one theatrical performance at the opera house that season during which the Prince of Monaco fell asleep and started snoring. To his immediate right sat the greatly offended wife of the playwright, Marcel Achard. On another occasion, while talking with the Queen of Spain at a dinner party, my uncle again fell asleep, and Her Majesty found herself talking to thin air.

During this period the crisis with France was beginning to wind down. After so much mudslinging on both sides, it finally became obvious to both de Gaulle and my uncle that it was futile to continue their struggle. What had seemed like a major crisis now looked more like a tempest in a teacup. An accord was reached in May. The ninety-page agreement provided that taxes on corporations with headquarters in Monaco would be increased to thirty-five percent if more than a quarter of their annual income came from outside Monaco. Frenchmen who had lived in Monaco for less than five years before 1963 would have to pay French taxes. For de Gaulle this was certainly a victory, although Uncle Rainier's publicity machine somehow contrived to make it seem a positive truce. A new minister of state was appointed. Jean Reymond took over from the controversial Emile Pelletier. And with the Constitution officially restored, parliamentary elections that gave women the right to vote in Monaco for the first time were held during my absence in the winter term of 1963. Jean-Charles Rey was one of the highest vote-getters among the candidates elected.

When I returned to Monaco for spring vacation, I was disappointed to learn that my uncle and aunt were traveling abroad. At the time, soccer became my main interest. I was very happy that as a special favor I was able to join the players of the Monaco professional soccer team, which was French First Division champion that year, in the Louis II Stadium, going through all their physical and technical training sessions with them. I even traveled with the team throughout France and as far as Lausanne, not far from Le Rosey. It was exciting for a fourteen-year-old. The captain, Michel Hidalgo, was fond of me and always strongly encouraged me. I would eat with the team before the matches and, dressed in the team's colors, would sit on the players' bench during the match. But Mother decided that when I went to football training, I had to wear a tie. I told her it was ridiculous, but she was insistent. On one occasion, when she drove me to the stadium, she saw I was tieless. She screamed at me, and, finally, after years of silently taking her abuse, I told her it was idiotic to expect anyone to wear a tie to go to practice. She muttered to herself over and over again, "He's got too much of the bad blood. Too much of his father's blood." This was the first time she had made any reference at all to Daddy since the day he left.

I returned to Le Rosey. The French soccer final would soon take place in Paris, and to my great joy, the Monaco team was to play against the Lyons team. I got permission from Mother to travel to Paris, provided Monsieur Johannot agreed. With my dubious academic and conduct record, I was reluctant to approach him, but I forced myself, and to my surprise he said that he understood the importance of the event to me. He agreed to make the necessary travel arrangements for me and to give me the money for the trip. I should come again to his office that Friday.

I couldn't sleep or concentrate on anything for the next few days. I spent every cent I had to purchase fireworks and a red and white banner to celebrate when I went to the match. At last Friday came around. But when I went to Johannot's office at the appointed time, he was out. The secretary told me that he was not at school that day, but that he had left a message forbidding me to go to Paris because my grades for the week were among the lowest in the school. I exclaimed that this had been so for the past five years and asked, why was it being used against me now? I was mad. I slammed out of the office and without wasting any time, I borrowed money for the flight from some of the rich American kids at school. Then I walked all the way to Rolle and bought a ticket for the train to Geneva, where I would make my way to the airport.

I sat in the carriage, barely able to wait for the train to start. Suddenly a huge hand slapped down on my shoulder. I swung around. It was Johannot. He asked me with slowly worded sarcasm whether he could contribute further to my trip. I was dragged back to Le Rosey, where I contrived to watch the match on TV. It was a draw. The match would be replayed the following Saturday.

I had nothing to lose—the previous term I had become the first boy in Rosey history to be caned, in public, after I had a run-in with an instructor—so I asked Johannot to let me go to the next game. His response was to have the Italian teacher, Signor Mastrelli, act that Friday as a round-the-clock guardian. He was never to let me out of his sight. That afternoon I went running around the football field circular track. It was bordered by a few trees. Mastrelli was reading a paper on a bench. When his attention was focused on some article, I seized the occasion to dart off into the trees. I climbed up one of them and sat on a branch. I watched with pleasure while the Italian teacher, noticing my absence, turned pale, began searching for me everywhere, and ran back to the school to inform Johannot, whom I saw jump into his car and drive off in the general direction of Rolle. I stayed in the tree for five hours while he searched for me and questioned the students as to my whereabouts. Then, at seven o'clock, I walked in during the middle of dinner. There was a ripple of astonishment. Johannot sent me to my room at once.

Next day he called me to his office and told me that at the end of the term I would be expelled. With the assistance of a friend, I embarked on my last anarchistic venture. I placed explosives in the different bathtubs that were located in cubicles in the communal bathroom. They blew up one by one, shattering the glass skylights. I literally went out of Le Rosey with a bang!

EIGHT

I N THE WAKE of my dismissal from Le Rosey, I had to face my parents. My mother decided to forget all about my having a Continental European schooling, thus making it impossible for me ever to obtain, in the unlikely event I ever reached the necessary standards, the *baccalauréat*. Without the "bac," the equivalent of the college boards in the United States, it would be virtually impossible for me to obtain a good job in France. Her decision was a mistake. The British education she had in mind for me would count for little across the Channel.

As usual, Mother created the grimmest picture of my future. She warned me that my reception at the palace would be cold. Grace and Rainier, she said, were angry with me over the expulsion, particularly Uncle Rainier, who had been a star pupil at Le Rosey. I realized that she was starting to use Uncle Rainier as a threat: that somehow he would be a menacing presence in my upcoming late adolescence. I was therefore all the more surprised when, upon our next family visit to the palace that summer of 1963, not a single thing that my mother predicted in fact took place.

To the contrary, Uncle Rainier could not have been nicer

to me. The first pool lunch with my uncle and aunt that season was as pleasant as always. I had expected Uncle Rainier to give me a stern lecture about my responsibilities as a member of the family, or even a loud bawling out for the embarrassment I had caused him regarding his alma mater, but he made no reference to my expulsion until he said casually that he was glad to hear I was going to be sent to a British public school; that it would be better for me there than at Le Rosey. I couldn't help but wonder whether his attitude was due to a desire to avoid a direct confrontation or to an authentic sense of decency that would prevent him from making things worse.

By contrast, Grace didn't hesitate to deal directly with my expulsion. I had always been struck by her capacity to grasp every situation in the family completely. She had a far keener insight about family affairs than Uncle Rainier.

We finished lunch in the garden; Grace, as usual, sat under her big sun umbrella. After we drank our coffee, she asked me to walk with her in the garden. Wearing her big floppy hat, her eyes shielded behind sunglasses, she said to me, "Buddy, I understand what happened perfectly." I listened while she told me that my behavior at Le Rosey was an understandable reaction to excessive discipline at home; that I was reacting against the years of sermons from my mother. She pointed out to me that my mother, whom she never spoke of with less than understanding, lived her life in anticipation of disaster. No doubt this was due to her childhood. Grace pointed out that if a boy is constantly warned of the consequences of any future malfeasance, and if he is always expected to behave badly, it is only natural that he will fulfill the worst that is expected of him. I had been brought up on the assumption I would break all the rules, and so as soon as I got the opportunity to do so, I did.

I looked up at Grace with surprise as we walked together. It seemed to me incredible that without a shadow of criticism of my mother, she had summed up my whole life. That brief conversation under the palace walls had more effect on me than fourteen years of endless instructions and dire prophecies. Nor did she finish there. She reassured me that, although the expulsion was serious, it wouldn't necessarily ruin my life. "Remember," she said, "you're hurting yourself more than the figures of authority you're rebelling against."

We returned to the table. I had always loved and admired Grace; now I appreciated her more than ever.

From then on I couldn't resist twinges of jealousy during those summer visits, as I observed Grace with her two children, quiet, fair-haired Albert, six, and brunette Caroline, seven, who looked like her father, while Albert resembled his mother. Both were attractive children, and they exuded the air of happiness that comes from being well-loved.

That summer I spent much more time with them and came to know them as a family. I noticed Grace raised her children with discipline, sensing that, despite their complaints, they basically longed for her authority. A child, she felt, needed a sense of direction. She was always tempted to spoil her children and was easily in the position to do so but stopped just short of that. She raised them bilingually, never emphasizing one language over the other. Uncle Rainier talked to Albert and Caroline in French. Grace spoke to them in English.

Caroline was high-spirited, imaginative, uninhibited, and unpredictable, and had a stronger personality than her brother. Albert was quieter and more subtle. He was also much more shy of people. The relationship between Caroline and Albert was very close, though for some time she used to bite him and only stopped when Grace bit her to show her what it felt like. They were looked after by their English nanny, Maureen King, who had worked for the playwright Jean Anouilh. Maureen was outgoing, open-hearted, and affectionate toward the children. But in no case was there a question of her usurping Grace's role, as Nanny Wanstall had replaced Mamou as the center of Rainier's life. Rainier and Grace often had funny exchanges with their children. At a party on National Feast Day, Albert was dressed as a carabinier. He walked proudly through the crowd in his uniform. When Grace reprimanded him for a small mistake, he replied, "Carabiniers do not come under your control, Mummy!" On another occasion Caroline said to Grace, "Mummy, there are many gods in heaven!" Grace replied there was only one. Caroline responded, "There have to be many gods, because there are so many churches!" Grace could only laugh and reassure her of the singularity of the Deity.

The children were amazingly self-assured when their photographs were being taken. They loved television and the books of Babar the Elephant. Except for official family portraits, Grace liked the children to be dressed unpretentiously: Albert in sweater and blue jeans, Caroline in simple dresses. Caroline was already coquettish, looking at herself in mirrors, constantly changing her clothes, fussing with her hair. Albert was serious and introspective. Caroline had a consuming curiosity about everyone and everything, an amazing memory, and a healthy appetite. Both children were very good sailors. Albert and I loved to watch soccer matches at the Louis II Stadium from the palace garden terrace that overlooked it. We would kick a ball round the garden together. Caroline liked dolls; her favorite was called "Poor Pitiful Pearl." Albert was keen on his collection of Dinky Toys: small toy cars.

The affection between parents and children was moving to see. Rainier wanted his children to have the secure, happy childhood he had never had. As he had during his visits with my sisters and me years before, Uncle Rainier behaved like a large child himself, chasing Albert, who was dressed in a feathered headdress, pelts, and moccasins, while Uncle Rainier was dressed as a sheriff in fast pursuit. Uncle Rainier had an elaborate electric train set that filled almost an entire room. He was fascinated with it, playing with it more than Albert. My sisters and I would watch him as he started the train and sent it along the tracks, through green papier-mâché mountains, around bends, through long tunnels, busily switching points as it moved from one track to the other. At the same time our uncle was busy propelling his toy train on its journey, he was with equal determination building a whole new underground route for the express trains that passed from Paris through Nice to Italy. Ignoring advice to the contrary, he had a tunnel put through a mountain of the Maritime Alps, providing a more direct route but at the same time keeping our principality in an uproar as explosions rang out by day and by night. In view of his love of his toy train, it didn't surprise me that this real-life railroad was my uncle's obsession.

Although most of the palace was kept immaculate by the hundred or more servants, my uncle and aunt's personal library was messy and disordered. When I walked in there, I would see piles of old newspapers, cuttings of articles relating to the royal couple, toys of Caroline and Albert, dolls, photographs of the children, and half-opened books scattered across the floor and tables. Grace's favorite pet, Oliver, had died, savaged by another dog at Schonreid, Switzerland, where they spent time in winter. She had acquired a number of other dogs, who bounded about the library, often upsetting small tables and spilling everything to the floor. But the new dogs never took the place of Oliver for Grace.

I would watch as Grace sat at her desk, busily typing with two fingers on a portable machine before passing the correspondence on to her private secretarial pool. She would also spend hours painting landscapes and flowers. She signed the paintings GDeM. Many of the paintings went unfinished. It seemed she would tire of them individually, make a final brush stroke, and then turn to another. The unfinished paintings were placed in the palace storerooms. Many of the finished ones were given away as gifts or auctioned for charity.

The rest of the private apartments were kept up considerably better than the library. In the royal bedroom, with its double bed, he on the right and she on the left, the bedside table was a clutter of newspapers, books, papers, and bottles of medication. When Rainier and Grace woke up in the morning, the children would come bursting in even before their nanny was ready to bring them. They would all have breakfast together at exactly 8:30 every morning, Grace always enjoying her grilled grapefruit and tea. She herself would make the toast, fix Uncle Rainier's café au lait, and boil an egg for each of them. The couple was determined to give the children as normal a family life as possible. At night there was usually a family get-together: my uncle would play with the children and Grace would read them to sleep with fairy tales by Hans Christian Andersen or Lewis Carroll. Whenever I visited with my cousins, I was impressed by the quality of time Rainier and Grace made for the children, despite their heavy schedules of public responsibilities and obligations and the innumerable personal appearances they were required to make. We all enjoyed going to Uncle Rainier's zoo, his private menagerie at the foot of the steps leading down from the private quarters. While we were at dinner, we would hear the growlings of a lemur from a cage in the corner of the dining room, and the days were filled with the squawkings of Coco the parrot, who could perform on request the Monaco national anthem and "Colonel Bogey" from *The Bridge on the River Kwai*. The one animal Grace did not like was Uncle Rainier's chimp, Tenagra, who had a habit of throwing excrement at distinguished guests at unexpected moments.

It was clear to me that Uncle Rainier and Mother had reacted differently to their unhappy childhoods. The episode in which she had fled from Pierre de Polignac's Paris house and had taken shelter with Louis II had marked her. Uncle Rainier's response had been to give his daughter and son all the love possible. One might think that Mummy would have reacted the same way, but she didn't. Grace's instinct sprang from her own typically Irish-American upbringing, in a family that believed in sharing in every way.

During that summer of 1963 my sisters and I first discovered Roc Agel, on Mont Agel in the Maritime Alps, as high up as you could get by road and directly under the huge antenna of Radio Monte Carlo. We would drive up to the farmhouse on weekends, with Uncle Rainier at the wheel and Grace seated beside him. The road would wind up and up around dangerous slopes.

Roc Agel was a haven for all of us. The Provençal-style farmhouse, with its sprawling living room, decorated by Grace with brightly patterned chintzes, its American kitchen and big swimming pool, was for my uncle and aunt much more enjoyable than the palace. Grace especially loved the flower garden, tending the flowers and cross-breeding them with dedication. She would feed the chickens in the coop and, with my uncle, grow vegetables, fertilizing the earth with cow manure from their own cows. Rainier would sell the cows' milk to our citizens in Monaco. Uncle Rainier enjoyed riding his tractor or making metal sculptures with a blowtorch in his workshop. The gates of Roc Agel were manned with guards, and no *paparazzi* ever got in.

Grace was fond of my sisters, now in their teens. She was concerned that they were cooped up at Mereze with private governesses and not allowed to attend a girls' school. Inviting them up to Roc Agel was her effort to expand their horizons and to give them at least for a while a taste of family life. Christine was especially happy at Roc Agel; Betsy was more under my mother's influence, more quiet and repressed, and was less given to spontaneity.

Late in the summer, as had become our tradition, we returned to Mamou at the castle. The pilgrimage to Marchais was, as before, a mixture of pleasure and discomfort. One day Mamou was under her hairdryer in her bedroom. Mother was there talking to her about nothing in particular. The notorious terriers were as usual running around the carpet, barking away. I was playing with one of them; as a result, the other dogs set up a terrific din, barking at the one I was having fun with. Mamou asked me not to play with the dog. I obeyed, but he continued barking, wanting me to go on. Mother began screaming at me, not pausing long enough to realize that I was not the cause of the dog's excitement, and after a few minutes I left the room. Her shrieks of anger followed me as she demanded I return and apologize. "How dare you leave the room!" she yelled. I made up my mind to leave not only the room, but the castle and her forever. I threw on a black leather jacket, persuaded Christine to give me her pocket money savings, took my passport from my mother's handbag in her bedroom, picked up my bicycle, rode to the village nearby, and took a train to Paris and then Monaco. My intention was to get to Monte Carlo Beach, where I knew I could find my half-brother, Lionel Noghes, Daddy's son from his first marriage, whom we had been forbidden to see all these years. He spent almost all of his time there in summer, pursuing girls and swimming. I would ask Lionel to lend me the money for the air fare to America, where I would turn up in Phoenix, to join my father at the Camelback Inn.

The train stopped at Nice. As I looked out of the window, I saw a man named Gaston Biamonti, a friend and business associate of Jean-Charles Rey's, walking down the platform looking into the carriages. My heart sank. Before I could hide, he caught me. I knew Rey must have sent him on Mother's orders. He told me he was under instructions to fly me back to Paris, from where I would be driven to Marchais.

I had had it. All my plans had blown away. When I arrived at the castle, everyone was gathered in the kitchen. Mamou was crying, still suffering from concern over me. Mother was a block of ice. No one took a step toward me. Mother shouted, "When are you going to apologize to Mamou and me?" Mamou was furious. She snapped back, "If there are any apologies in this house, they are due from the person who caused the boy to take such a drastic step!" That one remark made my entire excursion worthwhile. Mother was shocked, but dared not cross Mamou.

Mamou told me, as we walked out of the kitchen together, that she hoped my running away was not caused by any unhappiness with being at the castle. I reassured her that the only reason I had left was Mother. Mamou told me of the melodrama that followed my departure: Mother's critiques of my running away, Mamou's own deep concern when I wasn't present at breakfast or lunch, the search of the park, and the discovery of my bicycle at the station. I discovered from Mamou that Mother's real terror was that I had run off to see Grace and Rainier, that I would tell too much about the conflicts on our side of the family. During the rest of our stay that summer, Mother constantly begged Mamou not to let Rainier and Grace know that I had run away, or why I had done so. I noticed that in the future, our visits to Marchais grew shorter and shorter.

In September 1963 I went to Downside, a British public school, which was the only educational institution for my age group in Britain that would accept me. Mother wrote to virtually every school in England, starting with Eton and Harrow, but based upon the devastating reports on my behavior from Le Rosey, they all refused to take me.

I flew to London and took a train to the Somerset town of Bath. I had been to England before, staying mostly at Rugby, where Nanny had a house; this was the first time I had been to the West Country.

Downside was about thirty miles outside Bath, in open country with rolling hills and forests. It was a monastery run by Benedictine monks of sober demeanor wearing dark brown cassocks and habits. I was met at the station and driven to the school. The discipline was much more severe than at Le Rosey. Forty of us slept in a dormitory; a bell woke us at 7:00 A.M., summoning us to Mass. We would shower, put on our school uniforms—a white shirt with stiff collar and tie, blazer, and trousers—and go into the chapel for daily Mass. Breakfast was typically English, consisting of porridge or cereal, eggs and bacon or sausages, toast and tea. There were periods of study, gymnastics, and sports. We had to make our own beds, change our own linen, make sure our laundry was done, and be clean at all times. We were never allowed to walk with our hands in our pockets, smoke (as the senior boys at Le Rosey were allowed to do), or wear our blazers unbuttoned. We were forbidden radios and record players. Caning was the standard form of punishment. Compared to Le Rosey, this was a stern and harsh place. Yet surprisingly, I wasn't unhappy at Downside. In fact, I settled down and behaved myself. In the course of my three-year stay there, I was caned only twice. I did well on the house soccer team as inside forward, and on the cross-country team, one term finishing third out of three hundred pupils. Later I became trainer of the house boxing team.

Sports dominated British schools, and I was in my element. Moreover, Grace's words to me in the garden of the palace had influenced me. By making me understand the cause of my rebelliousness, she had temporarily exorcised the demons in me. Once I understood the reason I was so rebellious, I no longer felt a compulsion to be anarchic. And I think there was something about the rigidity of a British education that tamed me. At Le Rosey every pupil was rich and privileged, and teachers were not given much respect. They found it hard to control young boys who were accustomed to servants of their own, unlimited pocket money, and futures of wealth and power. At Downside I was one of the few foreigners. I was anxious to blend in with the other boys, to be part of the community and not be an odd man out.

I was back in Monaco in January for my fifteenth birthday. Uncle Rainier and Grace had invited me to the palace a few days earlier. Grace had asked me what would be my birthday wish. I replied, "Aunt Grace, I would like to wake up and find that this wasn't my fifteenth birthday but my eighteenth, and I could have a car and take off in it to lead my own life." Grace replied, "I find that sad, Buddy. It seems so unhappy to think that you would want your childhood to fly away." She added, "Most of us look back on our earliest years as the best of our lives." I replied that I could only hope that the future would be better than the past. At that moment, I think Grace fully realized how unhappy most of my previous years had been.

I asked Mother that same evening whether she would, when I was eighteen, buy me a car. She replied that she would buy me a very good car eventually, but only when I got a job. It was obvious to me that that could be a very long way off, so if I wanted an automobile, I would have to start saving for it right away.

Mother gave me a small allowance. Fortunately, unlike Le Rosey, Downside offered few opportunities to spend money because we were never permitted to leave the school grounds. I was therefore able to put away all of the cash that I received while I was there. During my vacations I was careful not to spend more than I had to. I filled my days playing football and stayed at home as much as I could stand to. I supplemented my savings by selling my Christmas and birthday presents to some of the boys at school. Each year I also added to the fund

Mamou's five-hundred-franc birthday gift, equivalent to about one hundred dollars.

When the school term ended and I returned home for the summer holidays, I became aware that trouble was brewing once more in our restless principality. This time Aristotle Onassis was at the center of intrigue. Although on the surface still friendly with Rainier, Onassis was now competing with my uncle in a protracted struggle for control of the state's tourist infrastructure. As early as 1953 Onassis owned about a third of the issued capital of the SBM, the Société des Bains de Mer, which owned the Casino, the Hôtel de Paris in Monte Carlo, the Sporting Club, and most of Monaco's other tourist attractions. Onassis still used the old Sporting Club as his headquarters, running his company Olympic Maritime from there and continuing to live aboard his yacht the *Christina*. Although there were repeated conflicts between Uncle Rainier and the tycoon, my uncle and aunt continued to socialize with Onassis until 1964, when the arguments between the two powerful men grew more acrimonious.

In the preceding years they had fought over Uncle Rainier's favorite railroad project, the way nightclubs were operated, the building of new apartment complexes, the additions made by Onassis to the Hôtel de Paris, land reclamation, and all of the problems that cropped up every day in running the principality. Uncle Rainier complained that Onassis was derelict in building new tourist facilities; Onassis complained that Rainier opposed the extension of his urbanization plans. For a while Onassis appeased my uncle by building the Sea Club. He also built a cabaret, an indoor swimming pool, a bowling alley, and a discotheque. He poured millions into the Summer Sporting Club. But Uncle Rainier was never completely happy with Onassis's various projects, finding fault with many of the details.

Uncle Rainier was of two minds about Onassis's presence in Monaco. On the one hand, he was pleased that Onassis's business interests gave the tycoon the incentive to carry out so many of his plans of improvement; on the other, he was irritated by Onassis's increasing power and influence in the principality. There is no evidence that Onassis ever wished to diminish my uncle's prestige and importance. But Uncle Rainier was never one to share the limelight in his country; nor did he like hearing opinions that contradicted his own. Indeed, at the time, some people referred to Monte Carlo as Monte Greco and to Onassis as "the other prince." This led to considerable friction. Further tension arose because Uncle Rainier retained veto power over the management of the SBM. In other words, he could at any moment rescind plans upon which Onassis had embarked at considerable expense. At the very moment that Onassis was pouring capital into construction and development, Rainier was discussing the possibility of nationalizing the SBM. Uncle Rainier didn't trust Onassis any more than Onassis respected Uncle Rainier's administrative ability and executive wisdom. Rainier complained that Onassis was concerned only with making money and not with the interests of the sovereign state itself; and Uncle Rainier worried whether Onassis represented an actual threat to his royal authority.

Yet another conflict arose in 1963 over the all-important question of gambling in Monte Carlo. Onassis had a surprisingly puritan attitude toward it. In one argument, my uncle remarked, "I do not think you are in a position to tell me whether gambling is moral or immoral." During this period Uncle Rainier was determined to democratize tourism in Monte Carlo, pull down old buildings, bring in package tours from overseas, construct inexpensive hotels, and build a convention center. Onassis wanted Monaco to remain an exclusive enclave for the rich, and whatever alterations he made, such as a rooftop restaurant at the Hôtel de Paris, were designed to appeal to them. But it would be two years before the final eruption took place. In the meantime the two declared an uneasy truce.

On a more personal level, there was new trouble at Mereze. Just before we left for our annual visit to Marchais that summer of 1964, my half-brother, Lionel, brought my sisters and me exciting news. He told us that our beloved father was coming to be with us once again. Nanny also knew this fantastic information, which had to be kept secret. Father had written to her at her home in Monaco in order to evade Mother's censorship and had told her in the letter that he was on his way.

We were all careful not to disclose even a clue of his arrival. We remembered too well the unhappy circumstances in which he had been compelled to leave eleven years before. We wondered what our uncle's reaction to his reappearance would be but were mollified by the thought that now that we were all welcome at the palace, Uncle Rainier would not wish to hurt us by interfering in any way with our father's return. On top of that, we learned that Uncle Rainier had conveyed through third parties to my father that he welcomed his return and would not in any way obstruct him or the resumption of his law practice.

Throughout our stay at Marchais, Betsy, Christine, and I kept our secret like a treasure. We couldn't imagine what effect the news would have on Mother. But we were soon to find out.

We were returning from Marchais by sleeper. Our car was on the train. When we arrived at Fréjus, on the Riviera, where we were to leave the train and drive the rest of the way, Mother turned up in our compartment and told us with a look of severity and barely repressed fury that she had an important announcement to make. She told us that she had found out something disagreeable. Our father was on his way to Monaco. She said that on pain of instant punishment we were not to be seen with him anywhere in public, that any arrangements for seeing him in private would be strictly laid down, and that until they had been made, we were to have no contact with him whatsoever. We all burst out laughing in her face. She was taken aback, asking us what was the matter with us. We told her in unison that we had known about this for several weeks and were overjoyed about it. She demanded to know how we knew. We didn't answer. She was beside herself. Now that we were a little older, we were much less intimidated by her gloom-laden prophecies.

Once we were back at Mereze, I told Mother I needed a haircut. I used that excuse to make a getaway. As soon as I reached the barbershop, I picked up a telephone and called the apartment of my Aunt Thylda, Father's sister Bathylde, with whom Lionel had told me Father was staying. Daddy came to the barbershop instantly. It was one of the happiest moments of my life.

The years that had passed hadn't changed him. He was exactly as I remembered him: handsome, robust, outgoing, exuding kindness and warmth. I walked with him to Aunt Thylda's flat, where we sank into chairs and spent hours in excited communion, exchanging news. It was just as well that we had this interlude, because once I was back at Mereze, Mother made it clear that the "special arrangements" she had in mind for my visits with Father were as formal as she could make them.

She began with a calculated invitation to Father and his third wife, Margot, a warm and attractive American, whom he had met in Arizona, to dinner at Mereze. After all my mother had done to hurt my father, this was certainly not to be the occasion for a happy family reunion. Especially when Father found himself sitting down to a table laid with silverware and china, which Mother and he had once shared. Conversation was awkward and restricted to trivialities. Mother's plan was to presumably make the occasion as stiff and unnerving as possible, in order to remove the spontaneous excitement that we children would normally express on such an occasion. She had no idea that her anarchistic son had already made contact with his father. Indeed, throughout that whole uncomfortable evening, with everyone trying too hard to be polite to everyone else, I caught my sisters' eyes in silent complicity, all of us trying not to give the game away. We succeeded.

At the end of the dinner, I happened to be passing through a room when I overheard Mother calling Aunt Grace at the palace. Mother was bragging that everything had gone magnificently, that she had succeeded in her purpose, and that her children were not especially thrilled by Father's reappearance. She boasted that she had so completely achieved this that now my sisters and I seemed quite cool about the visit. I knew that Grace would not respond to her announcement with the congratulation my mother hoped for. Through the palace grapevine she and Uncle Rainier had made it quite clear that they welcomed Father's return and wanted him to act as a guide to his growing son and daughters. That Mother, on the other hand, would wish to deprive a man, separated for more than a decade from his children, of all the pleasure that his reunion with them would provoke struck me as incredibly insensitive.

Her conditions of visitation were as rigid as we had feared. We were allowed to see Daddy only a very limited number of times a week and were never to be observed with him in restaurants frequented by the Monegasques. We had to have dinner in little places in the mountain regions. Always considerate of us, and realizing the strain it would put on us all if he had an outright quarrel with Mother, Father did his best to put up with these restraints. But they became even more extreme as time went on. We were to meet him at precisely seven o'clock, no sooner and no later. After a while we rebelled against these conditions, and at last they were relaxed somewhat. Had Mother not done so, I would have left to live with him, which would have caused her great embarrassment in Monaco. By the following year, 1965, we were allowed to see more of him. The greatest pleasures of all, our drives together when I was a small child, were miraculously restored. Now Father let me take the driving wheel, and we would speed around the Upper Corniche. I was in heaven. I would take off with him in his Chris Craft speedboat, water-skiing day after day, free for a few hours from the oppressiveness of home. Margot, of whom I grew very fond, often joined us in our outings. There were happy visits at father's new apartment on the Avenue Princess Alice, named for Grace's American predecessor.

Father had given up much to come back to us. Believing Uncle Rainier's reported assurances that he could reopen his law offices and recommence his business associations, including an interest in a bank, he had sold two flourishing art galleries in Arizona and surrendered his job as tennis pro. But Daddy was to be stung again.

NINE

HE SUMMER of 1964 ended all too quickly, and once again, as fall approached, I returned to my studies at Downside. The highlight of the term was news of the birth of Grace's third child, Stephanie Marie Elisabeth, born on February 1, 1965. Her birth, following two miscarriages, was a great joy to Grace and Uncle Rainier; like Caroline, she had her father's dark brown hair.

The birth of Stephanie was only a brief interruption in Grace's increasingly busy life in Monaco. There was a gala fancy-dress party at the Hôtel de Paris for the opening of its indoor pool, with Grace dressed in a rubber mask, straw hat, and flippers, and Uncle Rainier sporting a piratical mustache. Everybody, including my uncle and aunt, wound up in the pool, and the party continued until dawn. Grace, in fact, loved to stay up all night and see the daylight in. When Uncle Rainier and Grace flew to Majorca for the opening of a new hotel, Grace conducted the hotel band during the festivities and Uncle Rainier played the drums. On another occasion the following year, Grace was joint guest of honor with Jacqueline Kennedy at the Spring Fair in Seville, Spain, where Grace opened the fair in a magnificent Andalusian dress. After a week of constant partying, there was the Debutantes' Ball, hostessed by the Duchess of Medinaceli at her lavish mansion filled with antiques and classical statues. The event was somewhat marred when Grace's bodyguard, a squadron of helmeted soldiers, attacked the *paparazzi*. It was claimed that Jackie Kennedy was notably cool toward Grace and blamed her for arriving late at the party.

The year 1966 was nonetheless ablaze with one spectacular event after another. It was the centenary of Monte Carlo, a public display of gala events celebrating one hundred years since the foundation of the Casino. Party followed after party, each more opulent than the one preceding it. Uncle Rainier seized the occasion of the anniversary to outmaneuver Onassis, constantly giving interviews to the press criticizing the Greek's many alleged malfeasances in the principality. He made up his mind to dislodge Onassis from the SBM once and for all by in effect nationalizing it: he forced the SBM to augment its capital, creating six hundred thousand additional shares out of thin air, all of which would be held by the government. In June Uncle Rainier asked the National Council to pass a bill for the creation of the new shares; Onassis fought this in the Supreme Court and even found some support from dissident members of the Council. The battle continued, but it was clear by the late summer that Onassis was on the way out of Monaco.

Meantime, Grace never ceased in her dedication to social galas. She and Cecil Beaton jointly designed Monte Carlo's red and white centenary poster, which became internationally famous. Celebrities of the musical and theatrical worlds poured in for benefit performances, including the divas Joan Sutherland and Birgit Nilsson, the ballerina Zizi Jeanmaire, the pianist Van Cliburn, and the French actor Jean-Louis Barrault and his wife Madeleine Renaud. Nureyev and Margot

Fonteyn performed *Romeo and Juliet* in the palace courtyard. Grace completely redid the historic Hôtel Hermitage, making it one of the most beautiful establishments in the south of France.

I was invited to attend the biggest social event of all, the International Red Cross Gala, in the first week of August. Of all the charity events in Monaco, the Red Cross was the most important in the eyes of the rich and famous of Europe. Uncle Rainier himself had founded the Monegasque Red Cross; as president, Grace was required to provide the ultimate glamour of her presence as well as use her personal charisma to raise financial support. By 1966 she had made the event the most sought-after in all of Europe. That year she herself supervised the details, attending long meetings, holding interminable telephone conversations with society figures all over the world, helping with travel arrangements, and guaranteeing the presence of Sammy Davis, Jr., Frank Sinatra, Cary Grant, David Niven, and all of her other friends for the occasion.

The 1966 gala was one of the most glamorous ever, since it contained within it a double celebration: the centenary and the imminent defeat of Onassis. The rich and famous poured into the Hôtel de Paris and the Hermitage. From Nice notables motored along the Corniches in their Rollses, Mercedeses, and Daimlers. The hotel safes were crammed with emeralds, diamonds, and rubies, and the Sporting Club was filled with servants dressed in livery. Reservations had been made months before; hotel rooms were at a premium; vintage champagne was served day and night. Nobody thought of sleep.

That night, Jean-Charles Rey drove my mother, my sisters, and me to the palace in his Rolls. The royal party, consisting of Uncle Rainier's family and special guests, waited in a small private salon until the master of protocol, Colonel Ardent, told us it was time to proceed. According to form we would enter last. Most of the guests were jostling with each other to be the last to enter. The later anyone entered, the more noticeable they would be.

At last Colonel Ardent announced our entrance. Grace and Uncle Rainier came in first, followed by my mother. Protocol required that I and my sisters, as members of the family by birth, should walk in front of Rey. Status usually meant nothing to me, but I admit that I did enjoy the precedence I took in this case, seeing how much it upset Rey. At the last minute, just before we reached our table, he still managed to nudge his way in front of me.

The Summer Sporting Club was so constructed that all guests had to walk across the stage on which the gala performance would take place. This had something of the effect of a cattle show: all eyes were upon the person entering, examining his or her clothes and jewels; it was quite unnerving to be in the glare of the spotlight. As we took our seats, the caviar was served. The orchestra conductor invited everybody to dance. Once again protocol called for Uncle Rainier to open the ball with Grace. He disliked dancing, but naturally the royal image had to be sustained for the world's press. Tonight, however, something totally unexpected and embarrassing took place. No sooner had the conductor, Aime Barelli, struck up the band than Rey jumped to his feet and with a great show, making sure everybody was looking at him (they were), took Grace by the hand, and led her onto the dance floor to open the ball officially. This was unheard of. Of course Uncle Rainier was totally unprepared for that, and his face was a picture of barely concealed fury. If Grace had refused Rey, it would have been a public scandal. So she was compelled to see it through. Her face was masklike, frozen and detached. Colonel Ardent was clearly on the verge of a heart attack.

I looked at Mother. Given her background and understanding of protocol, I could see that she was dismayed and humiliated by her husband's impromptu gesture. This was a perfect example of how completely Rey had used her to further his position, and was a blatant expression of this purpose and of his colossal ego. He was triumphant. He nodded, grimaced, and smiled at the great crowd of local and international celebrities as much as to say, "Here I am, the most important citizen in Monaco, and I can get away with absolutely anything." The disappointment on the faces of the jet-setting crowd was all too obvious. Instead of seeing the world's last absolute monarch dancing with his famous consort, they had to settle for the sight of Grace being taken rather cumbersomely around the floor by her nobody of a brother-in-law. For me, however, the evening did have one special benefit.

Some weeks earlier I had embarked on a mission with my sisters to see Uncle Rainier and Grace. I phoned my uncle directly at the palace, the first time I had ever done that. I told him it was very important that I see him and asked him pointedly to make sure that only he and Grace were present. I meant that I did not want my mother and stepfather to be there. The call seemed to make Uncle Rainier nervous, but he did accede to my request. He said, "I'll see to it," and then, abruptly, hung up. It was typical of him that he didn't arrange the meeting himself but asked Grace to fix it, which she did with a considerable ingenuity that would have done justice to several generations of Grimaldis.

She must have spent several days thinking the whole thing through: how could she possibly make sure that my sisters and I were received without the omnipresent Rey and Mother? A week elapsed. At last she telephoned my mother late one afternoon. She had discovered, I learned later, that my parents had accepted an invitation to a dinner party that evening, an invitation they could not decline at short notice. Knowing they could not accept her own invitation, she phoned them up inviting our whole family to supper and the screening of a new movie. She carried the whole thing off very cleverly. Mother was disappointed to have to decline the invitation. She couldn't forbid my sisters and me to go to the palace, however, since we were not included in her official engagement. She and Rey dropped us off at the palace on their way to dinner, and we went directly to the converted garage that Uncle Rainier had set up as a private screening room.

We were warmly welcomed, and Grace hugged us. No doubt both she and my uncle were wondering what we were up to. Christine and I were very excited to see our uncle and aunt. It was the first time we were to be completely alone with them. But Betsy, who was more naturally cautious, was ill-at-ease given the conspiratorial nature of the occasion.

I was surprised to note that Colonel Ardent and his wife were there despite the fact that I had asked for an audience without outsiders present. After the movie was shown, however, and supper was over and coffee was served, the Colonel and his wife discreetly made an exit. Now I could speak.

Uncle Rainier turned toward me in his cinema seat. He said, "Well, Buddy, I understand you have something to tell us." I thanked him for making the arrangement possible, and also thanked Grace for her special part in it. I said I was glad that my mother and stepfather were not present, and began to explain why. I told him and Grace that it had been difficult until now to feel at ease when we were at the palace with our parents because at home Rey was always making a mockery of Rainier and generally doing everything he could to turn us against our uncle, while Mummy constantly referred to him as "nasty Uncle Rainier." I said I had been anxious to let him and Grace know that Mother and Rey had not managed to influence us and that I wanted to express my true feelings about my stepfather, whose antagonistic opinions we did not share.

It meant a lot for me to let my uncle and aunt know this,

so that in the future I could feel more comfortable and relaxed at official functions with Rey and Mother, knowing that Rainier and Grace knew the way we felt about Rey and the whole situation.

I could see how disturbed Uncle Rainier and Grace were. It must have been painful for them to hear that Mother and Rey, despite all appearances of a truce following their early intrigues, were still criticizing him behind his back. I could also see a look on their faces of relief and pleasure that we, Rainier's only nephew and nieces, were not in any way in agreement with them. Uncle Rainier said, "I am delighted to see that you have good insight and judgment." Neither he nor Grace proceeded to say a single word, however, that was critical of either our stepfather or our mother. Grace was visibly delighted by this unexpected and frank statement of support from her family, and she told me that my mother's behavior should be understood in the light of her own miserable childhood. Then she hugged us with all of her customary affection and sweetness. We left happy and secure in the knowledge that whenever we saw our uncle and aunt, they would immediately be assured of our true feelings, even when our parents were present.

It was to the memory of this visit that I returned on the evening of the Red Cross Gala. Because of Rey's conduct, I was glad my uncle and aunt knew the way we felt. When we looked at Grace and Rainier at the table, following the opening dance, they looked back at us, and I could see in their eyes the same memory of that evening some weeks earlier.

However, while Uncle Rainier expressed his appreciation of our support in an intramural conflict, even though he knew that we were opposed to my mother and stepfather's schemes, I came to understand that he was capable of certain intrigues of his own. My father, now settled back in Monaco, was still living on his capital from the sale of his two art galleries, waiting for the restoration of his lawyer's license. He was also considering the offer of an important position as director of a private bank that he had assisted in forming just after World War II for his friend Guy Weill. Time dragged on, however, without anything happening. He waited and waited. Although he had a lot of patience, after two years he began to wonder whether anything would happen. He asked his uncle, Paul Noghes, secretary of state, what was going on. Assurances were given that something would come through and that it was only red tape that was delaying the approval of the license. But pressure was seemingly being exerted to prevent the restoration and make it impossible for my father to work in Monaco again. If that was so, it was effective. The license never did come through.

As a result my father decided to accept the offer of Guy Weill to become director of the bank. Weill owed Father a favor: Weill was Jewish, and during World War II, when the French collaborators were trying to round up Monaco's Jews to send them to concentration camps, my father had hidden him in his apartment at great risk to his own safety. So it came as a severe shock to my father when Weill withdrew his offer. Allegedly, Weill told Father that he had been informed by a very high personage that if he wished to retain his banking license, he must discontinue any offers he might be making to him. Weill, much as he liked my father, had no alternative but to tell him that the position of director was no longer open.

This disastrous event, which resulted in my father's leaving Monaco for the last time and returning to the United States once more in 1969, made me aware that there were other sides to Rainier's character. Up to now I had seen him only as a kind relative who genuinely seemed to care about my sisters and me. Now I saw he could be weak, or at least indifferent to our welfare. If pressure from other quarters had indeed been applied to thwart my father's attempts to resume his legal practice in Monaco, Uncle Rainier, as absolute monarch, surely could have pressured back, or pulled strings to restore the license. If that failed, he himself might have made my father an offer of employment, thereby enabling him to stay in Monaco and be near us. Given the fact of Father's long exile after the divorce, that would have been the just and fair thing to do. As I look back on it now, I also have to wonder what sort of intrigue might have been behind the pressure put on Weill. As a member of the National Council and as president of the Finance Commission, my stepfather was, in our unique monarchy, capable of favoring or canceling a banking license. If Rey was in fact behind it—and my father denies to this day that he was—I have to wonder if Rainier had a role in countenancing it. He had no time for Jean-Charles Rey; more, he despised him. He had no time for my mother either: he had not forgotten her effort to depose him or her provocative marriage to his leading opponent. Appearances to the contrary, I came to think that Rainier could merely assume a position of reconciliation with them in order to provide a common front against France, and later against Onassis. Yet he had stood by and allowed the whole life and well-being of a decent man to be destroyed for a second time, thus depriving his nephew and nieces of their father's presence for the indefinite future, a presence we needed more than ever. I began to lose respect for my uncle.

If weakness was a problem of Uncle Rainier's, there was no indication of that characteristic in my mother. She seemed to grow even harder with the years.

My beloved Nanny, well into her seventies, finally began to succumb to the onslaught of old age. She had remained remarkably healthy and vigorous, but even her sturdy British constitution gave out that spring. It was obvious to everyone that she couldn't last more than a few weeks.

Betsy and Christine were with her constantly in her room at Mereze taking care of her. My father adored her, and Nanny's fondness for him had never yielded throughout the events that had resulted in his leaving Monaco, returning, and then being left high and dry. He was eternally grateful to Nanny for her efforts in smuggling his letters and post cards from Phoenix to my sisters and me. Christine informed him that Nanny was dying. I was in Marbella, Spain, at the time, taking lessons in Spanish toward my A levels in languages, an agreeable relief from the austerities of Downside. I suppose I shouldn't have been surprised that my mother didn't bother to tell me of Nanny's condition, even though Nanny very much wanted to see me, her undisciplined but beloved "child."

Daddy phoned my mother and said he wanted to come and pay Nanny a visit before she passed away. It was a simple request, one that surely Mother should have agreed to immediately, no matter what the circumstances of divorce and remarriage. But Mother again turned into steel. She responded that it was very complicated and she would have to telephone him back when the difficult arrangements were finally made. All the "arrangements" would have entailed was opening the door to him and letting him upstairs into Nanny's room.

A week later Daddy still had received no reply from my mother, and he worried, wondering if Nanny would die before he had a last opportunity to see her. He called Mother again, reminding her politely of his previous request to see a dying woman. She snapped at him, "Yes! yes! I haven't forgotten! I am making the difficult arrangements. It will take time!" After yet another week passed, it became obvious to Daddy that Mother had no intention of responding to his wish to see Nanny. He phoned her up and said he was coming to the house immediately. He walked into Nanny's room and found her only a short distance from death and, sadly, much too confused by now to know who he was.

I still had not been told about Nanny's illness. By the time my father and sisters got in touch with me, it was too late. I had no money to go to her, and there was little chance I would re-

Princess Charlotte, my grandmother, known as Mamou. The resemblance between her and Caroline is striking.

My ancestor, Rainier II Grimaldi, at the end of the Middle Ages, dressed in battle gear, probably to deal with family conflicts

The Royal Family of Monaco, 1929, with the founder of the Boy Scouts, Sir Robert Baden Powell. As usual, Mamou is standing as far away as possible from her husband, Pierre de Polignac, and is looking as bored with official functions as her granddaughter Stephanie would look many years later.

My grandparents,
shortly before their separation,
with their children,
Antoinette and Rainier

My great-grandfather, Prince Louis II. The only family heirloom I have is the ring he is wearing on his ring finger.

My mother

My father

On the boat with my father and sister Elisabeth

On our private beach at Les Galets at Beaulieu.
Nanny is sitting in the background.

With father

Dressed as a Monegasque carabinier

In the official royal box with Mother and my younger sister, Christine.
Mother at this time was hoping to topple her brother.

Nanny Wanstall

Rainier in the garden at Mereze, where he
used to visit us after my father's departure

The Villa Mereze

Father Tucker congratulates Rainier upon his engagement, as Mr. and Mrs. Kelly look on.

Grace's arrival in Monaco harbor on Rainier's yacht

The household staff greets its future mistress. The ever-present Father Tucker stands at the head of the line.

The wedding rehearsal

Uncle Rainier in full uniform

Grace before descending to the courtyard on her wedding day

The ceremony. I am sitting behind Grace, holding the ring on my velvet cushion.

After the wedding, the sovereign gets back to work.

At Villa Mereze

Presiding over the 1956 palace Christmas party

Grace and baby Caroline, 1957

At Caroline's christening, holding my candle

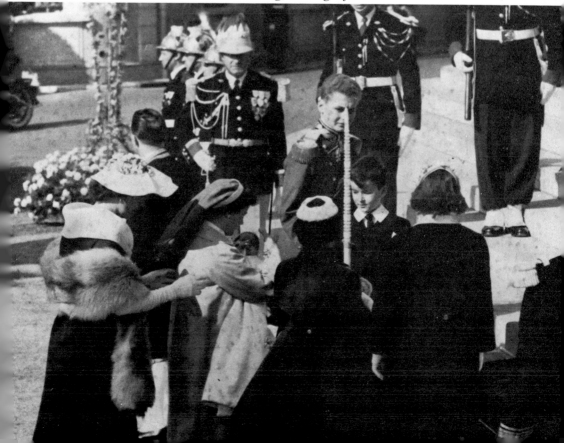

Mother and Grace entering a gala at the Sporting Club

Mother and Rey, just married

Posing for the press after the marriage. I was hiding, not wanting to appear in the same picture as Rey.

Mamou and her notorious terriers in front of the castle

Family lunch next to the pool at Mereze

Monaco centenary costume ball, 1966

Entering the Monaco Red Cross Gala ball
with Grace and my sister Elisabeth

Rey and his ill-advised dance with Grace

Portrait from the palace balcony

My mother, my uncle, and me at a Red Cross Gala

Grace and Rainier vacation with the children, 1973.

Brighton, 1969

Rhodesia, 1971

Back from Africa with the repaired Alfa Romeo

With my first wife at a fancy dress ball

Racing. The happiest days of my life

A view from my house at Saint-Laurent-d'Èze

My favorite doberman,
Cocaine

Scuba diving with plastic surgeon Ivo Pitanguy, Brazil, 1977

Driving to Gstaad in my Ferrari, with its provocative license plate

With girl friend Barbara and my sister Christine, going to an Arabian Nights dinner at the Grill of the Hôtel de Paris

The state of my Ferrari after it had slid 150 yards on its roof. I don't know how I got out of this one.

A dinner party with dear Paco-Paco, making people laugh, as usual

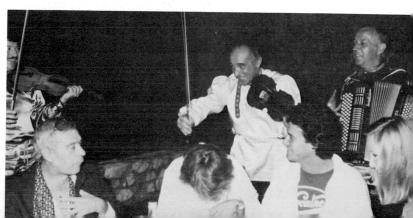

Caroline and Philippe at the time of their engagement

Smiling wanly, Grace and Rainier pose with their future son-in-law.

The guests wait in line outside the palace for the ball on the eve of Caroline's wedding.

The religious ceremony

The newlyweds

Caroline and Philippe.
Their marriage was starting to fall apart.

In front of my "headquarters" in Monaco, the Hôtel de Paris

With my second wife

With three-time Formula I champion Jackie Stewart

Rainier and the children at Marchais, January 1983

Mother and Rainier leaving a
commemorative Mass for her third
husband, Gilpin

Caroline with Stephanie, a few weeks
after her marriage to Stefano Casiraghi

1986

ceive any. I was just trying to figure out how I could make the trip when a telegram arrived from Mother saying NANNY PASSED AWAY PEACEFULLY YESTERDAY. I was shocked into tears by the news. I thought once again of all the things Nanny had done for me. I remembered her taking care of us as children, watching us swimming, taking us for walks, filling us with all of the English food she hoarded in the larder, making sure we were healthy, being a true mother to us. I thought of her house in Monaco, crammed with photographs of all of us, and of her complete selflessness, giving up all of her personal life so that she could take care of us. The last time I had seen her before going to Spain, she had expressed a premonition of death to me, saying that she hoped I would come with my family to visit her grave.

I immediately called Mother as soon as I received the telegram. I asked when the final rites would take place and told her I would leave for Mereze as soon as my air ticket arrived. I was anxious to pay my last respects to the finest woman I had ever known.

I expected Mother to say that the ticket was already on the way. I therefore could not believe my ears when she told me coldly, "I'm not sending an air ticket. It isn't worth it. Don't come to the funeral." I was stunned. Nice was only one and a half hours by air from Marbella. The cost was next to nothing. I was devastated. I felt completely powerless. I had no way of getting there; even if I hitchhiked the whole way, I would arrive too late for the funeral.

I was now seventeen, able to analyze and sort out my thoughts more clearly. I reasoned that if she was capable of refusing my wish to attend the funeral of the woman who had raised and loved her, and me, then I could hardly be expected to respect her decisions now.

After Nanny's burial in Monaco, her little house was disposed of. The vast collection of photos of the Grimaldi family, the largest on earth, a priceless record of two generations and the result of her dedicated years of taking and meticulously preserving them, was unceremoniously dumped by Mother in the basement of the disused gardener's cottage at Mereze. The winter rains flooded the cellar, and the water ruined the collection. Even Mother's own childhood pictures with her brother, Rainier, were destroyed. Perhaps this act of destruction was based on Mother's desire for a total removal of all memory of her past, of her mother putting her down and then abandoning her, of her flight from her father, Prince Polignac, and of other aspects of her early life. Nor, it seemed, did she wish to preserve any recollection of her own children's upbringing. She did not want to be reminded of anything; I remembered again how she always used to tell Nanny, when Grace and Rainier came to the house, that "souvenirs" or reminiscences of any kind were absolutely forbidden.

At last, when I reached Monaco, I was able to place flowers on Nanny's grave. I asked Mother why she had been so thoughtless in preventing me from coming to the sickbed or the funeral. As she had a thousand times before, she snapped back, "Mother knows best!" and the subject was closed.

After I passed my final exams and left Downside, I embarked upon a Grimaldi-like policy of intrigue. I had no interest whatever in going to university and therefore decided that rather than give the game away, I would pass in all subjects for entrance level except one. I chose biology as the one subject in which I would deliberately fail. I had little difficulty in scraping through my language exams, because I had a natural aptitude for picking up various tongues. My only real interest was in reaching my eighteenth birthday and buying a car with my savings.

My eighteenth birthday fell on a Saturday. I had laid down my plans for that memorable occasion by securing special permission to take the driving exam that day, even though it was a weekend and one would otherwise have to wait until Monday. Since I had had an enormous amount of illegal driving experience beforehand, taking the wheel from the age of eight, and I knew the handbook by heart, I passed the exam easily. That same afternoon I went to the local Renault dealer, and feeling extremely proud of myself, I plunged my savings, all seven hundred dollars of it, into a beat-up, ancient, fourth-hand Dauphine. It felt wonderful to drive off in it for the first time. I went directly to pick up my registration. However, I was told by the official that being a minor by Monaco laws, I had to obtain the signature of my parents. Fortunately Father had not yet left Monaco, and he was with me that day. He signed the document.

I was in paradise. Quite alone, ecstatically happy, I drove around the three Corniches as fast as the traffic allowed. The beaten-down red Renault was priceless to me. I tended to it as carefully and lovingly as if it were a Ferrari. I was in and out of garages having everything checked over: lubrication, oil change, and tune-up. The big question remained of how I was going to hide the car on the family estate. Luckily I was able to drive in unnoticed by Mother or Rey, and I hid the car behind a rabbit and chicken shed.

But after four days I was summoned to Mother's office. When I entered, I could see from her face that she was on to me. She rose dramatically to her feet, removed her spectacles, and went on and on about doing things behind her back and not asking her permission. I waited for her to end. No power on earth could have silenced her. I told her that I did not understand what was troubling her. I had bought the car with my own money, and I was in possession of a valid driver's license. What was her problem? She now responded that the registration was invalid without *her* endorsement. She claimed my father's signature alone was pointless and the registration was thus invalid, if not illegal. My car was confiscated on the spot.

I was devastated. I had waited four years, had denied myself much to scrape together the money, and had eaten, walked, and slept with only one dream. In an instant Mother had taken it away. I understood her motive at once. The fact that Father had signed the document was intolerable to her. Removing my car was her method of destroying every last link with my father. I shared with him an overpowering love of automobiles and fast driving. I had shared, in turn, so little with her. She didn't understand that if she had given her blessing to my new purchase, she might have earned back some of the affection she had gone to such extraordinary pains to lose. I was powerless. At eighteen, if I took the car and drove away, she would close my home to me, stop my pocket money. I was left with no choice.

Then at last Christine pleaded in my behalf with Mother, so passionately that she yielded. She agreed to co-sign the registration form as a Christmas present. But Mother decided to impose herself in a different way. The Renault, she pronounced, was unsafe to drive, and instead I must have a car that was reliable. Shifting from the repressive to the magnanimous with dramatic emphasis, she decided to present me with a brand new black and white Austin Mini-Cooper, an exciting car for my age. I was alive again.

The next year I went to what is called in England a "crammers." This is a special finishing school for boys and girls at which students can be pushed through their A and O levels for university when for one reason or another they have not been able to complete them at public school. The best in England at that time was Davies's. There were two branches, one in London and one in Brighton. Naturally I applied to go to the one in London, where the relaxed freedom of mid-sixties British life was unlike anything I had known before. I looked forward to partying away the nights in Tramps and the Saddle Room.

Mother saw through this plan, however, and decided to send me to Brighton instead. Little did she know that Brighton would offer me the same pleasures. I drove from Seville, where

I was allegedly studying Spanish, and proceeded with my car by ferry to England. By now the car was much improved: I had souped up the engine considerably, installed wide wheels, and built an instrument panel that would do justice to a Boeing 707. I liked Brighton very much. The other students, representing many nations, had all applied for London only to have their parents see through their schemes as mine did. I found a room in a house run by a sweet old lady who was tolerant of my life style and never fussed too much if I came back with a girl. I was happy to be away from Downside, Mereze, and Monaco. I was notably inattentive to my studies, seldom rising before 11:00 A.M. and seldom going to bed before the small hours, and I knew that when the exams came up, I would expertly fail in biology. My plan was to give the impression I was progressing, albeit slowly, so as to spin out my stay in Brighton as long as possible.

With my Greek friend Panos, I formed a foreign-born group of similar interests, and we hung out together at the Zambezi Café. The Zambezi had a bad reputation because of its noisy clientele and loud music. I would drive my group around with the girls from the English language Institute next door, parking the car wherever we saw fit. We knew that we would never pay the fines, as it would be impossible to trace us once we left for Europe. Soon our own crammers was filled with more beautiful girls from Europe, who were also in Brighton to learn English.

On the first day of each term, Alan Morton, the director, welcomed them, ending his speech by warning them of a Monegasque who drives like a maniac and of the Greek with the red pullover. Inevitably the warning only served to encourage them to meet us faster.

For two years Brighton was a haven of free living, and I didn't have a responsibility in the world. If only I could have hung on to that golden age forever!

T E N

Now that it was impossible for Mother to control my movements, I started to discover more of Monaco's possibilities. In my vacations in the late 1960s and 1970, I was able to enjoy the pleasures of Monte Carlo and its girls. I was not allowed to go to the Casino, because of my age and Monegasque citizenship. According to an old law dating from the foundation of the Casino in the nineteenth century, no member of the royal family could even visit the Casino during operating hours. I spent a good deal of time at the Hôtel de Paris bar, the Sporting Club, and all of the other famous places of that part of the south of France. At the palace I would assist in entertaining the guests as a full-fledged member of the royal family. I met a number of renowned figures there. One of them was Carl Gustaf, crown prince of Sweden and grandson of King Gustaf. A joyful man with a strong sense of humor, at one summer party he picked up several of his friends and threw them into the palace swimming pool fully clothed. To my surprise Grace laughed at the sight of her guests floundering about. She enjoyed Carl Gustaf's presence at the palace.

Frank Sinatra was also capable of wild behavior. One night

at the Paradis Nightclub, he lit fireworks that exploded across the room. Nonetheless, he and Grace remained good friends. Cary Grant was always a model of behavior, polite and gracious: he and his attractive wife, Barbara, came often to visit with Grace at different times of the year. David Niven was always a charmer, effortlessly relaxed, witty, and accomplished, very much the same as his screen image. I liked him very much. Years later, when I started a magazine, I phoned him and asked him to contribute an article. Distraught and anguished because one of his children was seriously ill in a London hospital, he still took time to explain the situation, and promised to write one later. I also liked the novelist Paul Gallico, whose wife, Virginia, later became Grace's lady-in-waiting after his death. Paul Gallico was the author of *The Snow Goose*, a classic and a best-seller of World War II.

While I was now beginning to enjoy being present at the palace's social occasions, Uncle Rainier seemed more bored than ever by them. Perhaps it was one thing to find him snoring through the opera, ballet, plays, and other public functions; but now that I was quite often at their small, intimate dinner parties in the palace's private dining room, Grace usually facing Rainier at the table, I could see how restless he was as the conversation went on around him. He was especially awkward in the presence of Grace's Hollywood set; uncomfortable with them perhaps because they were associated with a time when he wasn't with Grace. He didn't know much about film production or Beverly Hills gossip, and so all that chat about the latest movies being made or people whom Grace had in common with her visitors had little interest for him. Of Grace's set he liked David Niven the best. David had been a long-time resident of the south of France and knew my uncle separately.

I was struck more forcibly than ever by the fact that Grace, living out her role of princess, was more royal than her own husband. Her grooming in motion pictures, and the careful way she prepared herself to carry off her responsibilities as a royal person, proved telling in every instance of her private and public behavior. After Stephanie's birth, what had been a toleration for protocol and ceremony became a real interest.

She was somewhat Victorian in her approach to conversation. But increasingly Uncle Rainier showed a penchant for dubious jokes, which he related with a commingling of English and French. I watched Grace during these stories, and although they were delivered with a great deal of wit, I could see that she was upset by his brashness. As the stories went on and on, growing more and more questionable, she seemed to turn to stone. Everyone at our table would be convulsed with laughter at Rainier's stories. The laughter swirled around Grace, who sat like a beautifully sculptured rock in the middle of the gaiety.

She was similarly unresponsive when certain guests tried to monopolize the conversation. She would frequently cut across them with an announcement that dinner was served or it was time to leave the table. It was not that she lacked a sense of humor—nobody loved a party more than Grace—she simply had a sense of propriety and elegance that evoked an earlier and more distinguished century in royal circles.

I could see how Grace's children were developing. Caroline was twelve now, bursting with energy and curiosity, asking me about my life, about the nightclubs and discos I frequented. She was becoming a beautiful young woman. Her fascination with the outside world illustrated only too clearly how insulated the palace was for a girl of her age. Whereas my mother had used a spiked glove to rear her children, Grace used a velvet glove concealing a steely but considerate discipline. Caroline presented no problems to her mother at that time, but her father spoiled her as much as Grace would allow.

Grace wanted her children to understand that the real world was not soft, as her girls would later learn. If given a free hand, Uncle Rainier would have created a fairy-tale world for his children. It was as well that Grace controlled his adulation and indulgence. If, for instance, Caroline wanted to stay up late and was pleading with him to let her, he would tell her it was all right with him if Grace gave permission. Grace, on the other hand, never hesitated in saying no. He deferred to Grace as "the government" in almost every decision relating to the children; he disliked having to take overt positions.

Albert was the opposite of Caroline. Resembling his mother more and more with his sleek, golden hair, handsome features, and reserved manner, he had become handicapped by a stammer, which he later overcame, and while Caroline babbled on about everything, he shifted from foot to foot at public gatherings. He was very athletic, however, and later would make his mark in judo, earning a black belt.

As for Stephanie, she was much too young at the time to make much of an impression on me. Observing her today, it is hard to believe that only fifteen years ago she was running contentedly around the palace.

The children studied at the lycée across from the palace; Grace wanted them to have the opportunity to mingle with other boys and girls. Caroline was an especially good student. Intellectually she was the keenest of the three and the most interested in her school work. Albert did well, but perhaps more to conform to his parents' wishes than because he had Caroline's zeal. To supplement their learning, the children took private lessons from my former governess, Madame Alizard. She told me that she warned Grace more than once to be extremely cautious about Jean-Charles Rey and that he had made disparaging remarks to my mother in her presence. According to Madame Alizard Grace responded to her warnings by saying that because she had had to earn her living and had worked her way up, she had acquired a shrewd judgment of people. She could see through them at all times.

Grace took a special interest in Le Rocher, an ancient part of Monaco with cobbled streets twisting through archways in shadowy intricacy. She loved the ancient stones with which the streets were formed, the flowers filling the window boxes, and the fruit shops. She set up two boutiques to sell local arts and crafts; she always tried to preserve the beauty of the old quarter despite the constant rebuilding that went on. She fought against the cutting down of olive trees and fig trees, and she encouraged people to maintain their homes in bright pastel colors. She loved the Exotic Garden, the Jardin Exotique, filled with thousands of flowering cacti; she was constantly at the cactus nursery, and she encouraged Marcel Kroenlein, the garden's director, to show her the plants, all the way from seeding to development. She collected orchids from all parts of the world and filled the palace with them in her own flower arrangements. She devoted her time more frequently now to collage rather than to landscape painting, pressing fresh flower petals between book pages, forming designs with ginkgo, maple, and roses. The collages were signed G.P.K.

Grace suffered when she turned forty in 1969. As she told a reporter, she couldn't stand the thought of this transition into middle age. She gave a party for those friends who, like her, were born under the sign of Scorpio; Carroll Righter helped her to make the arrangements, and people came from all over the world to attend it. Among them were Hjordis Niven, Sam Spiegel, Richard Burton, and Elizabeth Taylor, who wore for the first time the famous Krupp diamond Burton had just bought her.

Of all Grace's interests, her children were central. She was proud of them and had committed herself totally to the demanding role of wife and mother, but she did not feel that it replaced completely the satisfaction of professional achievement—she was a gifted actress who could no longer perform. She very much wanted to play Alexandra, Queen Victoria's tragic granddaughter who married Czar Nicholas of Russia and died with him in the cellar at Ekaterinberg at the hands of the Communists. But the backlash of public opinion again prevented her from fulfilling her wishes. The satisfaction Grace gained from her artistic career could not be replaced easily, even by all of the duties that she carried out with total dedication. If the marriage lacked anything, it was the possibility for Grace to continue with her art. She loved her job as an actress but loved her life as mother, wife, and princess more and knew she couldn't have both. Her acting career had been the central focus of everything in her life. Now her life centered on her husband and family. What she wanted most was to make a real home for him and their children.

My interests at this time were far more parochial than Grace's. Beyond Monaco's nightlife and social occasions, there was one event that captivated me more than any other, the Grand Prix of Monaco, the most important automobile race in the world. My interest in racing had developed in those days when I had sped my mini-car around and around the pine trees of our garden at Mereze, living out the part of the great drivers of my childhood, Fangio in his Alfa Romeo, Marzotto in his Ferrari, Stirling Moss in his Maserati and Lotus, and Trintignant in his Ferrari and later in his Cooper. As a young boy I continued to follow the races passionately in magazines and newspapers and, intermittently, on the spot. I was just six when one driver, Alberto Ascari, spun his car into the Bay of Hercules and had to be rescued. Men like Bruce McLaren, of New Zealand, and Graham Hill and Jackie Stewart, both of the United Kingdom, were my idols. Now the

Grand Prix represented the summit of my interests and hopes. I dreamed of entering it someday.

The Monte Carlo circuit was exceptionally tight, with a maximum speed of 132 miles per hour in those days. Drivers had to use first gear a great deal; the track was completely hemmed in, so that if you cut one of its numerous corners too close, you crashed into a wall or a railing. On other tracks you could spin off into sand and grass and recover control of the car. But there were no such let-outs on the locked-in track of the principality. Two and a half miles around, winding through the narrow streets, the track was tortuous and difficult, and caused many multi-car crashes; in 1936 six cars were eliminated on the second lap, and in 1950 there was a nine-car first-lap pileup. It was in 1955 that three Mercedes Benzes failed and the brakes on Ascari's Lancia locked and he plunged into the harbor. Soon afterward he was killed on a practice lap at Monza in a borrowed Ferrari. He was only thirty-six years old.

I talked to the Grand Prix drivers as much as I could at the parties before and after the races. I identified with them. I knew how attached they were to their cars, and how the compulsion even drove them from their families in some cases, so intense was their love of racing. It was their life, because in action you and the car were one. The car was an extension of yourself. I understood what Moss meant when he said that racing was not only sensual, it was ecstatic. I wanted to experience that sensation as soon as possible.

On the day of the race, it was our custom to drive in a motorcade to the royal box. It was surrounded by velvet drapes and flourished the Monegasque flag. My uncle and aunt drove in a convertible car and performed a lap of honor to declare the race open. Then they joined us in the box. After ten laps we left the box and went to the top floor of the Heracles building, where, in the penthouse, we ate canapés and drank champagne and had a great view of the track before we returned for the award ceremony.

The race that year, 1968, was notable for a battle between champions Graham Hill and Richard Attwood. Attwood was a terrific driver: his BRM was one of the best cars in the world. Graham Hill, driving his Lotus Ford, was using aerodynamics for the first time, with wings on the front of the car and a wedge-shaped tail. The final laps became a struggle to the end. Finally, Hill said later, he could easily have moved out in front to build up a comfortable lead, but he was afraid that cutting half a second off his time would put too much extra strain on the car. The climax of the race came when he was almost overtaken by Attwood. All of us watching from the Heracles penthouse were in suspense as the cars approached a close finish. Even Grace, who had mixed feelings about auto racing, clapped with excitement as Graham Hill at last came in ahead, and then we all went down to the royal box, where he was presented with his silver cup.

After the race the drivers traditionally joined us for the Grand Prix gala. As the years had gone on, the Grand Prix brought a different crowd of people to Monaco: jet-setters, starlets, business tycoons, aristocrats, sportsmen, and hangers-on. The glitter, the champagne, the excitement went on and on. Moet-Chandon threw a party at the Grill on the top floor of the Hôtel de Paris, and other party-givers like Gunther Sachs and Countess Cicogna entertained elaborately. Figures such as Merle Oberon, the Beatles, and Mick Jagger would sweep down on the citadel and jazz it up even more.

Not long after, I became the beneficiary of an unexpected windfall. Mother got it into her head that I must go to Oxford or Cambridge. But by now she had caught on to my scheme of avoiding university by not passing the last biology exam. She asked me, if she were to present me with my dream car, what, within reason, would that be? I wondered what she had in mind; it seemed curious that she, who had begrudged me my first car, would now be coming around.

I didn't hesitate to tell her it was the Alfa Romeo 1750, which was a brand-new model at the end of the 1960s. It combined power and road-holding capacity; it had a good five-speed gearbox and a beautiful sleek look. It was probably the best car available for its price. I was amazed when she told me that if I could get accepted into a major British university, she would trade in the Austin Mini for it and pay the difference.

I immediately returned to Brighton and settled into passing biology, which I did, quickly. Once I was through, however, I still had one obstacle to overcome. I had to choose a subject before I could be admitted. Since I already spoke French, Spanish, and Italian, I chose modern languages.

First I applied to Christ Church, Oxford, where a don saw through me right away; he knew I had no interest in studies and said that there were enough playboys at his college as it was. I then turned to Cambridge, where I had an almost equally hard time. It was obvious that I had no knowledge of modern European literature, and therefore it would be difficult for me to be accepted. But surprising though it may seem, I managed to get accepted to Cambridge, and I was able to pick up the new Alfa Romeo from the Monaco dealer.

I broke in my Alfa slowly and conscientiously. I drove for a week, day and night, alone and in ecstasy, on the motorways of France, gradually opening out the engine from 50 to 55 to 60 and then to 110 miles per hour, driving in a country where there was no speed limit. When I left for Cambridge, the car went with me.

Cambridge was beautiful. The university somehow preserved its academic peacefulness in spite of the constant blare of traffic through the nearby city streets. St. Catharine's College, where I was to be a student, was open to the street, its courtyard enclosed by red brick buildings with dormer windows and red tiled roofs. By the law of the college, I had to meet my tutor right away. I had hoped to find the same kind of relaxed academic atmosphere that I had found at Brighton. But the tutor was severe, and I understood immediately that the discipline at Cambridge would be strict. I had undertaken this venture in education only to secure a car and wait for the day when I could begin my racing career. Never expecting to obtain a degree, and not having read the literary classics, I wasn't surprised that I failed the exams.

I tried to switch courses in midstream and read law instead. But when I went to see my tutor, he objected. He was used to this trick of changing subjects, which was a custom of inattentive students. He told me that because I didn't know Latin I couldn't possibly read law. He gave me bizarre alternatives: Oriental languages, or the equally improbable choice of a combined course of anthropology and archaeology. I could not imagine myself rummaging through arcane volumes on the origins of man and descriptions of the ruins of Greece, Rome, and Egypt.

I asked for twenty-four hours to decide between these unlikely choices. After I talked with a few fellow students, it became obvious to me that anthropology and archaeology would involve less work than trying to master the intricacies of Japanese grammar. I returned to my tutor and told him my decision. I saw it was going to be hard to hang on to the car I loved.

E L E V E N

TRY AS I MIGHT, I had no en-
thusiasm for life at the great university, and little aptitude for
it either. During the week I cut as many lectures as I dared,
but I had to attend my tutorials, one-on-one teaching sessions
with the dons. When they gave us books for assigned reading,
I would turn over the pages, thinking of how anxious I was to
escape to London. Discussions about the origins of a piece of
stone passed around the lecture hall, questions about its character and definition based upon its shape and size, seemed to me a
waste of time. There was life to be lived, fun to be had, and
these musty lecture rooms, hundreds of years old, seemed to
represent a kind of creeping inertia.

London, on the other hand, was alluring to me: fast-paced,
good fun in that era of the Beatles and Carnaby Street. I found
a small flat in Chelsea and spent four-day weekends away from
the Cambridge curfew. It took no time to find and befriend the
young foreign scions and the lively British group. Everybody
had money to burn, and, like me, most of the foreigners were
pulling the wool over their wealthy parents' eyes, telling them
they were in Britain to complete their educations. But few
of them had any interest in graduating or going to work in

their parents' offices. A few of our crowd were allegedly already employed in their fathers' businesses, but their "jobs" consisted largely of moving papers—and chasing secretaries—around the desks.

I would drive the Alfa Romeo back to Cambridge to attend classes in a desultory way. I also began to plunge into athletics again: I was left wing on the St. Catharine's soccer team and tried out for the university team. I also trained as a boxer with the university team. Despite my evenings on the town, I somehow amazingly managed to stay in condition. But then I was only nineteen years old.

I became interested in an Italian-born girl named Marisa, who was small, dark, and classically beautiful. She was as reserved and subdued as I was brash and outgoing. Over dinner one night at a London restaurant, I realized I was in love with her. I entered into the first relationship of my life that was romantic, despite our very different temperaments. Marisa disliked drunkenness, loud parties, noisy young playboys, and the fast lane. Never was the phrase "attraction of opposites" more applicable than in our case.

Christmas vacation came, and Marisa went to her family in Switzerland and I went home to Monaco. At the customary party around the Christmas tree at the palace, Grace expressed her satisfaction that I had been accepted at Cambridge. She told me that she could see that I was full of happiness for a change, and this naturally intrigued her. She said to me, "Buddy, if only I could believe this radiance was as a result of the pleasure you are taking in your studies! If I could believe that, I would be very optimistic about your future at St. Catharine's! But knowing you as well as I do, I am a little suspicious!" She laughed and went on. "Am I wrong in suspecting that something else is going on?"

As always, her instincts were impressively acute. Of the family members, Grace was the only one who had had a normal family upbringing and had been exposed to the realities of the world instead of the claustrophobic atmosphere of the palace, where flatterers supported every royal whim and said only that which my mother and uncle wanted to hear. This gave Grace a more realistic grasp of human problems in real-life situations. She could talk to me in the language of ordinary people since I had been educated and lived abroad most of the time. It was amazing to me how every time we met she got right to the heart of the matter.

I replied to her question about whether something "else" was going on, "Aunt Grace, believe it or not I'm having a wonderful life now, and I've been going out with the same girl for a month!" Grace smiled broadly with affection and understanding. She asked me, "Do you think you will have time in view of this romance to attend your lectures and other studies?" Then she became serious. She said, "Buddy, really, I do hope you'll be able to combine pleasure with study at Cambridge. I'm sure you realize that you have made a remarkable turnaround in your life by achieving entry there. You've managed to overcome the stigma of being expelled from Le Rosey. Be careful. You have a chance to remove those dark clouds over your reputation. You have it all now. Cambridge has given you peace and balance and order. Your mother is satisfied for the first time, and at last she isn't fighting you every minute. You have a good allowance. You have the car you always wanted. Don't risk losing all this!" she said.

I was deeply influenced by everything my aunt said to me. But wanting to do something to please her and actually being able to carry it out were two different things. I was badly behind in my studies. Moreover, I had disobeyed my instructions for vacation study. I was supposed to go to Périgueux, an ancient archaeological site, but the thought of slopping around through mud examining ancient stones in the rain turned me off completely. I returned late for term that January, having stopped in London for a party that stretched on to ten days, and found my mail stacked high with notices calling me to see my tutor.

Driving over to St. Catharine's to see him, I belted through heavy rain, and as I was making a turn from one street to another, I narrowly missed hitting the rear wheel of a bicycle. One more inch and I would have knocked the rider over. As he cycled past me in the downpour, I recognized him. It was Prince Charles.

The tutor's face was grim when I entered his study. He asked me how many nights of the autumn term I had been out of my rooms after midnight. I said I had no idea. He told me that I had been absent far too often and that in the future I must ask permission. The rules of the college required me to ask permission for an all-night leave no less than two days beforehand. I replied, how was I supposed to know two days in advance if I would "get lucky," meaning with an attractive girl. He did not find my attempt at humor funny. He asked me how many lectures I had attended, and I told him between forty and fifty. He then asked me sharply whether that estimate was accurate; had it in fact been any more than ten? I told him that I preferred to leave the exact count to his mathematical skills, which were no doubt better than mine. He went on to reprimand me for attending only one meal in the dining room, reminding me that all except four meals there a week were compulsory. He also mentioned having seen a car with Monaco license plates in Cambridge. If it was mine, I must get rid of it at once, as students were forbidden cars. I must use a bicycle instead. After all, what was good enough for Prince Charles was surely good enough for me.

He told me that either I followed the rules or I left. I replied that in view of those conditions, I preferred to leave at once. My tutor was so astonished he sat down in his chair. He said no one in his right mind would throw away a Cambridge education because he couldn't keep his car and recommended that I go home and think it over. I could give him my decision the following morning.

Instead of returning to my room, I took Marisa to the restaurant where my group of foreign friends was gathered, and we drank several bottles of wine. When the owner learned we were celebrating my imminent departure, he ordered us an extra bottle.

Next day I told the learned don that I had decided to withdraw. He shook my hand coldly and wished me the best of luck in his flat academic tone. He said, with more than a little obviousness, that I would not go down in St. Catharine's history for academic achievement but as the first student who had left because he couldn't keep his car. On that note we parted company for the last time.

The dean advised Mother of my departure and the reasons behind it. She was mad with rage, which I had expected, but all hell broke loose at the palace, too. Uncle Rainier was furious. Jean-Charles Rey was delighted. Not a word was heard from Grace. On the phone Betsy told me that Mother was cutting off my allowance immediately and wanted to see me as soon as possible. Now I was completely penniless.

Marisa and I did not want to be parted. We had our plan: I had sustained a good relationship with the director of Davies's. Marisa would write to her parents that she wanted to transfer there because she had heard it was better than her school at Cambridge. She went with me to the seacoast town, and we found a flat together in a Turkish student friend's house, rented for him by his parents. This new move of mine proved disastrous to our relationship. Whereas the atmosphere of Cambridge had put some brakes on our fast crowd, the Brighton set was just too much for Marisa. Her romantic dream of love dissolved in the din of our whiskey-swilling day and night existence. She fled by train, leaving a good-bye note. It was all very sad, and I felt guilty and depressed.

I had to work. Without a penny in the world, and without any qualifications, I had to get a blue-collar job. I went off with an Iranian friend, Shari, to the docks. He, too, had been cut off without money by his parents for not attending to his studies.

We left in the Alfa Romeo in a driving rain at 7:00 A.M. We stood in line waiting. The union men had first refusal. But we were young and fit, and there were plenty of jobs that winter, so we were hired on the spot without questions. We had hidden the Alfa Romeo around the corner several blocks away because we knew what would happen to us if any of our British co-workers saw it.

We started to unload parcels and crates from the cargo holds of various freighters, placing them in the loading bays for the trucks. Inevitably the dock workers found out we were neither English nor union members, and they picked on us until we got into a fight. They beat us, leaving us strewn on the wharf in the rain. On the third day we were told there was no more work. Once again I was without funds.

We drove back to my flat. The road plunged down a steep incline to a sharp bend fenced in by a thick stone wall. Driving at sixty miles an hour on a twenty-mile-per-hour curve, I was so worried and distracted that by the time I saw the red light, it was too late. I slammed on the brakes, but the road was awash, and I skidded in a desperate effort to avoid oncoming traffic and smashed head-on into the wall.

It was the worst moment of my life to date. Neither Shari nor I suffered more than mild abrasions, but the Alfa Romeo I loved more than anything in the world was totaled. I had no insurance to cover this kind of accident. Once again I had had it.

The police arrived, and we had to go to the station to fill out a report. Back home that night, with no idea how I would get through the next week financially, I drank an entire fifth of Pastis, a very toxic French anise-based liqueur of lethal impact when undiluted by water or ice. When my friends arrived to pick me up, I blacked out going down the stairs. I knew I was falling, falling ... then nothing.

When I awoke, I was in a police cell. An officer was screaming at me, "What's this nonsense about a diplomatic passport? Where is it?" Feebly, my head splitting open, I gave him my address. I realized bit by bit that my clothes were in shreds, I was black and blue and completely covered in vomit. I could recall nothing. My friends told me what had happened. After I fell down the stairs and hit my head, I had staggered into our local bar, collapsed drunk onto a sofa, then jumped to my feet and started hitting everyone I could get my hands on. The owner called the police. When the first one strode in, I kicked him in the testicles and smashed a heavy ashtray on the second policeman's head. Soon after, the police brought their van and shoved me into it.

There was no keeping the incident from reaching Monaco, even though it did not appear in the press. The palace was in a fury. When I was released from jail, Betsy called me and said that I was to come home at once, but I mustn't be worried: Uncle Rainier had found a solution to everything, and a way to give me something for the future.

I flew back on a rapidly provided air ticket, feeling like hell. Mother greeted me at Mereze with an ominous calm. She was so lacking in her usual harshness that I suspected the very worst was to come.

I went at once to the palace, where Uncle Rainier had arranged an appointment for me. This was the first time I had ever been received in his audience room, where he normally conducted official business. When I entered the imposing study, he stood up, and his stiff manner struck a chill in me. I feared the worst.

He said to me, "Please sit down, Buddy. I'm glad to see you're in good shape physically, at least." He sat down next to me in an armchair. And then he embarked upon the longest lecture he had ever given me.

Uncle Rainier went on and on about duty, honor, responsibility, and learning from one's past mistakes in a sustained sermon that matched my mother's moralistic addresses over the years. Then he said the obvious, that it was clear I was not going to have an academic future. In view of my total lack of interest in studies or in obtaining a degree of any kind, what did I realistically expect to do in life?

I knew that at this point, there was no use in my even approaching the subject of car racing. There was an alternative: I had a good knowledge of the workings of the Hôtel de Paris and of the other Monaco tourist facilities, and I thought that it might be a good idea if I went to the École Hôteliers; the renowned institution in Lausanne, Switzerland, where people were trained in every aspect of hotel management. A degree there would qualify me to get a post with the SBM, which owned all the major hotels as well as the Casino, and all of the other numerous tourist facilities of Monaco. I could thus be involved in the management of our greatest industry: tourism. After I made this suggestion, Uncle Rainier said nothing. He apparently couldn't find fault with it, but still he said nothing. Instead he coughed, took out a cigarette from his case, lit it up with a gold lighter, and paused theatrically before he delivered his "solution" to my unfortunate predicament. He said, "I have a very good friend, an Irish tea planter, Bill Igoe, who is farming in Southern Rhodesia. I think it would be a good idea if you went out and farmed with him. You would see a completely different world and way of life, and undoubtedly that would give you a stronger sense of responsibility and a clearer perspective on your own present and future."

I thought: what am I in for now? Southern Rhodesia was just about the least likely place in the world for a white man to go in 1970. To describe it as a trouble spot would be an understatement. Northern Rhodesia had already seceded from the federation set up in 1953 to unite it with Southern Rhodesia and Nyasaland. In 1964 the federation was dissolved. Nyasaland was granted independence and became Malawi. Northern Rhodesia became Zambia that year, with Kenneth Kaunda as prime minister. The controversial finance minister Ian D. Smith succeeded Winston J. Field as prime minister of Southern Rhodesia, and in 1965 he declared unilateral independence, breaking away from Britain. He banished without trial four African leaders, including Joshua Nkomo, president of the People's Caretaker Council, and riots and demonstrations followed. Then came the upheavals, tensions, and killings that made world headlines in the 1960s. With black guerrilla movements forming on a large scale and trade and arms embargoes being applied by the United Nations, it was only a question of time before there would be a violent struggle for majority rule. For Uncle Rainier to send me to that place at that particular time was tantamount to disposing of me.

He told me, "You must stay a minimum of one year in Africa. It takes a year, Bill informs me, to be able to understand the African spirit. People who return before a year is up come back with false impressions." I replied that until now I had never thought that an understanding of Africa and the Africans was essential in achieving success in Europe. How, I asked, could this experience possibly be of use to me in any kind of a career in Monaco? My uncle ignored my remark and continued puffing away at his cigarette, avoiding my eyes. He was not used to having his judgment questioned and was visibly annoyed. He went on, "A year in Africa will prove you have guts and discipline. On your return, if everything goes smoothly over there, and there are no serious problems, then I shall be prepared to review your entire situation and consider what dispositions could be made toward your future."

There wasn't much I could say or do after that. The prospect of a year in the middle of nowhere was hardly encouraging. But in the wake of my abandoning Cambridge and landing up in prison in Brighton, I realized that I was in the wrong and had run out of options.

That night I was driving into Monaco in a borrowed car when it crossed my mind that all of Uncle Rainier's careful avuncular statements about the educational value of the year abroad were perhaps a means of hiding his true intention: was it possible that this was a thinly disguised form of royal exile? I remembered that in the past it was a custom in aristocratic or royal families to send the black sheep out to the colonies. Often they never came back. I joined some friends at dinner in Monaco, feeling increasingly worried about that possibility. My passport would expire in less than a year and could be renewed only by sending it to Monaco. That renewal might never take place. I asked the people at the table if they knew anything about Bill Igoe. Someone said, "Oh, yes! I know him! He's a close friend and golfing partner of Jean-Charles Rey." I began to see daylight. In the same way that Uncle Rainier had indirectly made promises to my father and had then broken them, exiling him for a second time, due in part, as I believed, to the efforts of Rey, so he was now acting toward me. It was clear that Uncle Rainier and Rey—much as they disliked each other—were of one mind when it came to me. But at least Father was able to get to America. Rhodesia was a considerably less attractive prospect. Thoughts raced through my head as the others talked, their voices fading out as I was seized by a blind, all-engulfing sensation of betrayal. I had gone out of my way to express my support of Rainier against Rey; I had been close to Grace, and I had a good relationship with his children. Was it possible that I had been sold down the river not by royal ordinance but by the combined efforts of my uncle and a man whom Rainier detested and who was still, as he very well knew from my visit with my sisters, stabbing him in the back?

Abruptly I rose from the table and walked over to the telephone booth to call my uncle. I told him that I had thought the whole thing over and I was not going to go to Africa. He replied abruptly and with barely concealed anger, "Very well!" and hung up without saying good-bye.

After dinner I returned to Mereze, only to find my mother waiting for me on the doorstep. Before I could say anything, she cut me off. "My brother has called from the palace. He has issued an ultimatum: unless you are on the plane to South Africa tomorrow, you will be permanently expelled from the principality. Permanently!" She added that the expulsion would take place according to the sovereign ordinance of 1882 giving the prince's wishes the force of law in family matters. I could not refuse to obey an instruction from the throne. She added that if I went without giving further trouble, she would make sure the Alfa Romeo was sent from Brighton to Italy and repaired at the Alfa Romeo headquarters.

There was no sign of Jean-Charles Rey that evening or the next day, but I was sure he was enjoying his triumph. I decided there was nothing to do now but prove I could survive this ordeal. I thought of my twenty-first birthday on the veld, thousands of miles from my friends and a million light-years from London.

I remembered that night an incident that had taken place involving my sister Elisabeth. She had become romantically involved with the Monaco professional soccer player Michel

Ruelle. Mother and Uncle Rainier did not approve of Michel, and suddenly he found himself traded to the Rouen team in the north of France. There was a saying that spread through the principality in those days, "Watch out, you're going to be sent to Rouen!" The humor underscored the belief that Rainier had deliberately exiled a player of his own team because of his desire that the young man not date his niece. Elisabeth was also sent away as I was to be, but her situation was far different from mine: my mother arranged for her to be the house guest of the Princess of Bavière-Bourbon at her residence in Madrid. Inevitably the romance withered, and the palace was satisfied.

Piling whatever clothes I had into two suitcases, packing up my portable stereo and favorite records, I flew the next day to Johannesburg, where the Igoes met me with their son at the airport. After a prolonged struggle with a stubborn immigration officer who thought Monaco was Morocco and that I would thus be an Arab and consigned to the nonwhite immigration queue—I uselessly tried to tell the officer of Princess Grace, the Casino, and the Grand Prix, none of which meant anything—I at last got through, and we drove northward to our destination. Bill Igoe turned out to be surprisingly decent: short, stocky, jovial, pink-faced, he was a kind man, and his wife was charming. As we drove on, Igoe not only told me that Rey was responsible for this entire scheme, but he also revealed that he was not a personal friend of Uncle Rainier. So that was it! Once again Uncle Rainier had not told me the whole truth. By calling Igoe "Bill" and pretending that he was his friend, he had misled me.

After three days of driving through the rolling veld, we at last arrived at the isolated farm, situated one hundred miles from the nearest settlement, Umtali, on the border of Rhodesia and the then-Portuguese dependency of Mozambique. The large white farmhouse stood on top of a small hill sur-

rounded by the thousand acres of tea plantation. The design
was typical of that region: a long wooden white-painted ve-
randa fronted the house, there was a swimming pool at the
back, and guest bungalows were dotted about the property.
A private golf course could be seen in the distance. There was
a large staff of cooks, butlers, and "boys," and the cleaning
servants wore white coats or red jackets with fezes on their
heads. The estate was separated into divisions and was manned
by a private security force who carried handcuffs and night
sticks. Punishments were administered abruptly and with
colonial dispatch. Transportation around the plantation was
by Land Rover. I was assigned one, as well as a bungalow with
a small living room, bedroom, and bath. Although I felt angry
and betrayed, I had to admit that even in this Godforsaken
place, every condition had been made to allow for comfort.
But I was also aware of the conditions in which the black
workers lived, and I could well understand why that whole
region was just a step away from revolution or self-govern-
ment or both.

Much to the consternation of the white overseers, I got on
well and joked with the blacks from the first day; they had a
great sense of humor, a naturalness, and an open warmth that
I liked.

I tried to make the best of a bad situation. I couldn't spend
a whole year feeling angry and sorry for myself. The Igoes
were away for months on end, traveling around the world. I
organized a soccer team, which I named the North Shumbas
(lions, in the local dialect), and dressed them up in shirts and
shorts in Monegasque colors of red and white. Getting the
team into shape, I felt reasonably alive and able to cope. I
worked out with weights and built myself up. This gave me a
purpose and something to do.

Sometimes I would drive into the local mud hut village
after a match and invite my players for a meal of maize and

some drinks; I was the only white who had ever joined them in that way, and they were fascinated by my "magic box," the portable stereo on which I would play the soul music with which they could identify. They were crazy about James Brown and joined in with loud singing and dancing. As a result of my companionship with the blacks, some of the overseers charged me with being a Communist.

I drove around the dirt roads at the best speed my Land Rover could do, taking my players with me to the matches. Somehow the months went by. But there were also problems. Sometimes the football games got out of hand. Many of the spectators got blind drunk, and I discovered the ferocity that divided rival tribes. Even the players would fight among themselves. Brawls broke out, and broken bottles and knives came into play. I did my best to break up these fights, but there wasn't much I could do about it.

A few days a month I would drive the hundred miles to Umtali. The whites would often stare at me critically because of my long hair—I didn't cut it for a year in a token gesture of defiance—murmuring that I was some kind of Communist hippie. I went into Umtali to look for women: there weren't any on the plantation. When I asked a taxi driver where I could find some "action," he told me it was against the law to be with a black woman and that if I was caught, there would be trouble. I thought of being locked up once again and giving my uncle and Rey the evidence that I was a constant troublemaker and deserved to be banished. The driver told me to avoid the local brothel, and instead, he brought me some girls he knew who worked there. I parked the Land Rover behind some trees out in the country and with them relieved my frustrations on the passenger seat. I could only think of the contrast between these hasty encounters in the middle of nowhere and glorious nights with the girls I had known in London, Cambridge, and Monaco.

After ten months, Bill Igoe suggested I drive the Land Rover to Lourenço Marques, the capital of Mozambique. This was an ancient fifteenth-century city, filled with legends of pirates and slave traders, colorful colonial despots and their mistresses. The very name had the scent of Baghdadian pleasure and escape. It had been marked by riots, and in 1970 Mozambique also seethed with insurgency.

It was an exciting drive on sand roads through jungle, low-lying hills, and forests. The moment I crossed the border from Rhodesia, I noticed a drastic change. Whereas under Ian Smith's British rule the blacks were all either ragged or dressed neatly in English safari suits, in the Portuguese territory the blacks were a blaze of vividly colored clothes, jewelry, and fancy bracelets. I was going through a country in the grip of guerrilla warfare. At last, after three days' drive, I arrived in the capital, which was heavily charged with colonial atmosphere. The streets teemed with merchants selling everything from cheap costume jewelry to teenage girls. My twenty-one-year-old appetite was enflamed. I wound up that night at an exotic bordello-cabaret called Esmeralda's. It was a great place, dimly lit, clouded with cigarette smoke, and fans revolved slowly in the ceiling. The air was heavy with perfume, the pulsing rhythms of a marimba band, and the laughter of dozens of sailors off local ships with girls on their laps and money to burn. It wasn't long before I had a mulatto beauty on my lap and I was drinking with a crew of French sailors. We exchanged jokes in our native tongue, got blind drunk on Scotch, brandy, and wine, and talked about cities and places we knew.

One night, after leaving the bordello having had too much to drink, I got into a fight with some Portuguese military police. I was thrown into a van and once more found myself in a prison cell. There was nothing in there but a straw bed. Luckily I had no identification on me, as I had left my passport and other documents behind at the hotel. I lay there, in a cramped cell, thousands of miles from home, in suffocating heat, my head splitting with a hangover, thinking that once again I was in bad trouble. What was I to do? I did not want to get in touch with the French consul because he would convey the news of my imprisonment to Uncle Rainier, who would surely use this as an excuse to prolong my exile.

By some miracle I had heard that the Italian consul in Lourenço Marques was no less than my old friend Ernesto Morinacci, who had formerly been posted in Monaco and had now wound up in this seaport at the end of nowhere. I had always liked him, dubbing him Fornicacci because of his promiscuous adventures.

I was allowed to write to him. I asked him to get me out of this without Uncle Rainier finding out. While I waited for a response, days and nights went by slowly. Fortunately my black jailer and I got on well: he was intrigued by having this long-haired Frenchman in his custody. One day he surprised me. Saying "Dagga, Dagga," he handed me an object resembling a cigarette, made out of rolled newspaper. I realized this was a joint. I had never taken drugs before, even at the height of my London period. I inhaled the reefer, hearing from the jailer's radio down the corridor the throbbing rhythm of African and Brazilian music and the faint, melancholy pulse of the fado. I found that under these conditions, jail wasn't as bad as it might have been.

After some time Fornicacci responded to my note. At first he thought it was a hoax, but he finally realized the incredible fact that the nephew of Prince Rainier of Monaco was actually a prisoner of the Lourenço Marques police! He freed me at once.

I left the Portuguese prison without having to disclose my identity and resumed my life on the plantation. One day Igoe returned from a trip to Monaco and told me he wanted me to accompany him to a peach farm, which he had learned was for sale at a good price. I knew that Igoe's visit to Monaco was no accident and that he was under pressure to have me grow peaches and never to return home. When Bill said that Jean-Charles Rey would advance me the money, I politely explained that the idea was out of the question. It shocked me to think that Rey, Prince Rainier, and even my own mother were so indifferent to my welfare that they would for their own convenience not want me ever to leave this place.

Soon after that Jean-Charles Rey arrived in person, ostensibly for a golfing trip. Because I felt it necessary to ensure my return home, I took the diplomatic step of forcing myself to meet his plane at the Salisbury airport and of accompanying him to a reception at the local golf club. He was as brazen and self-important as ever. During the reception, in response to a question on his exact status in the Monaco government, he replied, quite seriously, "I am the power behind the throne!" That said it all.

Soon after that Rey and I were uncomfortably together on a tourist trip to see Victoria Falls, which David Livingstone had discovered in the 1850s at the source of the White Nile. I did not betray my knowledge of Rey's connivances. I did not want to take any chances of having my stay extended. I had kept my part of the bargain. Now I would be able to see what further purpose Rainier had in mind. Rey couldn't resist injecting a dark note into our conversation, however. He indicated that it would be valuable for me to have more experience abroad. I wondered, as I at last flew back to Monaco early in the spring of 1970, thirteen months after my arrival in Africa, what new experiences my uncle had in mind for me.

Much as I disliked being at Mereze, I was glad to be back in Europe that spring of 1970. I saw little of Rey at the time. He was obviously eager to find some way to get rid of me again, because I continued to confirm out loud what everyone else thought of him privately. I was pleased to find that at least Mother had kept her part of the bargain and my Alfa Romeo, now repaired, was waiting for me in the garage. Mother also granted me a modest allowance: I never found out whether it came from her own purse or from the Civil List. It was just enough to scrape along on.

Mother was in an awkward position now. After all, I had stayed thirteen months, one token month longer than we had agreed; I had worked hard on the Rhodesian plantation, and even she could not deny that I had made a go of things there. Quickly, however, I realized that she wanted me overseas again. In one of our early conversations she said to me meaningfully that all young Monegasques should start their careers abroad and that traditionally this was true of just about everyone in the principality who was now a major success. I asked her if she could name half a dozen who had started their careers overseas. She could not. I said that I could think of only one example, my father, but he had twice lost everything by his involuntary exile. Mother brought our conversation abruptly to an end.

I spent much of the summer driving around in my car. There were some invitations to the palace, the first of which was a call to a party before the Grand Prix. This was my first reunion with the whole family since the Brighton episode. No mention was made of that. When Grace saw me, she drew me aside to a corner of the salon. She told me, "Buddy, I was so sad to hear of the fact that you had left Cambridge so quickly. I remember how we talked about your plans, and everything seemed to be going so well. But I'm glad that you did make yourself go to South Africa, and that you didn't fall down on your promise to your uncle. I imagine that with your sense of adventure, you enjoyed the whole experience very much." I asked Grace how she had reached that conclusion. She said,

"We were all expecting you to come back one year to the day after you left. After all, we were aware that you would be missing the life in Europe terribly. However, when you stayed thirteen months instead, I asked your mother why. She told me it was because you were having such a wonderful time." I was forced to say to Grace that there was nothing enjoyable about being exiled to Africa. Grace responded, "I see. Well, Buddy, I'm delighted you at least took the occasion to make something of yourself." She smiled and asked, "Well, now. What are your plans for the future?" I told her that I was expecting Uncle Rainier to have reviewed my situation and to make a suggestion for my future, as he had promised to do. I went on to say that he had not yet broached the subject.

Much as I loved Grace, the conversation left me with little to hang on to in the way of hope. But at least I was reassured by Grace's sympathetic warmth that the episode in Lourenço Marques had not reached the palace. Fornicacci had kept my secret, and I would be eternally grateful to him. Grace parted with me on a final note: she suggested that I myself make a proposal regarding my future employment that would be acceptable, rather than waiting for a palace-inspired edict that could result in severe problems if I refused.

Time had not deflected me from wanting to pursue a racing career. I had dreamed of it, first in Monaco, then in England, and most recently in Rhodesia. I had no money, and no prospects of any, to finance it. Now that I was twenty-one and legally an adult, I was no freer than I had been before. The modest allowance my mother gave me was just about enough to allow me to fill up my car and spend an occasional evening out. I forced myself to ask her for a larger income, pointing out that it had not been increased since I was eighteen. She told me, point-blank, that if I would agree to go to another country, she would increase the allowance.

I reminded her of the conversation with Uncle Rainier preceding my departure for Africa just over a year before. I said that I was still waiting for my audience with him regarding my future. Mother said that he had reconsidered my position and I was no longer *persona non grata* in Monaco. I told her that I was expecting something more concrete to be proposed.

Naively I assumed that since I had done my term of penance, if I was indeed to be sent abroad again, it would be to a cosmopolitan center where I could do something interesting and valuable. I expected to be sent to London, New York, or Paris. I proposed to my mother and Jean-Charles Rey that since my only interest was in cars, I would find it logical to be involved in the automobile business, which, I hoped, would bring me closer to the world of racing.

During this period Monaco was in the process of reclaiming land from the sea. It was a giant project. The building of the new port district of Fontvielle involved huge sums of money and was being implemented under the supervision of S.A.D.I.M., a subsidiary of the giant auto firm of Fiat. After a time Jean-Charles Rey told me he had good news. How fortunate, how extraordinarily lucky I was that because of Rey's kind consideration of my future and thanks to his influence, he had arranged a job for me with Fiat. He added, after a significant pause, "In Argentina!" My heart sank.

I replied that surely there must be Fiat branches farther away than Argentina: perhaps at the South Pole? Rey did not answer. I asked myself once again why Mother was going to such lengths to secure my prolonged absence. I understood now that the first exile was no mere test of my character but a method of getting rid of me as quickly and cleanly as possible. Now that I had "proved myself," she couldn't wait to dispose of me again. Why? I kept remembering her demands of poor Nanny: *"Pas de souvenirs!"* ("No reminiscences!"). Suddenly it dawned on me: was she trying to bury her own guilt regarding the failed coup d'état of 1955, of which I was a painfully embarrassing reminder? Did my very presence bring back that ill-judged episode, as well as memories of my father, whom I apparently was starting to resemble and whom she still hated?

I began to think about South America. I knew that Buenos Aires was the closest thing to a European capital in South America. I now heard from friends that it was fun and filled with beautiful girls. Suddenly the prospect of the trip became less grim, and I planned the journey with more enthusiasm than I had thought I would.

Just before my departure for Argentina, Uncle Rainier chose the occasion of a lunch by the palace pool at summer's end to give me another one of his special addresses. He said how pleased he was that I had proved myself in Africa and that he hoped that my stay in Argentina would do me an equal amount of good. Before leaving the luncheon Grace asked me how I reacted to the prospect of going to Argentina. She said to me, "You always wanted to work with cars, didn't you?" I replied that I was going to be on the administrative and commercial side, and this was far from the kind of involvement I had hoped for, but at least it concerned cars. I let her know my disappointment as we walked in the garden. I told her that it was clear to me that whatever job or activity or plans for the future I had seemed totally unimportant to my uncle, Mother, or Rey compared with their desire to place me at the farthest possible distance from Monaco. I told Grace I was well aware that I was a reminder to them of painful times and was unwanted, and that without having given reason for banishment—especially since I had done my time in Africa—I was being exiled once again.

Grace looked sad. She said she completely understood my feeling of constant rejection by the family, but she added that later on I might not regret going to Argentina as since I was twenty-one years old and a bit reckless, I would undoubtedly get into some more "mischief" before long, and it would be preferable for me that this should take place far from the palace. As I listened to her wise words, I regretted once again the fact that the rest of the family did not share her insights; it was disappointing that Grace was the only one of us who, with a short phrase truthfully spoken, could let me see the positive aspects of a situation and not talk out of self-interest as the others always did. Soon afterward Rainier called me with the name and address of a friend of his, the well-liked Duchess of Tamames, widow of the Duke of Tamames, who had been the brother of the Princess of Bavière-Bourbon with whom my sister Betsy had stayed in Madrid.

I thanked my uncle for the introduction. A few days later I flew from Paris to Dakar in West Africa, and then to Rio and Buenos Aires. I found myself in the depths of the southern hemisphere's winter. But as I traveled by cab through the streets of the Argentinian capital, I could not help but be impressed by the wide, tree-planted streets, the handsome pearl-gray buildings, and the awnings and outdoor cafés that reminded me of Paris. I cannot say that my spirits were particularly exalted—this far from everything I cared about—but at least I hadn't found myself in the middle of the African veld.

I struck up a good relationship with a local Fiat executive, Dr. Umberto Damiani. Damiani introduced me to the pleasures of the city, and I quickly discovered that Argentinian girls were very beautiful and exciting to be with. My job with the automobile company could not have been more easygoing. All I really had to do was visit the local dealers scattered through the sprawling suburbs of the city and make sure that they were being run according to Fiat's policies. I joined the managers for drinks or meals, or talked with them in their offices, feeling that life could be a great deal worse than this. Then in the evenings there was the prospect of attractive dates, restaurants, and nightclubs. I began to enjoy myself.

After a few days I telephoned the Duchess of Tamames. She invited me to her home for dinner. In my Fiat I arrived at her family's luxurious apartment on the Avenue Quintana, which was named after her ex-husband Enrique Quintana's grandfather, who had been president of Argentina. Enrique Quintana himself was later to become ambassador to Russia. Tita Tamames greeted me at the door. She was extremely beautiful and impressed me with her graciousness, sense of humor, and energy. She introduced me to her nineteen-year-old daughter by her first marriage, Maria Marta, a quiet, refined, well-educated, and sheltered girl, and to her two sons, Diego and Martin. Over cocktails I watched the family and their friends together. They immediately made me feel at home.

As for Maria Marta, we became instant companions. She helped me locate an apartment not too far from the Avenue Quintana, and with her I traveled the length and breadth of the city and the surrounding countryside, where we visited the *estancias*, or cattle ranches, that her mother owned. The atmosphere of these estates was relaxing and comfortable. The houses were tastefully furnished with antiques and were situated in beautiful country, on properties that covered thousands of acres. Whereas at Mereze and the palace wealth only brought compression and restriction, here it brought a spaciousness and freedom in which a man could breathe.

Maria Marta and I were inevitably drawn together romantically. I found in her family a security and solidarity I had never found at Mereze. As we rode horseback across her mother's vast properties, and as I noticed Maria Marta's unselfish concern with my welfare, our friendship deepened. At that time, in an Argentinian Catholic family, more than a few dates between a man and a woman called for a clear announcement of the couple's future intentions. Maria Marta and I agreed to announce our engagement. I decided to inform both my father and my mother of my good news. I knew Father would be happy for me, and I expected that even Mother would be pleased. I knew that she very much liked the Duchess and that she was an intimate friend of her sister-in-law, the Princess of Bavière-Bourbon, who was a frequent visitor to Monaco.

My father was now living in Los Angeles, in the part of the San Fernando Valley known as Van Nuys, where he was still working as a professional tennis coach. He had managed to patch his fortunes together again, and I was eager to see his and my stepmother Margot's home. I flew to California on my way back to Europe. The house, set back from a long street lined with pine trees, was cool even in the heat, spacious, and comfortably furnished with antiques salvaged from my father's years in the art business. I enjoyed the two-day visit, and my father and stepmother were pleased with the news of my approaching marriage. I now expected to get a similar response from Mother.

I flew on to Paris and then to Nice. Arriving at Mereze without warning in the middle of the day, I found Mother on the terrace having lunch with my sisters. When I walked out of the living room into the October sunshine, Mother looked at me with astonishment. "What in God's name are you doing here?" she asked. "You're supposed to be in Argentina! You haven't been gone very long! What is this madness?" I replied that if she would only stop and listen to me for a moment, I would explain. I told her of the wedding plans for November. The news could not have elicited a more horrified response. She seemed to forget that the Duchess of Tamames was a personal friend of hers, much appreciated at the palace, and that Maria Marta's father was a fully ranked diplomat, at present ambassador to Lebanon. She seemed to neglect the fact that I was already over twenty-one. She said to me furiously, "One does not say to one's mother I am *going* to get married. One says to one's mother, I would *like* to get married and would you please grant me permission?" I reminded her that now I was of an age where no such permission was necessary. She in turn reminded me, her voice full of rage, that this was totally irrelevant since sovereign family law required Uncle Rainier's permission and that she herself would have to seek it from him in person, a very difficult task, she claimed. I responded that I would be asking for that permission myself and that my wedding plans had nothing to do with her or her husband: it was a matter between me and my uncle. Her words of anger rang out behind me as I got into the Alfa Romeo, roared out of the garage, and set off to the palace.

T W E L V E

U NCLE RAINIER was out that afternoon. Grace received me in her private salon, with its view of the garden and swimming pool, the room dominated by a striking portrait of her. We embraced. As we sat down to tea, I asked her if she had received a telephone call from Mother. She said she had not and asked me what all this was about: hurrying home to Monaco like this, suddenly appearing without warning from Argentina. I replied, "Listen, since you've heard nothing from Mother, let me see your reaction to what I have to tell you."

I told Grace of my plans to marry Maria Marta. "Oh!" Grace exclaimed. "How marvelous! What a good surprise!" She went on, "As you know, I am very familiar with Maria Marta and her entire family. I am especially fond of the Princess of Bavière-Bourbon. And I very much like the Duchess of Tamames as well. In fact, as you may know, I've seen Maria Marta only recently and was impressed by the way she has grown up as a young woman. She is so elegant and has perfect manners!" As she drank her tea, Grace continued. "Yes, there's no doubt about it. This is a perfect choice for you in every way, a most conservative and sensible decision. I com-

185

pletely support you. It will be an ideal match for you. It will make you settle down. I couldn't be happier."

Grace paused. I felt instantly relieved, because Grace's approval meant a great deal to me. She had always shown such an understanding of me that the fact she was happy for me now made me feel exceptionally optimistic. Grace came to the inevitable difficult subject when she continued, "All right. Very good. And now . . . don't tell me your mother is making waves over this? I simply can't believe it!" I told Grace about the confrontation at Mereze and how my mother was making such an issue about my getting Rainier's permission to marry, and about the problem she claimed she would undoubtedly face in approaching the palace.

I knew, of course, that Grace was in a delicate position regarding my mother. Although she had maintained an impeccable outward appearance of never criticizing Mother, she had continuously felt tense and uncomfortable where Mother was concerned. I knew from the times I had seen them together that Grace couldn't suppress a degree of envy over Mother's calculated and carefully preserved relationship with the citizens of the principality, whereas she had had to work constantly at earning their approval. It wasn't in Grace's nature to be recriminatory or jealous, but the contrast was painful to her and would remain so. She knew also that in her position it would be unwise for her to take sides in family quarrels. She could no more overtly support me against my mother than she would support my mother in her behavior with me. And then there were the added factors of our dislike for Jean-Charles Rey and the fact that, given the present apparent solidarity of the family, it would be counterproductive to raise old ghosts by bringing up disagreeable episodes.

With my great empathy for Grace, I could see these conflicting thoughts moving across her mind as she leaned back in her chair and sighed, carefully composing the words she was about to speak, as she always did. She said, "Well, it's been a long time since we have talked about your mother. Now that you are over twenty-one, I imagine you have a more mature understanding of your mother's particular problems. I realize how difficult it is to have to try to deal with her behavior. But, and we have talked about this before, she was preconditioned to these problems by her youth. She was deprived of the right of succession to the throne by her own mother, Mamou, who hated her. In turn, your mother hated your grandmother. Then Antoinette also hated her father and ran away from him to your great grandfather. With her parents separated, and neither having any affinity with her, knowing that she would never rule, she was deeply insecure as a young girl, as you can understand. And naturally, with this broken home and no family life to speak of, she would likely try to overcontrol, overdiscipline her own family. It is typical of people who have had no security early on that they try to dominate and rule over their children. Try to understand this if you can."

Grace then went on to reveal to me the details about my mother's past, of which at the time I had no more than an inkling. I was flabbergasted at Grace's matter-of-fact disclosures, and when I told her she was the first person to tell me about them, she was amazed. She asked me how the family could have kept all these secrets about the past from me. How much worse it was to have to find them out now, and how much I had been lied to. At one stage she stopped herself in the middle of a sentence, realizing apparently that she may have said too much. This was when she was trying to answer my question concerning the reasons that my sisters and I had been deprived of our family name and given the patronymic of de Massy, one of many titles possessed by my uncle.

I prodded her gently to continue, reminding her that Mother deliberately closed off the past so that her childhood would never be recalled.

Grace went on to say that the trouble Mother was making now could not be because of my choice of a bride, who was certainly more than acceptable, but was due to her wanting to be in control of everything, a function of an extreme superiority complex which, like most of such complexes, sprang from a sense of inferiority. I had to agree with Grace's interpretation of my mother's complicated psychology. Finally Grace said that she would be happy to convey my news to my uncle that evening and that she was sure there would be no problem in obtaining his approval. Then Grace did a very ingenious thing, showing me once again her capacity to deal with family problems in the most subtle way.

Without telling me what she was up to, she picked up the telephone and called Mereze. When my mother came on the line, Grace said, "Tiny? I am so pleased to have received a visit from Buddy. You must be thrilled by his news! It's exciting, isn't it? What an excellent choice he has made! Maria Marta will make a perfect bride for him! What a match! I can imagine how pleased you are, especially since you're such a good friend of Marisol Bavière-Bourbon!" She paused. I could imagine Mother's face at the other end of the line and could barely suppress a laugh. Grace added, "At last, Buddy has brought you a surprise . . . you can appreciate!" The thrust was perfectly timed. This was a side of her very few people knew: a witty shrewdness in achieving objectives. Of course, Mother had no alternative but to agree with Grace's view. Not wishing to rub salt in Mother's wounds, Grace concluded the conversation with, "Well, my dear, I'd better let you go. You must be so busy writing letters informing all your many friends."

I asked Grace whether she would be coming to the wedding

in Buenos Aires. She replied that she was sorry it wasn't going to be in Monaco and that it would be difficult for her to undertake the long air trip to Buenos Aires with my uncle in November. However, she assured me we had their sincerest blessings, and as we parted, she hugged me again and wished me all the best for my future with Maria Marta, and sent her love to her.

When I returned to Mereze, I wasn't surprised to find Mother conspicuously absent. Over the next few days we barely exchanged half a dozen words. She was completely deactivated by Grace, as Grace had planned, and since there was no disapproval from my uncle, there was nothing more she could do. My sisters were excited at the prospect of going to Argentina for the religious ceremony. As for Mother and Jean-Charles Rey, I didn't care whether they attended or not. By this point they were seriously disaffected from each other. Their marriage—or what there was of it—had deteriorated into a pattern of ferocious quarrels, recriminations, and name-calling. They were always screaming at each other and were living in separate parts of Mereze, their marriage in effect over.

I flew back to Argentina to a great surprise. The Duchess wanted to make sure that Maria Marta and I would be comfortable, and as a wedding gift, she rented us a magnificent house facing the Rio de la Plata with a large garden, swimming pool, and staff. Located in the suburb of Martinez, one of the most pleasant districts of Buenos Aires, the house was everything anyone could desire.

The wedding ceremony and reception that followed took place in the garden of Tita Tamames's apartment on the Avenue Quintana. Over two hundred guests, including my sisters but notable for the absence of my mother, milled through the garden and around the tables. The orchestra played, and the atmosphere was very festive. Maria Marta's father, Enrique Quintana, had flown in from Beirut, and greeted me warmly, although when he saw I was wearing a white suit instead of top hat and tails, he expressed a slight disapproval.

Uncle Rainier and Aunt Grace sent a gold and silver cigarette box and matching ashtrays inscribed with their signatures. Mother did not send a gift; presumably the fact that she paid my sisters' air fares was considered sufficient.

We honeymooned in Rio, before settling down in our new home. We entertained and were entertained a lot; Tita was a dream mother-in-law, and the job with Fiat was undemanding. Next year Maria Marta gave birth to our beautiful daughter, Laetitia. She had golden hair, gray-blue eyes, and pink cheeks, and we adored her.

Inevitably I grew restless again. Agreeable though the life in Buenos Aires was, I wanted badly to get back to Europe and get on with my long-dreamed-of career as a racing driver. I knew that I was now in a stronger position than I had ever been before where my mother and the palace were concerned, since I had not gotten into trouble since leaving Africa and my marriage was well regarded by my uncle and aunt.

Just as I was making plans to return home, I received a telegram from Mother saying that Christine was about to marry Wayne Knecht, the young cousin of Grace herself! This was a surprise. The last I had heard was that Christine was going to marry another of Grace's cousins, John Lehman, special assistant to Henry Kissinger in the State Department and later to become secretary of the Navy in the Reagan Cabinet: It turned out that she had broken off her relationship with Lehman and had fallen in love with his first cousin Wayne Knecht, whom she had met when they were in Washington.

There was nothing in Mother's telegram to indicate that I was being invited to the wedding. I phoned her to ask why I hadn't been invited. In view of the fact that she certainly would not think to invite my father, I was, apart from my grandfather Anthony Noghes, Christine's nearest male relative. I knew that my sister would want me present. Her answer was a cool, "Come if you can."

I decided this occasion provided the perfect time to return home. Grace was happy to see us and eager to see her grandniece, fond as she always was of children, she couldn't have been more sweet and welcoming. She made a big fuss over Maria Marta. Mother, who was always looking to find fault, remarked sourly to me about the extravagance of a young couple traveling with a nursemaid, despite the fact that she had been raised by Nanny Wanstall and so had her own children.

Mother made sure Christine's wedding took place at the palace. Interestingly enough, the press never picked up on the fact of Wayne Knecht's family relationship to Grace. Grace was upset with Knecht because he refused to cut his long hair for the wedding. Mother was out of her pro-British period and was now in a pro-American period, so she welcomed the idea of Christine marrying an American, particularly Grace's cousin. Grace, of course, was pleased at the family link. The ceremony was simple; I gave the bride away. Wayne and Christine went to Philadelphia, where they would have a son, Sebastien, and I was to see little of them for the next years. Now Elisabeth was the only one of us who was not married.

My interest now focused entirely upon preparing my career as a racing driver. In the late summer of 1972, I entered the Winfield Racing School located at Magny-Cours in the Loire Valley of France. The Winfield Racing Schools have produced the greatest number of Formula I drivers in the world. Formula I, the most highly developed and fastest type of racing car in the world, represents the ultimate racing category and is every driver's dream. The current world champion, Alain Prost, along with a dozen other Formula I drivers, started his career at one of the two Winfield Schools.

About four hundred students attended the fifteen-day course that year. Many of them had had previous racing experience. We were all given one-seater Formula Renaults. We were instructed by a former racing driver in the most efficient ways of shifting gears and braking, finding the best trajectory for cutting across corners, and how to negotiate them. We then drove ten laps in a row, starting at a deliberately restricted engine speed. If we drove to the satisfaction of the instructors and under a fixed time, we qualified to do another series at higher speeds, and so on until we reached the maximum engine power. Those who still qualified after that stage did more laps until the twenty-four fastest drivers qualified for the annual semifinals. From that group just six would be admitted to enter the finals. The winner would receive a fully-sponsored season in one of the leading teams of Formula Renault-Europe.

It was with an equal mixture of nervousness and anticipation that I joined the other drivers. I had waited so long and had so willfully disregarded my academic future for this one opportunity to prove myself in the only field I really cared about that I never expected to find myself surviving one elimination heat after another, winding up among the twenty-four semifinalists. I now started to believe that my childhood dream could finally come true and that I had been right: it had been worth the wait and the struggle.

The day before the semifinals there had been a rainstorm, and the track was very slick. I was well used to that track, with its many varied corners, by now. At Magny-Cours, as at most tracks (Monaco was an exception), anybody who spun off would not crash into a wall but instead would spin onto the surrounding grass, from which he would be able to recover control of the car. Since every car was identical, every tenth of a second clipped off one's time was crucial. I took off, feeling extremely tense. I had the first lap to get ready and warm the car up, and then six laps to perform my best time to try to qualify for the finals. At this stage, to crash or spin off the track meant instant elimination. Entering a corner on my third lap, I braked too late, locked the wheels, and skidded off the track. I was angry with myself. Although I was able to recover and wound up seventh, I was still eliminated according to the rules. René Arnoux beat me by six-tenths of a second and went on to win; he eventually would race for Ferrari in Formula I. I was encouraged by being one of a dozen surviving four hundred eliminations. That I had managed to get this far was both surprising and gratifying. Racing was now more than just a dream; now I began to believe I could make it.

If I was to go further, I would have to obtain sponsorship. While I was trying to figure out how to get it, somebody told me that my results in the semifinals at Magny-Cours had been signaled to the directors of Philip Morris-Europe and that they were interested in me. For the next few months, I hung on to the possibility that Philip Morris might sponsor me, trying not to get my hopes up too high, while Maria Marta, Laetitia, and I rented a house of our own. It was located at Saint-Jean-Cap-Ferrat, near the Villa Mauresque, the home of the late Somerset Maugham, and Lo Scoglieto, David Niven's residence. Overlooking the Mediterranean and the port of Villefranche, it had four bedrooms, a large living room, and a formal dining room. Built in the 1920s it still had the original Art Deco fixtures, with tubular steel stair rails and fluted decorations of glass. The original wall and ceiling lamps had been preserved. Our cook-housekeeper from Argentina stayed with us and proved to be a continuing treasure.

I had by now resigned my job with Fiat, and Tita, my mother-in-law, proved very supportive of my racing ambitions. Most of my time during those months was taken up with training at the gym for my possible future racing. Meanwhile, several afternoons a week, my wife would take our daughter up to the palace to have tea with Grace, who showed a keen interest in Laetitia and had given her a belated christening spoon and silver cup.

Time went on. Much as I hoped for the Philip Morris contract to come through, I didn't really believe it would be possible. Then one day a telegram arrived from Lausanne, headquarters of the Philip Morris European corporation. I nervously tore it open. I could hardly believe the message, which invited me to Switzerland to discuss the company's possible sponsorship of me. I was wild with joy. The recently created Formula I Philip Morris Marlboro team, sponsoring British Racing Motors (BRM), was already among the best on the international circuit.

A chauffeur driving a Mercedes with the Philip Morris coat of arms met me at the Geneva airport and drove me to the corporate headquarters on the Avenue de Tivoli in Lausanne. The meeting with the directors was one of the high points of my life. They invited me to join the team and said they would provide me with a sufficient budget to buy a Martini MK-11 one-seater Formula-Renault-Europe racing car. I was ecstatic. My professional racing career was beginning at last. From it, if I was successful and sponsorship was continued, I could move up in class to Formula III and II, and eventually to the impossible dream of Formula I.

Two big problems remained. The first of these was that Marlboro's budget would cover only the car, two engines, and a set of wheels. They lent me a station wagon, but I had to pay for the trailer to put the car on. In order to participate, I also needed to have both engines prepared and regularly overhauled by a specialist. I had to have brake linings, tires, extra wheels, gas, oil, spare parts, and traveling expenses. For these I would have to pay out of my own pocket. I also had to pay the track for practice sessions, and above all I had to have my own mechanic. I had very little knowledge of mechanics; and even in situations where there was no accident calling for repairs, hours of work were involved just in order to keep the car in racing condition after qualifying sessions. The constant wear and tear on the engine inevitably resulted in a loss of horsepower. After an overhaul an engine could stand up to two qualifying sessions and a race, but it would then need overhauling again if one wanted to be among the serious contenders. Without money I would not be able to practice. That year there were ninety-eight of us trying to qualify for twenty places. We would qualify on the basis of our fastest lap times; the time spent in the pits to adjust the car to the track was crucial. Therefore, a mechanic was indispensable.

The second problem was serious, because now I would have to involve my family. Until now I had managed to keep my racing a secret, confiding only in the handful of people I could trust not to leak word to the palace. But now I would need an FIA, or international racing license, if I was to compete in a European championship. I knew that as soon as I applied for one at the Monaco Auto Club, the palace and my mother would be alerted at once. The president of the club had told me he would not issue me a license unless my mother or the Prince authorized it. It was frustrating to me that I would have to obtain permission for a license from anyone. Being subject to the laws governing the sovereign family and without financial independence, I had no way of fighting the palace's power. Born in a state in which everything depended on my uncle, I was forced once again to face certain realities. Having come so close to realizing my life's goal, there was no way that I would risk blowing it.

At this difficult moment I didn't feel I could turn to my uncle, and to go to Grace would have put her in an awkward position with him. Surprisingly, it was to my fifteen-year-old cousin, Caroline, that I turned. Despite her young age, I knew that her counsel would be valuable. Since my return from South America, we had grown much closer. She had turned into a beautiful, dark-haired, cheerful, and warm young girl. She was very mature for her age, and strong-willed, and always seemed to be happy. She was not at all pretentious or self-important. I always looked forward to being with her at parties at the palace. Moving from group to group, she would invariably liven up the atmosphere by her presence. I always had fun with her. She was the only one at the palace to see the funny side of my misadventures. She called me her "big bad cousin." Later we would laugh together over the newspaper stories about her and the pictures that would make her parents furious. I felt I could trust Caroline and regarded her as my ally: smart, fast-thinking, bright. She disliked trivial and superficial salon small talk as much as I did.

Months before, I had found the occasion to confide in Caroline during yet another party at the palace. I drew her aside to a spot where we could not be overheard and told her of my plans for a racing career. She was very excited for me and promised she would say nothing to either her parents or mine. Her encouragement meant a great deal to me, and through this confidence between us our friendship grew. She did keep the secret. Now I went to her to ask how she thought I should approach her father about the license. She advised me to go to my mother and obtain her approval. She didn't think that Rainier would object if Mother approved. I knew at once that difficult though this would be, Caroline was right.

I drove to Mereze, past the lawns where I had once driven my kiddie-car around the trees as a child, dreaming of the future. Mother received me saying she was in a great hurry and didn't have much time. She listened while I delivered an impassioned plea asking her not to impede me in obtaining my license. I feared the worst but was astonished when she replied in terms that seemed to me, for the first time in my life, to make sense. After a silence she asked me the length of the contract with Marlboro. I told her it was for three years.

She said to me that if after that length of time I was placed among the first three of the European championships or had shown I could make a living at racing, she would not interfere with the license renewal. She would give me those three years in which to prove myself.

Mother finished the conversation by saying that I would also have to obtain my uncle's permission. This was necessary, she told me, because a member of the family would in effect be advertising a brand of cigarette, and my uncle could possibly object to this form of exploitation of the family name. Relieved and surprised by her attitude, I realized I had another major hurdle to cross.

I braced myself to see Uncle Rainier. He received me in that same office in which he had announced I would be leaving for Africa. I was greatly relieved when he said he would make no objections to my plans, nor would he stand in the way of a license, provided that my mother did not object. I assured him I already had her consent. Then he relaxed and to my surprise asked me the particulars of the make of car and engine, and many technical details of which he had some knowledge. He actually seemed interested in my racing and told me to keep him informed on how I was doing. I drove away from the palace feeling on top of the world.

I hired an Argentinian mechanic named Luis and purchased tools and a second gearbox and tires. Traveling to races all over France was costly. So was racing at Snetterton in Britain, Hockenheim in Germany, Spa in Belgium, and Monza in Italy. But ahead lay the biggest challenge of all: the Grand Prix of Monaco. Just before that race, I was so pressed for funds that I was compelled to let Luis go. I was now without a mechanic. I could afford to have my engine overhauled only every three races. After the third race that year, I had to go from race to race without being able to practice because I lacked the money. Between each event I would take the Martini to a garage at Cagnes-sur-Mer in the south of France, where a mechanic named Franconi became a good friend to me. Franconi and I would work on the car and afterward together often went to soccer matches in Monaco.

It was a serious handicap to have to race without my own mechanic. Whereas some drivers had a crew of them in the pits, I had none. I had to remove my safety harness, wriggle free, pull off my helmet, select the necessary instruments from the tool box, make the modifications, put the tools away, and climb back in the car, losing precious time. The other drivers simply instructed their mechanics to make the necessary adjustments.

Among the ninety-eight drivers racing in my category that year was the winner at Winfield, René Arnoux, as well as other racers who would go on to Formula I, such as Didier Pironi, Patrick Tambay, Jacques Lafitte, and Jean-Louis Schlesser. Also racing with me were Jean Rondeau, who would win the twenty-four hours at Le Mans in a car of his own design, Rene Metge, who would win the Paris-Dakar Rally three times, and Marc Sourd, future French Mountain Road National Champion. The competition was extremely intense.

In spite of everything, I managed to qualify for most of the races, sometimes with two or three others within the same tenths of a second. I didn't win any races: there were too many problems, and I was up against many outstanding drivers. But it was good for my training to drive under adversity that first year, so that when better conditions were obtained, I would be able to profit from them.

I remember two events in particular. I had arrived at Hockenheim, Germany, the night before the trials. Following a crash during the qualifying heats, hours of work lay ahead of me that night. It was then that I learned the meaning of sportsmanship among racers. A driver who would take every risk to get himself a better position in a race, even at a rival's peril, could be a real friend off the track. Following the accident I turned to the French driver Philippe de Henning, who, like myself, was short of money and lived in a truck. Since I had no truck of my own to shelter my car, Philippe helped me with the repairs in pouring rain. Deep in mud, using flashlights, we worked hard until after midnight while Philippe's girl friend fed us hot soup. He needed two tires for the upcoming race, so I gave him my spares. The next day we were at the same point on the departure grid. We fought hard with each other during the entire race. No outsider watching us in our struggle on the track could possibly have believed that we had spent most of the previous night side by side in the rain repairing my car.

At Snetterton, after leaving in twenty-second position following the elimination heats, I came in eleventh. It was my first time racing in rain. The race was extremely dangerous for all of us, driving surrounded by a dense pack of cars and with virtually no visibility. Although my eleventh position didn't qualify for any prize, and would not even be noticed, I had seldom felt so happy as I crossed the finishing line. I knew I had at last done something about which I could feel really proud. Now it was on to Monaco and the trials before the Grand Prix.

As a Monegasque, as Prince Rainier's nephew, and as the grandson of Anthony Noghes, founder of the Monaco Grand Prix, I knew this was personally as well as professionally the most important race of the season. If my heat times were good enough to qualify me for the race, I would have the opportunity of doing what I had been striving for over the years: proving myself in front of my family and compatriots.

I scarcely slept the night before the qualifying trial on May 31. Three days before the race, I had just repainted my Martini MK-11 with the red and white Marlboro colors, coincidentally, the same as those of Monaco. As I got into my car that morning, I thought of the cocktail party in Geneva at which I had been presented to the press along with other members of the Marlboro team. I had felt proud that the publicity release Philip Morris issued referred to me as a young and promising Monegasque driver and not as the Prince's nephew. I wanted to make it on my own. My main thought that night, as I tried to get some sleep, was a strong desire to justify Marlboro's faith in me and to earn a good starting position in the June 3 final.

I had never been around the difficult Monaco circuit in a racing car, as the streets were always in use. Despite the fact that I had driven those streets in everything from Alexander Onassis's kiddie-car to my present Renault Alpine, it was impossible to get to know them in advance under racing conditions, as driving an ordinary car couldn't give anything approaching a true picture of what would be involved.

Now that I didn't have a mechanic, I decided to save time by not adjusting the car constantly at the pits during the thirty minutes in which we tried to qualify, but instead using the time saved to do extra laps. I also planned to take the first five laps slowly to warm up my tires, and, more important, to get to know the track properly. But two laps into the trials I could no longer hold myself back, and I opened up and went flat out to qualify. Tense and nervous, I lost patience. As I was driving down the sloping track from the scaffolding of the new Loew's Hotel, I came out of a sharp corner close to the sea edge leading into the tunnel that goes under the hotel and emerges in full sight of the port. I came out too wide and oversteered. I managed to control the car, but I couldn't prevent my back left wheel from touching the guardrail. I heard a loud snap, which told me I had bent the axle. As the attendants hauled my car over the guardrails, I realized it was all over. One of the attendants sympathetically told me not to worry: it would go better for me next year. But something inside me said I would not be back.

T H I R T E E N

$\mathcal{N}$EXT DAY, Jackie Stewart
won the Grand Prix. I had gotten to know Jackie and his wife,
Helen. I liked him personally as much as I admired him as a
driver. That night at the gala ball at the Sporting Club, I
joined everybody else in celebrating his victory.

At the ball I ran into a friend of many years, a prince whom
I will call Rafael. He was well thought of at the palace, and a
friend of Uncle Rainier's. We talked at the gala and at Regine's
afterward. During our conversation Rafael told me, "I have
some advice for you, Christian. If you want things to be all
right with your uncle, stop racing." There was something
ominous in his tone. I immediately said, "No, you're completely mistaken. He's in support of my racing career." I told
Rafael of the meeting with my uncle at which Rainier had
given me permission to race and had seemed to show an interest in my progress. Rafael shook his head. He replied, "Unfortunately, Rainier this afternoon made himself quite clear
about his adverse feelings regarding your future in racing."

Knowing as I did how Monaco seethed with rumor and gossip, I didn't take the well-meaning prince seriously. Only the
night before, at the traditional cocktail party at the palace

preceding the gala, Rainier had been cordial and had made a good-hearted joke about what had happened. Caroline had been sweet and comforting to me over my accident, feeling for me in my disappointment. Albert had talked to me at length and was interested in my plans for upcoming races. Grace did not like racing but was happy to see me finally content with what I was doing.

I mentioned all this to Rafael and assured him that he was wrong. Again he reiterated Uncle Rainier's negative attitude. He told me of something disturbing he had witnessed after the race, when Rainier had overheard members of his staff and officials in the royal box talking sympathetically about my accident and hoping that I would have better luck the following year. Something about my uncle's reaction to the conversation had worried Rafael. He sensed that Rainier seemed jarred by their concern and genuine affection, and by their expression of my growing popularity. It seemed to Rafael that Rainier was troubled by the idea that if I was successful as a racing driver, I might attract too much attention. I did not want to think that Uncle Rainier could possibly react in this manner. But I couldn't shut the thought out.

Rafael's revelation of my uncle's attitude toward me was not my only problem. My money had drained away completely in racing expenses. I barely had enough to repair the damaged Martini. Nor could I afford to have my two engines reconditioned. It would take a financial windfall to enable me to continue to the end of the season. My bankers were kind enough to provide me with one more overdraft so that I could enter a few more races that summer. But then, in September, Philip Morris wrote to me saying that Marlboro would not be picking up the option on my contract for the following year. This was a devastating blow.

Now I had to find a new sponsor for 1974. Budgets were normally voted in September or October, and the late arrival of Marlboro's news left me little time to obtain backing. I weighed my alternatives. I could try to race in the four remaining contests of the season, hoping to raise a small budget that would allow me to continue in the following year with what equipment I had. If I had had difficulty scraping by with no mechanic or practices in 1973, what would it be like next year, racing against the new car models with the same handicaps and two badly overdriven engines? I knew that in the second year I really had to get results; in the first year allowances were made because it was considered an apprentice year, but in the second year nobody was interested in a driver's problems. He was expected to win.

The other option was to stop immediately, sell the Martini, and repay most of my overdraft. I could use the time during which I would not be driving to shop around for a sponsor. After thinking it over, that was the alternative I settled on.

With the help of some friends, I drew up a list of forty-seven potential candidates, French companies that were important advertisers with Monaco's local radio station and other firms that might be interested in becoming sponsors of Grand Prix racing. With this list in hand I prepared a brochure filled with facts and figures and photographs, putting forward the advertising advantages of racing. Covering letters were attached, and the forty-seven proposals were sent out to the firms.

I was about to leave for Paris to see the various advertising directors who had indicated an interest in discussing my proposal further, when a friend, a man connected to the Monaco Auto Club, told me that he had learned that Uncle Rainier had had something to do with the Marlboro decision against me. I found this impossible to believe. It seemed just another example of Monaco gossip. But my friend insisted he had heard that Uncle Rainier had indirectly conveyed to the cigarette people that he would prefer it if my option were not renewed.

It was hard to shake off this extraordinary allegation. I reminded myself yet again that Rainier had not objected to my racing career.

Uncertain and worried though I was, wondering whether there might be some truth in this, I left for Paris. I went from meeting to meeting, finding the general response sympathetic. At the outset, everything seemed to be going well.

Four of the firms were especially interested. At one meeting two out of the three directors responsible for the advertising budget told me they intended to propose my racing under their colors at their upcoming general meeting. I returned to Monaco with a degree of confidence that when the plan came to a vote at the general meeting a few weeks later, the outcome would be in my favor. It was therefore an unhappy surprise to me when I received an abruptly worded telegram from that company, even before the meeting was held, telling me to forget the whole thing. I would not be included in their proposed campaign.

The three other firms that had shown an interest in me also advised me that their decisions were negative. Before investing a large sum in any driver, it was logical that a company would obtain as much information as it could on a candidate. In my case the most obvious source would be the Monaco Automobile Club, which I now understood received instructions from the palace to discourage potential sponsors from backing me.

I was never able to prove my suspicions, and I knew that if I were to confront him with it, Uncle Rainier would deny it. Not only would I gain nothing by a confrontation with him, but by bringing the matter up at all, I would also distance him from me still further. For obvious reasons I could not take the situation up with my mother. I was back to square one again.

I found myself at a kind of dead end, uncertain of the future. In the meantime, Mother's marriage to Jean-Charles Rey finally caved in after more fierce quarrels and mutual recriminations about the other's impossible character. For once I agreed with both of them. If Mother had thrown Rey out, she might at least have satisfied her pride, but when he left her, it was humiliating to her that he would have dared. When he got married again just a month after his divorce, she was injured still further.

I sold my racing car and repaid most of my debts. Because I had no equipment now, my driving career effectively came to a standstill. I set about improving my mechanical knowledge of cars and went to work with Franconi at Cagnes so that if I ever was to have a chance to race again, at least I would understand more about the cars I was driving. I spent long hours covered in grease in Franconi's company.

I found another interest that helped to make the waiting a little easier. Mother had set up a fund, which would go to each of her children when they got married, to provide each of us with a house. She had already bought a house for Christine in Philadelphia, where my sister was living with her husband, Wayne Knecht.

Wanting to create my own environment, I bought some land and started to build on it. The land was on the steep slopes of the foothills of the Maritime Alps, just under the Middle Corniche at Saint-Laurent d'Eze, standing on a cliff between Cap d'Ail and Cap Estel, overlooking the sea, about ten minutes' drive from Monaco. It was worth the time I had taken to find this setting, and I made sure that the house would be an exact reflection of what I wanted: freedom. I happened to see in an architect's office a photograph of a Frank Lloyd Wright house, and I drew much of the inspiration from that. My intention was to reflect the ocean and the sky in the flow of the house's design. The swimming pool was crescent shaped and ran the whole length of the front, which from floor to ceiling was walled in glass. As one woke in the morning, one could see the pool seemingly flowing into the Mediterranean itself. The illusion was harmonious and complete, so that one seemed to be on the edge of the sea, gazing into infinity without restrictions. My bedroom and the guest bedroom opened out through French windows onto the pool.

The daybreaks and sunsets were beautiful. Yet despite my love of the house, life seemed fairly meaningless to me now that I could no longer pursue my passion for racing, and there were problems at home as well. My marriage to Maria Marta was falling apart. There were no ugly scenes between us. My wife was considerate and understanding. The fault was entirely mine that I yearned to be free, that the obligations of marital responsibility were too great for me to handle at that age. While I was racing, I was fully satisfied with my life, but now I was restless again.

Grace was fonder than ever of our baby and was not aware of the disintegrating relationship. Grace continued to see Laetitia as often as she could to watch her progress. She appreciated Maria Marta more than ever for her sensibility and flawless education. Grace respected the polish that had come to my wife from her childhood years spent in the embassies around the world. Whereas Grace had had to learn all the complexities of protocol as she went along, my wife had been born to that world. The two shopped together from time to time in Monaco. I myself saw little of Grace in that period.

Maria Marta increasingly sensed my restlessness in our marriage. She realized, as I did by now, that there was no hope for our relationship. One evening she said to me, "You're not happy, are you?" I told her the truth. She went on, "All right, I understand. There's no point in dragging on like this. I will leave tomorrow." And she did, with our child, without a single recrimination. She went to stay at her grandmother's house in Biarritz; she agreed that although she would have custody of Laetitia, I could see our daughter whenever I wanted. Maria Marta and I remained on the best of terms.

I had not told anyone in the family that I was going to end my marriage, although Caroline had almost certainly sensed it. I didn't tell Grace what I was considering because I knew she wouldn't find my desire for freedom a sufficient motive. As a Roman Catholic, and because of her strong sense of family, she found the idea of divorce unacceptable. And I knew that she wanted the marriage to go on, not only because of her affection for Maria Marta, but because she felt that it would keep me out of what she still called "mischief." Finally, however, I had to tell her the truth, and I drew her aside at a palace party to break the news. She was very upset. I also told her of the problems I was having, not racing and not sure when I would start again. I could tell from the expression on her face that she knew nothing about the alleged suspension of my racing future by her husband. I told her that the only thing I wanted was to get my career off the ground again and that I was working hard learning auto mechanics and was in training, working out at the Monaco Boxing Gym.

I was tempted to come right out and tell Grace about the allegations that had been made about Uncle Rainier and my racing. But I didn't. It would have been unfair to put her on the spot that way with my uncle, forcing her to ask him some awkward questions which, if I were wrong, could only embarrass her and enflame him. And moreover, even if the charges were true, I knew that he would deny them. In either case I had little to gain.

I found consolation in my new house. For many hours I was happily alone there, listening to music. I redesigned the interior, knocking down walls to create even more space. With a talented young Italian designer, I changed the off-white and beige motifs to pure white, with white carpets. Combining modern Italian and Japanese influences, the rooms achieved a new degree of openness, with arrangements of plants, stones, and asymmetrical designs of twigs. We painted the ceiling a grayish blue so it would blend into the sky, which in turn blended into the sea. Maria Niarchos, who at the time was writing for *Vogue Homme* of France, featured the house in an illustrated article on Monaco. I had finally created the environment I needed, surrounded by nature, alone on a hill, able to see with no obstructions the sun rise and set into the Mediterranean. There were speakers in every room and around the pool, and from midday on the house would resound with modern jazz and rhythm-and-blues.

One August day Aunt Grace telephoned me to invite me to dinner at an outdoor restaurant at Roquebrune called the Hacienda, which served Provençal cuisine in a Mexican setting and had a mariachi band. She said to me, "This is to be a birthday party for a special guest. You'll be seated to her right. Buddy, for heaven's sake, this time try to be punctual. Make an effort to get there before our party from the palace arrives." Grace was very mysterious about the name of the guest of honor. I asked her if it was to be a formal evening, and she said no, but that I should wear a jacket. She seemed in an exceptionally good mood, warning me because she knew that I invariably turned up at the last minute. It was obvious that on this occasion she wanted me to be at my best. When I arrived punctually at the Hacienda, I realized I was the only guest present not wearing a tie.

As I walked into the main room of the restaurant, I saw an enormous birthday cake decorated on the top tier with a replica of a horse jumping over a wooden hurdle. That should have given me an idea, but I still didn't guess in whose honor the party was being held. It was not until I took my place at the table and the palace party arrived that I found out why

Grace was so concerned. The person who was to sit next to me was Princess Anne of England.

I saw Grace smile at me in recognition of the fact that I had come early. As I began talking to Anne, I could see Grace checking on me with a twinkle in her eye, relieved to see I was behaving properly. It was obviously important to her that I represented the family correctly. I did my best.

Anne asked me politely what my interest in life was. She must have regretted her inquiry because I launched into an interminable monologue on the subject of automobile racing, in which, of course, she had no interest. She never betrayed her boredom, but instead, with all of the patience required in her royal position, never stopped smiling until I had finished. Naturally I had to ask her what her chief interest was, knowing it in advance. She embarked on an equally protracted account of horses, horse training, and horseback riding, interests as far removed from my life as racing cars was from hers, and as predominant in her life as they were in her mother Queen Elizabeth's. When Anne was finished, she said to me, "Everybody who meets me for the first time thinks I can only talk about horse riding. So they make that the sole topic of conversation." She laughed and added, "I do know how to talk about other matters." Jokingly I replied, "I didn't feel like taking any risks, Your Highness!" I smiled as I said that, and she responded with an official half-smile as the cake candles were lit and she blew them out.

That same year, my older sister Elisabeth followed me and Christine in marrying; her wedding to the extroverted young Swiss Baron Bernard Taubert-Natta, an avid student of royal genealogy, was held in the palace chapel. As had been the case with Christine's marriage to Wayne Knecht, there was no question of my exiled and long-since-remarried father being

invited to Monaco to give the bride away. Normally, by the
rule of protocol, if the bride's father was unavailable or dead,
her grandfather would perform that office. But Anthony
Noghes, despite his background as former president of the
Assembly and founder of the Grand Prix, his age, and his distinction, was required once again to take a spectator's seat,
and I was told by my mother that I would be standing in.
After all these years could she still be so full of prejudice
against my father as to ignore an old man's feelings?

Stephanie, now age nine, acted as a flower girl. Because of
the age difference between us, I saw much less of her than of
Albert or Caroline. She always seemed to be sulking. She
never stopped sucking her thumb and barely resisted doing so
at the wedding itself. It was a habit she would not give up
until she was fourteen. She seemed to be several years younger
than her actual age. The baby of the family, she was spoiled
and deeply dependent on her mother. Although shyer than her
sister at first meetings, she, too, shared what seemed to be the
common denominator among Grimaldi women, a very strong
character that exploded in flashes of willfulness. She argued
frequently with her mother to the point of intransigence. As
I came to know her better, though, I discovered her to be
genuinely sweet and vulnerable. Less intellectual than Caroline and less thoughtful than Albert, Steph was more artistic;
she became fond of drawing, painting, and designing clothes.
She cared nothing about her role of being a child princess and
was far more interested in doing gymnastics or, later on, speeding about on a motor scooter than being a member of a royal
house. On her cousin's wedding day, she looked very cute
dressed up in her white flower girl's ensemble.

Caroline was as independent and generous-spirited as ever.
I noted at this time her strong physical resemblance to Mamou
when my grandmother was a young girl. She had much the
same strong will and temperament that marked Mamou, yet

nothing like the conflicts of Mamou and her parents existed between Caroline and Grace. Despite her light-hearted character, she remained surprisingly scholarly, doing very well at her studies both at the Sisters of St. Maur convent school in Monaco and at St. Mary's Convent at Ascot in England. In July 1973 Caroline passed the second part of her *baccalauréat* in Paris.

Caroline's position and good looks made her, even in those days, a natural target of the columnists, who were always linking her with this or that eligible bachelor from wealthy or aristocratic families of Europe. She was even linked with Prince Charles, despite the fact that she scarcely knew him. Caroline laughed over this gossip with me. She was always able to see the funny side of the columnists' stories. Grace was of course more seriously offended by them. Preoccupied with Caroline's welfare, Grace experienced the tensions of any mother seeing a daughter come to adulthood. With her usual discipline and sense of balance, she tried to be as free and even-handed with Caroline as she could, not chaining her in any way but still keeping a certain degree of control over her life, asking her to be home at certain hours, meeting the young men who wanted to date her. She was afraid that if she allowed Caroline too much freedom, there would be trouble. Uncle Rainier played little or no visible role in exercising any discipline upon her, leaving that difficult job to Grace.

My cousin Albert was very different from his sisters. He was quiet and subdued, almost as if the duties and obligations he would one day inherit were already beginning to weigh upon him. He was also far more self-controlled than his sisters. In his conscientiousness, reserve, and politeness, he was, more than the other children, reminiscent of Grace. I saw him mostly at palace receptions. We got on well; he was friendly and easygoing, and, like me, he loved soccer and car racing. He went to every football match he could, and later, when the

Monaco team reached the Paris finals, he went there with my uncle to see the match. He attended football school in the principality twice a week and played on the palace team. He later formed his own team and played against the other teams in the principality. We often discussed the European Cup matches, which we both followed.

I would run into him at the Monaco Grand Prix, joining him in walking around the pits and meeting the various drivers. Although he didn't drive at that time (now he has twice taken part in the Paris-Dakar Rally), his passion for cars was real.

During the mid-1970s, Albert was away much of the time, visiting the United States, staying with his cousins at Ocean City or in the Pocono Mountains in Pennsylvania. He continued to be slightly handicapped by his childhood stammer, which, with great determination, he overcame. He became very American in appearance, and his speech was so completely East Coast that no one could tell he had not grown up there.

Uncle Rainier's Jubilee year arrived in 1974; it had been twenty-five years since his succession to the throne shortly after I was born. April, May, and June were given over to a series of spectacular events in which the immense wealth that the principality had acquired since Rainier's marriage was fully apparent. The Grand Opera House, scene of my childhood boredom and Uncle Rainier's snoring naps, was now the site of an important concert, performed by the Monaco National Orchestra. Rainier himself had founded the orchestra in 1953. Among the guests in the royal box bedecked in red and white flowers were the Count and Countess of Barcelona and King Juan of Spain and his wife Sophia.

The performance was followed by a party at which the Begum Aga Khan, Princess Marie-Gabrielle of Savoy, and the new Mrs. Stavros Niarchos were present. Another guest was the Princess Ghislaine, the former actress who had married my great-grandfather Louis II.

There was another grand dinner in the Empire Room of the Hôtel de Paris, which was lit by magnificent chandeliers, some of them brought out of storage and specially hung for the occasion. The floral decorations were made of 2,500 roses brought in from the Loire River Valley. Prince Albert was performing for the first time an official function as co-host at the dinner. Initially he had not been scheduled to appear, but then at the last minute his parents decided that now that he had just turned sixteen, he should take part in the event. Bespectacled, reserved, and self-conscious, he acted out his part with great concentration, while Caroline played hers with more effortless and authentic relaxation.

There was also a Te Deum at the cathedral in honor of Louis II, at which Cardinal Krol, Archbishop of Philadelphia, acted as special representative of Pope Paul VI. The Bishop of Monaco, Monsignor Abele, presided in happy contrast with the banished Father Tucker. Also present were delegates of the Greek Orthodox Church, the Russian Orthodox Church, and the High Church of England. The floral decorations of red anthericums and white irises were a product of Grace's own Garden Club. The pillars were covered in red and white roses and lilies. The cathedral resounded with the music of Bach, Mozart, and Haydn. It was a relief for me to see that for once the antagonism in the family ranks was overcome by the majesty and solemnity of the occasion.

The festivities of the jubilee year ushered in a period of unrivaled growth and financial well-being. Monte Carlo was more than ever now the undisputed playground of the rich and the super-rich. The very look of Monaco changed radically. Through Grace's influence the entire principality was a blaze of flowers. She gave instructions to decorate the bases of trees with displays of red and white primulas. She personally supervised plantings of mimosa on the cliffs and walls of the palace. Her flower arrangement competitions brought contestants from all over the Riviera. Monaco had never looked more beautiful, and neither had the palace's public and private rooms, all awash in vivid color. In fact, you could scarcely move through the royal apartments for the quantities of tulips, carnations, and roses.

Simultaneously, the enormous building and extension program that had begun in the mid-1950s was reaching its peak. Reclamations of land increased the waterfront by over ninety acres. In addition to the Loew's Hotel, there was a new Holiday Inn with a huge swimming pool. The SBM and the Casino achieved unprecedented gains. Under the guidance of my grandfather's first cousin, Prince Louis de Polignac, president of the Administrative Council, the SBM announced a profit of $2.5 million and a forty percent rise in its stock. Half a million people had visited the Casino that year. Work was done on it so that the gilded, richly muraled ceilings and gold and velvet curtains of its theater were fully restored. Under the influence of Prince Louis, Regine, whose Paris nightclub had made her legendary, opened the first of her clubs outside the French capital. The Monaco Tourist Office also opened in New York.

Grace always tried to extend the public celebrations of that period to her people. She had some time before initiated the practice of serving Thanksgiving dinners in all the hotels and was responsible for the decree requiring the Casino to close on Good Friday. She threw a Texas-style picnic-barbecue for every citizen of Monaco, all four and a half thousand of them, at the Louis II stadium, receiving them in the traditional Monegasque costume of flowered hat, white blouse, and red and white skirt. She cemented her country's relations to the United States even more than before, launching the Monaco-U.S.A. Foundation. In addition to hosting an American week, she helped Rainier establish the International Circus Festival. Years before, in January 1961, she had also created the International Television Festival; and in 1963 she had become honorary president of the World Association of Friends of the Children. When Grace saw there was no day nursery for working mothers, she founded the Garderie Notre Dame de Fatima and personally saw to the decorating of the building. She did not do these things out of the obligation of being a princess, but more from her "mother hen" instincts, an extension of her love for her children. She didn't just join organizations, she created them, reflecting her interests and the need to solve the problems that came to her attention. Among many others was the Princess Grace Foundation, created to help young performers of various arts. She helped Josephine Baker and her twelve adopted children to get a house and financial support. She launched the International Ballet Festival and founded the Académie de Danse Classique Princess Grace, and launched the annual flower show. She presided over more than twenty organizations. At last, after all her efforts, she became known not merely as "*la Princesse américaine*" but, "our Princess."

While Grace's life at this time was fulfilling, crammed with activity and social obligations, my own existence seemed fairly meaningless. For a while I thought of going to America to continue racing in a place where Uncle Rainier would not be able to influence potential sponsors, but unluckily I did not. Feeling frustrated at every turn, I gave up all hope of a racing career and no longer even went to the garage at Cagnes. Instead I plunged into the seductive pleasures of Monte Carlo with all of the zeal of a now-single man in his mid-twenties.

FOURTEEN

HE FOCUS of my life became the magnificent old Hôtel de Paris. I received most of my messages and telephone calls there, and I was very fond of the staff, as they were of me. The interior was as familiar to me as that of my own home: the immensely high ceilings, the marble floors, the ornate baroque mirrors, the leather sofas, the chandeliers, the statue of a horse with its left leg raised, its hoof touched by gamblers for luck. I took many of my meals there, either at the beautiful Grill on the top floor, with its sliding roof that opened to the stars, or in the Salle Empire, on the terrace overlooking the Casino. I was as happy as my circumstances could allow. After the constant pressures and arguments of my childhood at Mereze, I enjoyed living alone. I sold my Alpine and bought a gray SM Maserati. I also bought two female dobermans, Cocaine and Cannabis; and later I bought a male, Igor. Three of the puppies joined the other dobermans until I had six in all.

Each night during the summer season, which started in July, I would drive from my house to the hotel. There was always a large crowd of tourists at the foot of the steps leading up to the foyer, staring at the wealthy and famous of the world. They would gaze from behind the police cordon as each Rolls, Mercedes, Daimler, Ferrari, or other expensive car slid to a halt.

I would go through the richly appointed lobby to the oak-paneled and mirrored bar. There the international jet set gathered night after night. Among the new residents in Monte Carlo were Ringo Starr and Lord Michael Pearson. I liked Ringo for his typical north-of-England humor. It was always a pleasure to have him at my table at the Hôtel de Paris bar; I could count on him to liven things up. He would come to parties at my house, as would Bill Wyman of the Rolling Stones, who lived down the coast near Grasse. Ringo and Michael had become residents of Monaco and were living there on a semipermanent basis.

I was the youngest of the Hôtel de Paris set, and by far the least affluent. But I always managed to have a good car, and I could sign my bills everywhere I went. I didn't receive these bills until the end of the month, and it was only after several months of not paying them that I began to feel some heat from the restaurant and nightclub offices.

Aside from the fashionable crowd in the bar, I had a friendly relationship with the bartenders themselves, Louis, Petit Louis, Roger, Jean-Pierre, Laurent, and Dario. I was the only member of the royal family to go casually to the bar alone.

Beyond the activities at the hotel, there were great parties each year. One of these was given at her magnificent estate at Cap Ferrat by Lynn Wyatt, who used her Boeing 727 to fly in from Texas a country-and-western band, T-bone steaks, and baked potatoes. We all came dressed in cowboy clothes. This was among the very rare private parties attended by Rainier and Grace. I remember seeing Grace square-dancing and having a great time. She was a fine dancer, but Uncle Rainier was self-conscious and stayed at the table.

Anja Lopez, a woman of great extravagance of style and

presence, gave her dinner parties on the terrace of the Hôtel Hermitage overlooking the Monaco port. On each occasion the terrace was decorated with the color of the evening's theme. I also went to a fantastic party given by Carlo de Chedid, who had reserved the entire Hôtel de Paris Grill for the night, and who had an orchestra and belly dancers brought from Egypt as part of an Arabian Nights gala. There were many others, but Hans and Cardy Smith outmatched every-one in their entertainments. They had a magnificent house known as the Villa Trianon at Roquebrune, not far from the Villa Tebba of the Princess of Bavière-Bourbon and the home of Helene Rochas.

One night the Smiths gave a gold party. Many of the women were completely covered from head to foot in gold sequins and jewelry. One girl even appeared in a gold-painted body stocking, giving the initial impression she was nude.

Another soiree the Smiths gave was their Great Gatsby ball. We were all dressed in 1920's clothes, and the orchestra played Charlestons, black bottoms, two-steps, and other music of the period. There was a show with transvestites imitating famous female singers. The dinner was prepared by the chefs of the famous three-star Michelin restaurant the Moulin de Mou-gins; and when the ball finally ended as the sun emerged at dawn, fresh croissants were baked on the premises. Even the servants were dressed in 1920's uniforms, and the terrace and garden overlooking the Mediterranean were lit by glittering silver candelabra.

On most nights "our crowd" would inevitably wind up after midnight at Jimmyz, D'Été, Regine's magnificent new night-club. The club was about two miles from the Hôtel de Paris and was situated in the Summer Sporting Club complex out on the peninsula, with grass lawns overlooking the sea. It is generally agreed that Jimmyz is the most beautiful nightclub on earth. Although the club did not require a membership fee, as Regine's was to do in New York, nobody could be admitted of whom Regine would not approve. During events like the Grand Prix, when people poured into Monte Carlo and too many tried to get inside the club, guards were posted at the door with German shepherds.

Once inside Regine's, one walked down carpeted steps to the bar on the right, or to the dance floor, surrounded by tables, on the left. I was usually greeted by one of the two maître d's, Luciano or Bernard. I would join one or another of the large parties that was always seated on the first two banquettes on the right. With their adjoining tables they could seat as many as thirty people each. These two banquettes were often fought over, and there were angry scenes from time to time when a party arrived a few minutes late, only to find that their reserved places had been given away to others. Behind these banquettes, which made up an elite zone, was an artificial pond with waterfalls and a fountain, and a display of tropical vegetation lit up with colored light bulbs. On warm and rain-less summer evenings, the roof would slide back, and we would sit under the stars looking out to the sea. The waiters moved about with red sequined jackets glittering under the lights.

During the summer season Regine was always present at her own table. She made a commanding impression, with her red hair, white skin, strong features, and dynamic personality. She knew everybody and their secrets, and was the friend of the rich and powerful. Often she would sing in her strong, vigorous voice. These were memorable nights, enlivened by Regine's colorful presence, by beautiful, bejeweled women, by music and champagne. Despite my sadness over my lost racing career, I was enjoying life more than I'd ever done before. These were the best years in Monaco: they were Regine's years.

I often ran into Caroline at Regine's, when she was on vaca-tion from her school in Paris, where she lived with Grace for part of each year. We enjoyed dancing together; she was still as fun to be with and sweet as ever. Many times she invited me and my date to sit with her at her table, and we would laugh together. When I got out of hand and caused criticism at the palace by my night life, she warned me of the impending trouble. She often interceded on my behalf and calmed things down for me.

After Regine's I would drive my date of the evening to the Tip-Top or the Bistroquet, restaurants that stayed open until morning, where we ate breakfast before speeding up the winding Middle Corniche to my house. My faithful valet, Tacconi, who worked part of the day as a cleaner at the Café de Paris, would come to my house, which I now called the Villa Iemanja, after the goddess of the sea in Brazilian legend, at 12:30 to wake us up. He would bring us coffee and me a glass of water with three Alka-Seltzers in it, and then prepare us breakfast. I would stagger toward the pool for a swim, and then, feeling somewhat more awake, my hangover beginning to clear a little, go to the garage to check the car. It always relieved me to see it hadn't been damaged on the way home.

I would drop my date off wherever she was staying, most often the Hôtel de Paris, and have an espresso at the bar as I picked up my mail and my phone messages. Then, feeling considerably better, I would make my way to the beach and mingle with the same crowd I would see later in the bar, laying out plans for the evening. And so the merry-go-round would start again at eight.

In the winter off-season, I would still spend much of my time at the Hôtel, often dining first at the Privée, the restaurant of the Casino, although I was not supposed to. The food was good, and reasonably priced in view of its quality and surroundings. The restaurant was situated up five steps on a raised dais overlooking the private gambling salon with its chandeliers and tables surrounded by high rollers. The fact that I went to the Casino, even though I didn't gamble, annoyed Uncle Rainier, as a member of his staff told me. He was irritated by the fact that I was friendly with many of the croupiers and other members of the Casino's staff. They often would discuss controversial issues regarding the management of the SBM and the principality, giving opinions with which I would often agree and which no doubt further enflamed my uncle. Perhaps, I thought, Uncle Rainier was remembering my mother's carefully planned public relations campaign where the locals were concerned. If that was so, then the comparison was absurd.

My uncle was, in fact, sensitive to what his subjects thought of him, sometimes overly so. One example of this was the case of a teacher at the Monaco lycée and a member of an old Monegasque family. The police stopped his car one evening because a headlight was not working. It turned out he wasn't carrying his identification papers. In such a tight little community, where everybody knows everyone else, his name cannot have been unfamiliar to the police. Nevertheless, he was brought into the local precinct until his identity could be verified.

The police were aggressive to the point of provoking the man to remark, "What can one expect from a place with a comic-strip picture on the wall?" He was referring to the official photograph of the royal family, a photograph that was present in every shop and office of the principality. The police were furious and charged him with making "utterances against the crown." He was immediately dismissed from his job at the lycée. Also present in the car that night was a friend, a member of a labor union. From the point of view of the palace, these facts no doubt constituted the equivalent of leftist sedition. The day of trial, police surrounded the courthouse, concerned about a possible demonstration. The teacher was given a one-year suspended sentence. After that he couldn't get another job except, finally, as a truck driver.

There were other incidents of police-statelike controls. Ringo Starr's manager, Adrian Green, wore pigtails, gilded earrings, and a nineteenth-century opera cloak. He told me over drinks at the bar of the Hôtel de Paris, where we would often meet in the evening, that he could not set foot on the sidewalk to stroll home to his apartment seven minutes away without police stopping him and checking his ID. Adrian jokingly shrugged off their menacing him by wearing his resident's card around his neck on a string.

I saw my grandmother Mamou on and off during those years, when I visited Paris after the Monaco season was over in September.

Mamou's home was part of the Monaco legation to which my mother had fled with Nanny Wanstall in 1936. It was a handsome apartment, maintained without redecoration in the style of some forty years before, with a huge dining room and a bedroom lined with pictures of the family past and present. I would go to have lunch with her. She told me that she had grown fond of Grace's children, especially Caroline, who stopped by to see her quite often. My mother's long-ago wishes notwithstanding, Mamou had reversed her original critical attitude toward their "American" upbringing and now took a grandmotherly interest in all three. When she mentioned Grace it was without the criticisms of the past. Mamou had mellowed with time.

The official in charge of the running of the legation was Monsieur Caruta. Prim and correct, possessed of a puritanical spirit, Caruta, like everybody else in the legation, seemed terrified of Mamou, and when she descended in the small elevator, he would always wait for her to assist her into her car. One afternoon I saw a typical example of Mamou's dry wit. When she made her usual descent, and was greeted by

Caruta in his customary deferent manner, she said to him, "I have a book for you. I couldn't put it down last night. It's fascinating. I recommend it strongly." I saw at a glance that the book was *Emmanuelle*, the best-selling erotic novel in Europe at the time. Caruta tucked it under his arm without looking at it; he probably fainted when he started to read it.

A friend of mine at the time was a British member of my swinging circle affectionately nicknamed "The Rat," or "Ratty." He was a *bon vivant* with no determined means of support. One winter at Gstaad, I went to the Gringo, the discotheque of the Palace Hotel, and found my friends greeting me in laughter. Somebody surprised me by saying that Ratty was embarked upon a campaign to become Caroline's husband. Several of my friends told me in concert that the night before, emboldened by a few drinks and encouraged by his friends, he had summoned up the nerve to invite Caroline, who was at another table, to join him on the dance floor. Next day he was invited to have tea with her at her parents' chalet at Schonreid, not far from Gstaad. Ratty then took up the story. He said that when the door of the chalet opened, he was taken aback to see my Aunt Grace standing there. He thought that the Caroline he had danced with the night before, introduced to him only by her first name, was Caroline Kennedy!

Once in the living room of the chalet, Grace ordered the tea brought in. Ratty didn't realize it, but he was about to become the object of Grace's custom of inviting her daughter's new dates to tea so that they could have "a little chat." He told us he tried to make the conversation as bright as he possibly could, but the atmosphere began to cool after Grace asked him what he did for a living and Ratty mumbled something vague. Although Grace was too polite to say what was really on her mind, he could see from her expression that she didn't see him as husband material. That, however, was not the last Grace was to see of The Rat. A year later he was with a group of us at Regine's. It was Grand Prix season, and we were all having a great time. Grace was a couple of tables away. Suddenly someone in our party dropped a popper, and it rolled out along the crowded floor. Ratty began crawling on his hands and knees, looking for it in near-darkness. We were so busy with the champagne and conversation that we didn't follow his journey, and therefore we were amazed to see him coming up from the floor beside Grace's feet, not knowing whose table he was under, smiling and holding up the popper. Grace jumped when she saw his face; her expression made it hard for us not to double up with laughter.

Grace spent much of her time now in Paris with Stephanie, at her house at 26 Place de l'Avenue Foch, decorated with eighteenth-century antiques and looking out onto a small garden. She had bought the town house chiefly to be near Caroline, who was completing her studies in the city, while Albert was in Monaco. Steph was also at school in Paris but found her Catholic school too strict. Grace put her into a more liberal one. She eventually refused to go back even there, and Grace had to find her a private school (Charles de Foucauld) in Neuilly.

After her Monegasque and English convent school educations, Caroline was determined to prepare her "bac" in Paris. Grace opposed it, fearing that Caroline would be unable to handle the temptations that life in Paris would offer. Caroline's experience of real life was nonexistent; so far it was limited to the inside of a palace and a convent school. And Grace thought Caroline was vulnerable because her father was a reigning prince and people would be watching her closely now that she was of eligible age. In fact, she was now being portrayed as a disco habituée who fought with her parents. The *paparazzi* staked out the Paris town house day and night, trailing her relentlessly. Caroline "speculation" became a cottage industry.

Isolated from the real world for sixteen years, Caroline was suddenly attacked by it. It weighed on her. "Why do I have to be a princess? I hate it!" she would exclaim. Grace underwent a certain change. In Monaco she was not overstrict or worried about Caroline. Now, alone with two girls in her Paris town house, missing her husband and son and with few occupations to fill her time, Grace clung more tenaciously to Caroline. Against the background of the press and her mother's new shielding presence, Caroline also changed. She began to discover "*la vie mondaine*" and liked it. She would say to me that if the press was reporting she was having a ball, she "might as well have one."

She was most frequently photographed by the *paparazzi* with French singer Philippe Lavil. In one shot, taken at a nightclub, she was wearing a very open blouse, exposing much of her breasts. Caroline said to me, "I didn't notice that button opening up and popping out as I fixed my collar!" Grace was very angry with Caroline over the incident. As usual, Uncle Rainier allowed my aunt to convey their mutual displeasure.

Not only did Caroline's behavior undergo change, so did her personality. She became harder and less concerned with her mother's opinion. Grace would sometimes say that Caroline was becoming "impossible." Caroline would complain that Stephanie was getting away with more than she had been permitted at her age. Grace was firm; Caroline was willful. Grace was not prepared when Caroline began to neglect her studies and wear overtight jeans and see-through blouses and too much make-up. At the end of her first term in political science, Caroline did poorly for the first time in her exams. Because Paris discos and high living seemed to be interfering with her studies, Grace and Rainier managed to persuade

Caroline to have a change of scene and attend Princeton. She was scheduled to begin the following fall. Then, in the summer of 1976, she started dating Philippe Junot and refused to go, proposing instead to enter the Sorbonne and take a degree in psychology.

I had met Philippe Junot a year before. Through Regine I had met Lauretta, a successful black model for Yves St. Laurent, who, years later, would run Regine's in Rio. Lauretta, in turn, introduced me to Philippe. He had dark brown, wavy hair, sparkling eyes, and a prominent nose. He was clever, energetic, and full of charm. Generous and quick-witted, he was the life and soul of any party. A good all-rounder at sports, Philippe was captain of the football team sponsored by the Paris nightclub Castel's, for which Jean-Paul Belmondo also played, and he was an excellent sailor. Frank and outspoken, he, like me, had spent much of his childhood and youth on the Riviera. He shared my love for pretty girls and fast cars. We hit it off at once.

I would bump into Philippe all over the place, at Regine's and Castel's in Paris, as well as in Monaco and Saint-Tropez. My first real memory of him and Caroline as a couple was when I went to a party at Regine's in Paris with Suzy, my girl friend at the time, and with the British actress Cleo Goldsmith. Caroline was already seated when I saw Junot take his place next to her. She wore an off-the-shoulder evening gown that displayed her arms. Junot squeezed one of them and said words to the effect, "Caroline, you could stand to lose a few pounds!" Later, as they were leaving, he said, "Come on, fatty!"

To please him she lost ten pounds in the next four months. I suspect that this was the first time a man had addressed her as an equal, or at least displayed a strength of will that matched her own. He presented her with challenges instead of empty compliments. He was the first real man she had met:

a leader, not a mere attendant to her. Until now the men she had been seen with were known as "Caroline's latest date," but now, in Parisian nightclub circles it was, "Philippe, who is now dating Caroline." Their romance blossomed quickly. Philippe taught her to relax with the press. They spent a lot of time in his apartment and with friends, and Caroline was exposed to a life different from the restricted one she had known.

Neither my uncle nor my aunt was happy about the relationship. Junot was seventeen years older than Caroline and was identified as a playboy. Rainier thought Philippe was a seducer and a fortune hunter. My uncle did not approve of Caroline's life under Philippe's influence, and both he and Grace thought Caroline was too young to marry anybody. They were puzzled and embarrassed by the scandal surrounding Caroline's behavior, which contrasted with the flawless image of the family Grace had always projected. Grace had dreamed of a "good match" for her daughter and was disturbed by the thought that Caroline's actions were motivated by rebellion against maternal authority. She feared Caroline would make herself unhappy in the long run. Pictures in the press of Caroline and Philippe kissing and hugging only made a bad situation worse. Although Junot's family was quite prominent in politics, and although he had served on the New York Stock Exchange and worked for various European banks, Philippe was still not at all my aunt and uncle's idea of a son-in-law.

Nevertheless, he and Caroline dated steadily, turning up to the inevitable glare of flashbulbs, whether it was at Maxim's in Paris or skiing in Switzerland. Grace never warmed to Junot. In an interview, when asked what he did for a living, Grace said, "I think he works with banks. . . . " As time went on, she became more and more unhappy, worrying about Caroline and dreading the moment when Junot would ask for

Caroline's hand in marriage. He did, in the beginning of 1977, after having gone alone to ski in Canada.

Rainier was ready to use his sovereign authority to forbid her to marry, but then he was afraid of losing his strong-willed daughter, who would have to break openly with her family and marry outside Monaco. Grace initially wanted Rainier to use his authority in that manner. Caroline said she would bow to her father's will if he withheld his permission but would live with Philippe out of wedlock. Rainier might have preferred this to marriage, but certainly not Grace, who recognized defeat and reluctantly gave in. In March of that year Rainier allowed Caroline to go to Ibiza with Philippe, and he and Grace received him at Roc Agel for Easter. He accompanied the family to the WCT Tennis Tournament, where he sat behind Grace. He came back for the Grand Prix and was seen with Caroline at the French Tennis Tournament at Roland Garros, and in July he joined the family on a cruise to the Galapagos Islands so that Rainier, Grace, and the children could get to know him better. On their return to the Riviera, an enterprising *paparazzo*, who had been relentlessly following the couple everywhere, spotted them in a boat off the coast near Cap Ferrat.

In the photographs Caroline was seen removing her bathing suit top, taking the sun with her head thrown back. Caroline in a bikini and Junot in white striped shorts were photographed necking. In one shot Caroline was lying on top of him. These pictures sent shock waves through the palace, which was warned of the debacle a couple of days before publication. Palace rumors flew around that Junot had deliberately engineered the shots to try to force Rainier to approve his engagement to Caroline. I didn't believe this for a moment, however.

Grace and Uncle Rainier did succeed in slowing things down. They would agree to the engagement, but the marriage was to be contingent upon the stipulation that the couple wait for a year. If Caroline was still determined to go ahead, they would not stand in her way. Grace asked my mother up to the palace to announce the news, and my mother noticed that Grace's eyes were still red from crying. She was very distressed, saying over and over again that Caroline was young and inexperienced and that Philippe's history and way of life did not promise a lasting marriage. Grace, in fact, gave it a maximum of two years, remarking to her husband as late as the night before the wedding ceremony, "Well, perhaps it's for the better. This way she'll have a successful second marriage!"

To make things worse, *Paris Match* succeeded in scooping the palace on August 25 by announcing Caroline and Philippe's engagement on the front page before Nadia Lacoste, the palace's press agent, sent out the official release.

On the night of the decision over the engagement, I was in Regine's with a group that included Junot's set. Philippe was conspicuous by his absence. At last he turned up after midnight. He was alone. He smiled, rubbed his hands, and said triumphantly, "It's in the bag, my friends! We've taken the town!" In other words, he had stormed the citadel of Monaco, which was so much opposed to the engagement. I knew that this was his way of making a joke, but he was not aware of how rumor and gossip immediately made their way back to the palace. The remark reached Rainier, further prejudicing my uncle against him.

In a 1985 interview with Barbara Walters, Caroline said that she became involved with Junot only in order to escape from the restrictions of life at the palace; but I am sure she was deeply in love with him. I may have been the only member of the family who was genuinely happy for them. Philippe's feelings for Caroline, and hers for him, were constantly under threat because of pressure exerted at the palace. But what none of us realized was that Philippe would get more than he bargained for. From the outset, despite the official approval of the forthcoming wedding, there was no real acceptance, and Philippe was made to feel this constantly. How could any marriage work under these conditions? Ironically, this unpleasant situation turned out to have a hidden advantage for me. Now, at last, I was no longer the principal black sheep of the family. Junot had unwittingly taken my place as the number one target of Rainier's royal displeasure.

F I F T E E N

*I*N THE WAKE of Caroline and Philippe's blossoming romance, my own future looked bleak. I had lost a lot of money that winter in Brazil, where I would go regularly during Monaco's winter season, and I was really broke; I had even had to sell my car. Then one evening the phone rang. It was a flamboyant character known to everybody as Paco-Paco. A self-styled Spanish hidalgo, always dressed in a long, flowing cloak with a trailing white scarf flung around his neck in the mode of Toulouse-Lautrec's famous poster figure Aristide Bruant, Paco possessed outrageous wit and inimitable charm that made him the life and soul of every party. I liked him very much. Paco told me that I must come at once to the Hôtel de Paris. I said I didn't feel up to it, that I wasn't in the mood. Soon after, he called me back and said he wouldn't take no for an answer, that if I did come I'd be doing him a special favor. He wanted to introduce me to a particular woman, whose "lady-in-waiting" he was by his own definition, who had expressed an interest in me. I asked him who it was. He replied, "Laura Alfa." I knew who she was immediately. I had run into her on and off at the Hôtel de Paris but had never really met her. Although she was several years older, with her auburn hair and striking figure, she was sexy and attractive, strongly resembling Sophia Loren. Yes, I thought, it would certainly be intriguing to spend an evening with this woman. She was married to a prominent Swiss business tycoon, and she was known to be obsessed with gambling. In my rented Peugeot, I drove down to the hotel.

I wasn't disappointed when I saw Laura with Paco at the bar. She looked stunning, and I could see in her eyes that she was attracted to me. All three of us went off to dinner, and then we proceeded to the casino at Beaulieu. I was staggered by the amounts of money she threw down for chips. She liked to play roulette and told me she had an arrangement with every casino on the Riviera—a sixty-thousand-dollar nightly credit line on a special account authorized by her husband. I noted an interesting detail that night: she was even more excited when she *lost* money. She played on until 6:00 A.M. I didn't play the tables myself; I couldn't afford to.

Next night we met again. We had a few drinks at Regine's and then drove in one of her Rolls Royces to Beaulieu again. I watched her play for an hour or so, and then told her I was bored and going back to Regine's. She asked me why I didn't like to gamble. I explained I didn't have the money, whereupon she tossed twenty thousand francs at me—about four thousand dollars—and said I could pay her back from my winnings. I asked myself, what happens if I lose? But as it turned out, not only was I able to pay her back, but I walked out with three thousand dollars in my pocket that night.

Although I had been exposed to the casinos all my life, I had never gambled seriously before and had certainly never met anyone as obsessed with roulette as Laura. She was known to everybody at the casino, and the croupiers were all on the alert the instant she arrived. She was amazingly extravagant and reckless. She would have as much as thirty thousand dollars' worth of chips placed across the table, covering a very large quantity of numbers. It was typical of her that just as the croupiers would call, "No more bets," she would, before the last word had been said, suddenly call out a batch of numbers to them. Sometimes she would insist that she had called out a number when it was clear that she had not. But because of the vast amounts she gambled, and because the casino benefited considerably from her presence—indeed, other customers were often drawn to the roulette table to bet themselves simply in order to see her in action—her eccentric method of placing bets was indulged. I remember one instance where she insisted that she had made a bet on the zero when she hadn't, claiming of all people our drunken Paco as a witness. Anywhere else this might have created a scandal, but once again she got away with it.

Every night with her was memorable. I remember her with her bracelets and necklaces flashing in the multicolored lights at Regine's, half-lying on me on the banquette, watching Paco screaming and, on top of the table, tap-tapping his way through a flamenco, or laughing hysterically as he kissed the waiters, who put up with this because they liked him so much. He was an institution. Laura loved to shock old-fashioned Monaco society by flaunting her relationship with me. With Paco, we never went unnoticed. One night we made one of our rare visits to the Monaco Casino. Monaco, as always, was different from everywhere else on the Riviera, and the Casino was no exception. In most casinos the directors were deferent to the high rollers, but in Monaco they were known for their imperiousness. They were not about to make an exception with Laura. She used her usual technique of calling out random numbers at the very last second, and the chief croupier informed her after the ball settled into the notch that she had not placed a valid bet on that number. In fact, this time she had. Both Paco and I testified that she was correct, but she was flatly refused her payoff. She flew into a temper, grabbed up the wooden scoop that was used to pull the chips across the table, and hit the chief croupier on the head with it. When she finally received the disputed chips, she contemptuously threw the entire amount in his face, crying, "This is for the staff," and then she stormed out.

It was now the summer of 1977. My winning streak with Laura was so strong that I never left the casino without at least doubling my initial stake. I remember one particular incident in Cannes. I began with the equivalent of five thousand dollars. It swelled to the equivalent of twenty-five thousand dollars as the night wore on. Laura was furious with me because she was losing, and many high-rolling Arabs were following my choice of numbers as my luck incredibly went on and on. After I had won three successive spins of the wheel, I asked the croupier what number I hadn't played up till then. He told me he couldn't recall me asking for 25. I put two thousand dollars on the 25, spreading the chips around the margins of the half dozen or so numbers surrounding it. As a result, I made about sixty-five thousand dollars with one spin. It was an ecstatic night.

Laura could never sleep. We closed nightclub after nightclub on the Riviera. Normally we would eat breakfast at dawn at the Tip-Top and would get to my house just as the sun was coming up. We were always accompanied on our nighttime adventures by her three French bodyguards and Paco. They would wait in their car as she parked the Rolls in my garage. Paco would sit in the living room dancing by himself to music while Laura and I went to my bedroom. Finally she would return to her villa, where she would call me, waking me up, day after day, still unable to sleep, and insisting that I myself sleep with the receiver on the pillow so she could hear me breathing—or snoring.

By early summer I had not only paid off all my bills, but I was now comfortably in the black. I fulfilled a lifelong dream: I bought a new dark metallic brown Ferrari 308 GTB. It was the best car I had ever owned, and it became the love of my life. For some time I had had a James Bondish A007 license plate on my former cars. Now I changed the plate to M001. When Uncle Rainier got wind of this, he supposedly exploded, "Now he is trying to usurp my position!" The fact was that the official palace license plates, with MC as their prefix, used higher plate numbers in order to avoid ostentation. Of course the police regarded my M001 as a gag, appreciating the fact that the sportiest and sexiest car in the royal family bore such a flashy appendage and had such an unconventional owner. Laura loved my speeding and screeching around corners up and down the Corniches; she screamed as I took every turn but loved the thrill of it.

In August her husband arrived at their villa from Zurich for a month's stay. We had to cool the relationship. I felt embarrassed and awkward when she invited me to a party at the house, where I met her husband: a distinguished old gentleman. My feelings of guilt were only made worse when he innocently asked me to join him and Laura for dinner. It wasn't easy. I grew to like Franz Alfa more and more. He was a great gentleman, and he savored good cars as some people savored fine wine. Alfa was also the most generous of husbands to Laura. When she asked him for a Ferrari exactly like mine, he gave her one the next day. Soon her brand new car could be seen making its presence felt around the streets of Monaco.

I had no indication from Franz Alfa that he was aware of what was going on between his wife and me, but everyone else in the principality certainly knew. Uncle Rainier was very intrigued by my affair with Laura; surprisingly, he didn't take nearly such a dim view of it as he did of my license plate. I realized that the heat was off me and focused on Junot when I was told that his only comment on learning of the relationship was, "Well, at least the woman's attractive!"

Grace, by contrast, was extremely upset about it. My sister Christine told me that when she, Grace, Caroline, and my mother were leaving a gala at the Summer Sporting Club together, Grace turned to Mother and asked, "What do you think about this business of Buddy and Laura Alfa?" Mother, whom I almost never saw, knew nothing of my private life and thought Grace was referring to a make of car, possibly a new version of the Alfa Romeo. She replied by asking what that was. Grace said sharply, "Tiny, you must know perfectly well!" Mother responded that she did not. It was all Caroline and Christine could do to suppress their laughter. Grace told her chidingly, "Laura Alfa is your son's present Swiss romance." By this stage my mother had given up on me completely and no longer cared what I did or did not do. She replied indifferently, "So what?" Grace didn't stop. Growing more irritable by the minute, she said, "But Tiny, Madame Alfa is a *married* woman." Mother shrugged. "Well, these things happen!" Grace went on, "I repeat, Laura Alfa is a married woman. Buddy is having an affair with her. And I don't appreciate your indifference to this, so why don't you do something about stopping it?" Mother said she would try to exert her influence, but of course she knew there was little she could do.

Not long after, I accompanied Paco and Laura to dinner at the small and fashionable Pinocchio's Restaurant, situated on the Rock of Monaco. When we arrived, the room was as crowded as always, and we had to thread our way through the tables to find our place. I saw that Grace was seated with friends on the right, facing our table. She smiled at me and nodded, but knowing her as well as I did, knowing how subtly she could convey displeasure, I could see from her smile that she was annoyed with me. Her eyes were like ice. I was reminded of her expression when she danced with Jean-Charles Rey at the opening of the Red Cross Gala Ball years before.

I knew that her strong sense of propriety and morality were offended by her nephew's involvement in an adulterous situation, and I felt a twinge of embarrassment.

During dinner I became aware that Laura wasn't feeling well and hadn't touched her food. She disappeared into the common toilet used by both men and women. When she did not return, Paco chose a moment when everybody's attention was distracted to slip in after her. I was left alone, facing Grace and feeling increasingly uncomfortable. After a few minutes the toilet door opened, and Paco pleadingly beckoned me to come in. I knew Laura was snorting coke in there, and I didn't want to get involved. With Grace directly facing me, Paco was making more and more desperate gestures. Finally, convinced there was something really wrong, I strolled over to the bar to get a drink, and when Grace was not looking, I managed to slip through the door into the toilet. Laura was seated on the bowl, and Paco was standing in the corner hysterically laughing. He said, "Madame has got diarrhea from snorting too much. There's no toilet paper left in the box. She expects me to go and ask Enzo"—the owner of Pinocchio's—"for paper for Madame's bottom. And in front of everyone. Including Princess Grace. I refuse! I may be Madame's poodle, but I am not a retriever!"

Between Paco's shrieks of laughter, Laura picked up her Hermes handbag and opened it. She threw five hundred dollars at Paco, telling him it was his tip to get the paper. Paco said to her, "If you can afford to give me five hundred dollars to fetch the paper, you can afford to wipe your ass on the money." Which she proceeded to do, contributing a small fortune to Monaco's sewage system.

It would seem as if Grace had the misfortune to be completely surrounded by couples not to her liking: Laura and me, Caroline and Philippe, and there was even the unlikely pairing of a government minister and a high-class prostitute.

The government minister in question was my old friend Xavier Carriere, the only open-hearted, unpretentious member of Rainier's government. He delighted in shocking the Establishment and rejoiced in a free-wheeling life style of drink, fine food, and women that never followed the rules obeyed by his more orthodox government colleagues.

On the evening of the next Red Cross Gala, he was dating a girl named Liliane, who, along with her sister and mother, arguably comprised Monaco's most notorious trio. Under their mother's skilled guidance, the girls specialized in picking up well-to-do older men at the bar of the Hôtel de Paris. Primly dressed, the alluring sisters expertly entrapped their prey. When the victim took one of the two back to his apartment or hotel suite, their mother would suddenly turn up at the door and mention in one breath that the man could be charged with seducing a minor, that his action could ruin him, but fortunately for him, at that moment she happened to have pressing financial problems. The result usually was a heavy payoff. But after a couple of years of playing this game, the girls had to forget the "minor" act, and actually "perform." This little trio seemed to have some unexplained ability to survive even the investigations of the Monte Carlo police, who did not tolerate prostitutes and who checked up on everyone in every bar or club in the state.

So when Liliane, of all people, appeared on the arm of Xavier Carriere at the Red Cross Gala, heads turned. In our principality, everybody knew everyone else. For a minister of the crown to dare to bring the most notorious of prostitutes to the biggest social event of the season was considered a deliberate slap in the face for Uncle Rainier and Aunt Grace, especially since Grace had gone to such lengths to clean up the image of her small kingdom.

I will never forget that night. I watched, along with just

about everyone else in the room, frozen with astonishment, as Carriere, drunk and stumbling, swayed with Liliane across the stage toward the government table. I looked at Grace. It was clear that she was doing her best to pretend not to see what was happening. She continued talking politely to the guest of honor on her right with a look that betrayed only to those who knew her very well her extreme unhappiness over the new arrivals.

When the couple finally reached the table, Carriere demanded that two extra chairs be brought, one for Liliane and the other for her mother, who had now also made an appearance. Soon I noticed Liliane's mother leaning across her daughter, saying something to Carriere and gesturing in the direction of Uncle Rainier, who was seated at the next table. She was suggesting that he present his prostitute girl friend to none other than the Prince. I could hardly believe my eyes when, under the astonished stares of the assembled, Carriere struggled to his feet, took Liliane's arm, and wobbled over to the royal party. He said to Uncle Rainier, "*Monseigneur*, I want you to meet somebody very special who wants to meet you!" Uncle Rainier, forced into a situation he could not escape, with every eye in the room upon him, coldly put out his hand in a form of greeting, and Liliane took it, dipping clumsily to the ground on one knee in a curtsy. Then she and Xavier began to make their way toward their next target: my Aunt Grace.

They were just about halfway there when Grace looked at them directly, her eyes conveying the unmistakable message, don't you dare make one farther step toward me. The pair stopped dead in their tracks and wobbled back to their table for the rest of the evening.

Two days later Carriere told me that he had finally blown it. He wasn't actually fired, but Uncle Rainier suggested to him in his usual roundabout way that he needed a long rest and should remove himself to a spa outside the principality to take care of his overworked kidneys and liver. An interim minister would be appointed in his absence. Carriere understood right away that his presence was no longer desired. Had he been asked to resign point-blank, he could have embarrassed the monarch considerably by disclosing certain information he had acquired during all the years as the head of his important ministry.

Quite ignoring the suggestion he should leave town, Carriere would often join me, Laura, and Paco-Paco at our regular table at the Hôtel de Paris bar. It must have annoyed Uncle Rainier to see his unregenerate minister, night after night, in the company of the flamboyant "lady-in-waiting" and would-be flamenco dancer, the most notorious adulterous millionairess gambler, and the black sheep of his own family, in direct defiance of his desires.

These evenings were always fun. I continued to see Laura constantly. Incredibly, she continued to succeed in keeping the true nature of our friendship a secret from her husband, even keeping him to some extent a prisoner in his own home in order to do so. She screened his appointments, allowing him to meet and entertain only those she personally considered safe—guests who would talk about the weather or the latest social events rather than betray her adulterous carryings-on. She even monitored Alfa's incoming phone calls. In the meantime, I grew increasingly remorseful over cuckolding this decent man, whom I had grown to like and who liked me.

One evening we were at the casino of the Hôtel Ruhl at Nice when Mr. Alfa told me about the new twelve-cylinder Jaguar he was adding to his stable of five Rolls Royces. We began an animated conversation about automobiles, and he said to me he was surprised that, given my passion for cars, I wasn't racing anymore. I told him it had been three years since I had last driven in competition. He asked me why. I explained to him my difficulty in finding a sponsor to cover the high cost of racing; I didn't tell him of my suspicion that Uncle Rainier had been behind my problem. Alfa looked genuinely startled when I told him of my difficulties. He said that many of his businesses had advertising budgets of considerable size and asked me how much I would need. I told him the equivalent of $100,000 for one year. Alfa did not flinch at the mention of the figure; indeed, he smiled as I mentioned it. He said he would make a couple of phone calls the next day. He told me to come to his house the following afternoon, as he hoped he would have news for me. I could hardly believe my ears.

Needless to say I arrived promptly for our meeting the next day. Alfa told me that he had been in touch with his business people in Zurich and that the $100,000 I had asked for would be no problem. His directors had found one subsidiary that would be ideal for me and under whose colors I could race.

But he added that he had a condition. He said he knew how excited and eager I was to get back into action on the track, but he didn't want me to try for spectacular results in the first year. He wanted me to use the twelve months as a training period so I could have all the practice possible to get back into top form. If I agreed, he said, not only would he put up the $100,000, but he would raise it to $150,000. As a look of astonishment crossed my face, Alfa quoted the maxim "Who goes slowly goes far."

In my wildest dreams I never could have imagined anything like this happening. I had given up all hope of racing again. My heart beat loudly in my chest. Alfa suggested I go as soon as possible to Zurich, where I would be met at the airport and driven to his office. He had made an appointment for me with his publicity directors a week from that Thursday.

That evening I started a health program to prepare myself for my renewed career. I was more high on Evian water than I could ever have been on champagne. I went to bed early.

The next day was the first in many months that I woke up before twelve. I got out of bed at nine, without a hangover and entirely alone for a change. Instead of my usual Alka-Seltzer, I had fresh orange juice. I threw away my cigarettes. And I went out jogging.

In the afternoon I went to the gym and worked out, and took a sauna after a round of boxing. Then I went to the local health food store and bought vitamin pills, fresh fruit, and vegetables. Once again I went to bed early. As the days went by, I felt better and better. The future looked brighter than I could ever remember.

At last, Thursday approached. I had my air tickets for Zurich, and I was counting the hours when, on the afternoon before I was to leave, the telephone rang. It was Alfa's secretary calling from Switzerland, telling me that he wanted to talk to me. When he got on the line, Alfa told me, "Hello, Christian! Please don't come to Zurich tomorrow. Instead, meet me for dinner on Friday evening at eight at the Privée of the Casino." I hung up feeling anxious. Was it possible something had gone wrong? I called Laura at her villa. A maid answered the phone. Laura, who usually took my calls immediately, took forever to come on the line. At last I heard her voice. I told Laura I was worried and puzzled. What could possibly have happened to cause this change of plan? I could tell from her voice that she was uneasy. She said she knew nothing about any problems but suggested that I wait the forty-eight hours until Friday, when I would find out the truth. When I hung up, I was certain she knew much more than she was letting on.

Somehow I got through the next two days. When Friday evening came along and I took my seat at Alfa's table, he offered me a cigarette. I refused it and declined a cocktail and asked the waiter for some water. Alfa watched me with a look of sadness. He clasped his hands together tightly, slowly shook his head, and measuring his words carefully, said, "Christian, at my age and in the position of responsibility I am in, running as I do a large number of corporations employing hundreds of people, there are many problems that arise every day with which I must deal. But I am now faced with one of the most disagreeable duties I have ever known." He paused, taking a long puff on his cigarette, obviously uncomfortable but compelled to speak on. "I know how you have built your hopes and dreams of racing again. I know how you have put faith in me to advance your career once more. And certainly, I wanted nothing more than to be of help to you, because I like your eagerness." He frowned. The words were growing harder and harder to speak. At last he said it straight out: "It is my painful duty to tell you that I cannot go ahead with our arrangement." I was dumfounded. He went on: "I know how bitterly I am disappointing you at this moment. But I want you to learn something from this terrible setback. I must tell you, Christian, to forget racing from now on. You will never be able to race again. And I will tell you why. Your uncle has made it known to me through another party that he is totally opposed to your racing career, and he made it clear that he would be grateful if I would not in any way facilitate it financially." Alfa now got down to the bottom line. He said, "Christian, I am sure I needn't say that as a guest in your uncle's nation, with considerable business interests at stake here in Monaco . . . I need say no more. Please understand. If you have any other projects of any kind, I would be happy to consider them and give them my most careful attention."

There is no way to explain what my feelings were at that moment. When you give up your dream, you die inside. The Evian water was quickly replaced by wine, and that soon by vodka. When the meal was over, I walked out unsteadily from the Casino to my car, where Cocaine and Cannabis were sitting waiting for me. In a state of shock, disappointment, and fury, I made my way drunkenly to Regine's and walked up to the door with a doberman on either side. Claudie at the door could hardly believe her eyes, and as for Felix, my favorite maître d', words could not describe his expression. He was used to my antics, but for me to invade the most celebrated night spot in Europe with two big dogs was beyond his wildest nightmares. To say that I created a stir as I walked in with my dobermans would be an understatement. It was the first, and probably the last time that dogs were seen in Regine's. Felix pleaded with me to leave, telling me that this time my behavior was really impossible. After a few more drinks I left, my head splitting open with one of the worst headaches I have ever experienced.

I spent the next week in turmoil. I tossed the thought around my brain hundreds of times: should I go to the palace and confront Uncle Rainier directly? All my suspicions about his interfering in my previous sponsorship seemed close to confirmation. This time I was certain I had proof of his intentions—although to this day Uncle Rainier absolutely denies any involvement in these matters. As I had so often before in my life, I turned once again to Lionel Noghes for advice.

Lionel agreed with me that there could no longer be any real doubt about my uncle's attitude toward my future. However, he warned that creating a scene with Rainier could only result in an ultimate rift. And I had to consider that at least my position in the family was better now than it had been. Philippe Junot had replaced me as the most visible target of royal displeasure. Nor had my income been threatened. It had remained the equivalent of what it had been when I was married. I owned a beautiful house, and I had open expense accounts throughout the principality. I could afford to go to the Hôtel de Paris, Regine's, and all my other favorite haunts as often as I wanted. If I were to rock the boat with the palace now, I could be stripped of my income and be back to square one before Junot's advent.

I had no choice but to keep my counsel, but I was deeply disappointed and frustrated. If only Uncle Rainier had made clear to me from the beginning what his intentions were, I would have known where I stood, would have accepted my fate in regard to European racing, and would have gone to the United States to pursue my career without the possibility of his interference. At least I would not have wasted all those years on something that my uncle condemned. I found it despicable that he would smash someone's lifelong dream for reasons that to this day I still do not understand.

In the early fall my relationship with Laura Alfa also ended. True to herself to the end of our affair, she acted with all of the extravagance that I had found so irresistibly appealing in her character.

Before meeting Laura, I had a brief relationship with a young French-Vietnamese girl who was physically exciting and sensual. I met her again that autumn, and as so often happens after an affair is resumed, the pleasure of the reunion was very intense. We spent the night together at my house. The next morning the telephone rang at 6:30 A.M., waking us. I knew at once it was Laura: no one else would call at that hour. I was not in the mood to listen to her usual recapitulation of everything that had happened during the night at the gambling tables. As she talked on, it soon became obvious that I was in a hurry to end the conversation. Instinctively she snapped at me, "Who's there? Who's there? Is anyone with you?"

I put my hand over the receiver and gestured to the girl not to make a sound. But she began deliberately coughing and talking loudly. She knew it was Laura and was happy that she was making her jealous. Laura became hysterical, calling me every name in the book. Finally she slammed down the phone.

Fifteen minutes later a car drove up and the dogs started barking loudly. I threw on a robe and went outside. Laura's bodyguards were in their car. One of them called out to me, "Excuse me, Baron de Massy, but you know how Madame is. We have no right to do this, but she insists we check up to see if you have a girl here in the house and what her name it." I told them it was no business of hers or theirs. They shrugged, liking me, caught awkwardly between our cross fire. "What do you want us to say to her?" they asked. I told them to tell her to go to hell. "Tell her I have a whole harem in here!" When they finally drove off, I returned to bed. But soon afterward Laura was on the phone again, sobbing and insisting that I meet her at 1:30 at the Hôtel La Reserve at Beaulieu.

I arrived just minutes after 1:30 and left my car parked at the main entrance. Thinking she was already there, I told the attendant not to take my car around to the parking lot, as I would be picking her up in the lobby. I intended to take her to a restaurant in the port area of town where we could talk.

I walked into the hotel to look for her but didn't find her, despite her insistence we meet exactly on time. I walked back to the driveway and saw her pulling her white Rolls Royce up behind my Ferrari. She left the motor running. She got out, looking beautiful in a flaring red dress, her eyes red from crying. She walked from the Rolls to my car, her bracelets jangling, carrying an Evian bottle. She opened it and began pouring the contents over the Ferrari's hood. I wondered what she was doing. Almost immediately I could smell gasoline pouring out from the bottle, and she took out her gold Cartier lighter and snapped it open. I grabbed the lighter from Laura's hand. The doorman, who had been at La Reserve for decades and had seen just about everything there, stood transfixed. Then, with all the passion of her temperament, Laura broke down, screaming abuse, crying, falling into my arms, embracing me, then pulling free and screaming that I was a bastard, telling me she loved me, kissing me, and then slapping me violently, scratching me and releasing a fury of blows on my chest and face. Suddenly she sat down on the hood of her Rolls and burst out crying again.

More insults, more screams and slaps followed, while the distinguished guests of the hotel tried to slip quietly past with their Hermes and Vuitton luggage. I suppose I could have walked away, but there was something incredibly sexy about her anger. I suggested instead that we go someplace for lunch and discuss the whole thing over a drink. She screeched, "No! No! We will have lunch here!" She stamped off into the lobby and demanded the hall porter immediately give her a suite overlooking the sea. She told him to have the kitchen send up a bottle of Cristal champagne and smoked salmon, and pulled me into the elevator with her.

No sooner were we in the suite than glasses began to fly about and shatter against the wall, so that the floor was covered in fragments. When the waiter arrived with the champagne and salmon and asked if we wanted a maid sent up to clear away the debris, Laura literally pushed him out the door.

As I ducked some more glasses, Laura picked up the phone and called for Paco, her indispensable "lady-in-waiting," to come at once. When he swished into the room half an hour later, he said the entire hotel was in an uproar over our violent scene and he could barely make his way through the lobby for the hubbub of commentators milling about. Laura told him to shut up, wound his Toulouse-Lautrec scarf three times around his neck, half strangling him, and launched into a series of complaints against me. Paco clapped his hands to his ears and said he couldn't bear it anymore, as he had just got out of bed with a hangover, and if she continued, he would throw himself out of the window. Couldn't we simply light up a joint, settle down, and discuss the matter like civilized people? he asked. It really was about the only thing in the world that could calm her down.

She stopped long enough to light up. We all began laughing, and then Paco began dancing his flamenco. Laura dragged me into the bedroom and told me, "Make love to me the way you made love to that Chinese whore!" With the stereo turned up full blast, and with the thudding of Paco's feet on the floor outside, I did. But by the time I left and went home, I knew the relationship was over.

SIXTEEN

THINGS WERE NOT too bad. I no longer had a possessive woman around my neck. I had paid up all my bills. I had my house and my Ferrari, and my accounts at the bank were firmly in the black. I was still doing very well at the gambling tables. I would bet four thousand dollars a night, and I never lost. I usually doubled my money in the course of an evening.

I would go to the casino often, enjoying my run of good luck. I preferred the Beaulieu casino, under the direction of Monsieur Carletti. He would always take a personal check from me or let me sign a house blue check, which was in effect an IOU.

I went there one night with an English girl I was dating named Suzy, and for the first time that I could remember, I started to get on a losing streak. My numbers continually failed to come up. Wiped out after the first twenty minutes, I went to Carletti and he issued me chips against my personal check. Soon that, too, was gone. Then I went back to Carletti again. I recovered slightly, but finally I was down twelve thousand dollars. I went to Carletti for yet another four thousand dollars, and he reminded me that this was the third time I had gone back to him for an advance of chips.

With no further luck, Suzy and I went to Regine's. I woke up the next day, had my daily Alka-Seltzer, and fell into the pool. As usual, after checking out my car, I went to my jacket to see how much I had made in the course of the previous evening. Then I realized through my hangover that I had lost sixteen thousand dollars. Suzy told me she remembered that Carletti had said, as he issued the final advance, "It's the third time, Christian." Suddenly I remembered what a fortune teller in Brazil had said to me the previous winter. She had told me, after she correctly predicted that I was going to lose a lot of money in a business venture, that she saw me suddenly acquiring a great deal of money without working very hard, and I would do so while surrounded by well-dressed people in elegant settings. However, she issued two predictions. She said to me that I would receive three warnings, and that I was immediately to stop whatever I was doing or I would lose all the money I had made. I realized I had just gotten my three warnings. I never gambled again.

She also told me to stay out of the path of a girl with cat's eyes, who would ruin my life if I was to get involved with her. Later, unluckily, I was less careful about heeding this second prediction.

Having given up gambling, I opened an office in Monaco for public relations, advertising, and publishing. My real office was the bar of the Hôtel de Paris, where I was able to use my social contacts. In time I began a magazine, expensively printed and designed, which I called *Prestige de Monaco*. Later, having launched it, I extended its range and renamed it *Prestige Internationale*. The magazine was given away free, and I had it placed in the thirty most luxurious hotels across the world and aboard the French Concorde, as well as in Regine's in Monte Carlo and top-class golf and polo clubs. It was appealing to the makers of luxury items, who wanted to advertise in it because of the very rich clientele who would automatically read it. My advertisers included Boucheron, Buccellati, Bulgari, Cartier, Moet-Chandon, Rolls Royce, and Van Cleef & Arpels. Because I knew many people in the jet set, it was not a problem to persuade them to contribute articles. Caroline did a piece on UNICEF's work for children. Björn Borg, whom I always liked, was a great help and contributed a story about his life the same day I asked him to, as I was missing an article and the deadline was approaching. From that day on we became very good friends and saw each other often, as he was a Monaco resident. Omar Sharif had the kindness also to write an article. Regine contributed an article on Paris nightlife, and when she gave it to me, she said, "I don't usually help out in this way, but I'm glad to see you working at last." Grace was also pleased that I had found an occupation, and she liked the quality of the publication. Rainier seemed satisfied that I appeared to be settling down with no more thoughts of racing. He suggested that the magazine be oriented toward attracting more of the jet set to Monaco.

A whole section of the magazine was devoted to the social scene, with many photographs of celebrities at parties. Knowing as I did that a main topic of conversation among the jet set was who was going out with whom and how was so-and-so looking, I was sure that these layouts would appeal to them. I worked long hours but didn't mind because the work was satisfying. However, there were problems that began to undermine the magazine's success.

Because of my lack of experience, I made a number of mistakes, the first one being not having a person with publishing experience to work with me. My plan of making the magazine the highest quality possible led to crippling overheads. My graphic artist was flown in from Milan, the printer was the best in Italy, and the finest-quality paper was used. I made

the disastrous mistake of distributing the magazine by air-
mail. I didn't research top-scale advertising rates, nor did I
bill my advertisers promptly enough. Within a year I was
forced to fold the magazine.

After I gave that up, I retained my office and began a new
venture, creating advertising spaces in the best locations of
Monte Carlo, such as on the sidewalks near the entrances of
the Hôtel de Paris and other SBM institutions. Those entering
and leaving couldn't fail to have their eyes caught by these
posters advertising various luxury items.

I also involved myself in assisting foreign businesses to establish themselves in Monaco. My address book was my chief as-
set, my main office becoming more than ever the bar of the
hotel. When I ran my magazine I had worked for twelve hours
a day and made nothing. But now I learned the law of my particular world: more money could be made over lunches and
drinks with business contacts and social connections than I
could ever have achieved working round the clock.

This was how I met Salvatori Dozio, who came to Monte
Carlo in the summer of 1977. About thirty-five years old,
newly rich and ostentatious, he had reportedly made over
$100 million in the previous six months from various mys-
terious dealings that had intrigued the Milan business community as well as the press. He arrived in Monaco on his yacht,
which was accompanied by two motor launches and four Rolls
Royces, which were always parked in front of the Hôtel de
Paris. Heretofore unknown to most people in our community,
Dozio was notorious within a week.

Through mutual acquaintances at the Monaco Casino, he
got in touch with me. We arranged to meet one evening at
the Hôtel de Paris "office" bar so that I could explain to him
what he could personally and professionally gain from investing in Monaco. My usual table was strategically placed
on the right of the entrance so that everyone entering or leav-

ing had to pass by it. When I arrived at the bar with my date, Salvatori characteristically asked me what was the most expensive and exclusive restaurant in Monaco. I told him it was the Salle Empire in the same hotel. We walked over there, accompanied by his chauffeur-bodyguard, who never left his side.

Over dinner I discovered that he was basically a good guy, unpretentious and amusing. After leaving the equivalent of the price of our dinner as a tip for the flabbergasted waiter, we went together to Regine's. During the course of the evening he spotted Adrian, Ringo Starr's manager, complete with pigtail, earrings, rings, opera cloak, and cane. Not understanding English, and having heard somebody at the next table commenting about Adrian and mentioning Ringo's name, he said, "That's Ringo Starr!" I told him that it wasn't Ringo but Ringo's manager. Salvatori maintained, "I tell you, Christian, it *is* Ringo!" I responded, "It is *not*!" Salvatori said, "Well, what do you want to bet on this?" He added, "You're very proud of your Ferrari, aren't you, with that M001 number plate? I'll bet you your Ferrari against any one of my Rollses that that man over there is Ringo Starr!" I asked, "Does that include the bottle-green Corniche with the beige leather seats?" He responded, "It does!" Obviously I couldn't lose. I called over Felix and René, the maître d's, and asked them the name of the man in the cloak. They both said immediately that it was Adrian. Salvatori proved to be a very good loser; without hesitation he asked me what the most expensive champagne in the club was, and I told him Louis Roederer Cristal. He ordered it, and we drank a toast to the Rolls as he handed me the keys.

I soon learned what it meant in France to drive such a car. Next day I went to Cannes with my friend Hervé Fontaine. As we left the car to enter a nightclub, a woman spat at us. Then, while we were in the club, someone scraped the side of it. We saw evidence of envy everywhere. Thereafter I kept my doberman Cannabis in the car whenever I left it. The sight of her ferocious face would ensure the car's security. Unfortunately I did not muzzle her and she ate away the back of the driver's seat.

There was another disadvantage in having the Rolls. I heard again and again from members of the palace staff that Uncle Rainier was annoyed by his black-sheep nephew's new acquisition. As usual, he never broached the subject with me. When I saw him at parties, he was very cool, making only superficial polite conversation. I suspected it was he who made it known to customs officials that I hadn't paid duty on the car. After a glorious summer driving around in the Rolls between Monte Carlo, Cannes, Saint-Tropez, and Biarritz, I was told that I would have to pay one-third of the cost of the car, or the equivalent of about forty thousand dollars. It had been a lark to be in possession of a Rolls as the result of a bet. But that's all it meant to me. I had had a good laugh and lots of fun in it, and I sold it without much regret.

I was in Paris that fall of 1977 when I heard that my mother was in town at the bedside of Mamou, who was suffering from a terminal illness. As soon as I learned of Mamou's condition, I went immediately to the legation to see her. I had seen little of my mother for the past few years, bumping into her only occasionally at palace Christmases or birthdays, or at the occasional official function. We had had little to say to each other. Now, as we stood next to the bed, where Mamou barely recognized me, Mother said, "She's sinking. They've sent for Rainier and Grace." I could see from Mamou's expression how terrified she was of death. It was humbling to see this very proud woman reduced to fear. A nun who was keeping vigil held her hand and said to her over and over again, "Death is perfectly normal. It's going to come anyway. It's nothing to be afraid of."

My uncle and aunt appeared the following day. Of the children, only Caroline was there. Albert was in America, and Stephanie was probably considered too young. I couldn't help remembering Mamou's initial contempt for Grace, as a movie star marrying her son. After the marriage Mamou never set foot in the principality again or had anything to do with Monaco. I thought more as the hours went on about Mamou's history. How she had been so severely maligned because of her early elopement with the Italian doctor, how distanced she had been from her own daughter, how isolated she was from the nation of which she was dowager princess, and how lonely she had been over the years. I thought how unfair the criticism of her behavior had been, and today it seems especially harsh compared with the scandals that have enveloped her granddaughters.

She passed away one November afternoon, and her final wish was to be buried at Marchais. Her death had been preceded by a Balzacian spectacle of family members who had come to pay their last respects in the hope of being favored in the will. I had noticed how Mamou had looked on them with skepticism and disdain. Mother, who seemed surprisingly relaxed for a change, asked me to accompany her for a walk in the Trocadero Gardens one afternoon. As we strolled with her dogs, I was astonished when, for the first time in my entire life, she opened up and said how afraid she was that Uncle Rainier would in effect cheat her out of her full inheritance, which should have been very substantial. Before Uncle Rainier had gradually raised his income from the privy purse to the equivalent of nearly $8 million a year, Mamou had been the wealthiest of all the family members. According to French laws of inheritance, under which Monegasque law also fell, he and his sister were to share the estate equally. I did not understand why Mother thought that Uncle Rainier would treat her unfairly.

The Château de Marchais, a priceless example of medieval architecture with its hunting grounds and small farms, was worth a fortune. Mother amazed me by confiding that Uncle Rainier was so determined to have it all to himself that he had made her an offer to buy out the bedrooms, sitting rooms, and bathrooms that she had occupied with Elisabeth, Christine, and me whenever we visited there. He would pay her a sum proportionate to their value against one-half the total worth of the castle. This was scarcely a fraction of the worth of the castle, farms, and grounds to which she was entitled under French law. It was a deal of total inequity, quite apart from the fact that it was also insulting. She replied, "He's always been like that! He's always wanted everything for himself and his own children! And I don't want you to say one word about this at the palace under any circumstances whatsoever. The matter is closed, and I am agreeing to the arrangement." Ever since her abortive effort to bring about the coup d'état all those years before, my mother had lived in constant fear that someday he would cut off her Civil List income. She was not about to provoke him now.

The mass for Mamou was celebrated in Paris. It would be followed by the interment at the castle. We all came dressed in black with the exception of Junot, who irritated Uncle Rainier by wearing a suit of medium-gray that was not considered sufficiently somber for the occasion. I was sad to see that only Caroline cried at the ceremony. Shortly before Mamou's death, Caroline had come to the apartment in Paris to introduce her to Philippe. Mamou had often said to Caroline, "Be sure to make a love marriage." She was clearly remembering her own unhappy past, in which she had been forced into marriage to my grandfather. She had liked Junot, sensing a free spirit and enjoying his sense of humor. She probably also enjoyed being in contradiction with Caroline's parents. After the ceremony there was a reception at the legation for all the guests at the funeral. I was happy to see my old friend Xavier Carriere, as well as several members of the Polignac family. Later, as Mother, Grace, Rainier, and the lawyers began to convene for the reading of the will, I overheard in the corridor Uncle Rainier saying, "I want them to stay in the family or he'll blow them all on his cars." Did he mean me? I wasn't sure to what he was referring. Could it possibly be to Mamou's jewelry and other family heirlooms? I did not know. But later I was informed that Mamou had left nothing to her grandchildren.

According to her desires, Mamou was buried near the château, very close to a special annex building that had housed her beloved terriers. Rainier and Grace, my mother, and I were present at the burial; no other family members were there, Caroline and Philippe having stayed in Paris. It was very touching that all the village of Marchais turned out to pay their last respects in a clear indication of their affection for Mamou. She had given aid to the sick and impoverished, had contributed generously to local charities, had helped the unemployed find work; and in running the family's several farms, Mamou had always been a considerate employer, helping not only the farm workers but their families as well. People would come to the château to discuss their problems with her, easily and without formality. Like my own, their sadness at her passing was deep.

It was clear that Caroline was not going to waver in her determination to marry Philippe. The months went on, and I could see that my uncle and aunt had accepted the fact that the relationship was not going to disintegrate before the stipulated year elapsed. Whenever I saw Caroline, I could tell that she was radiantly happy. When Prince Charles of England was visiting Monaco, pictures were taken of Charles and Caroline seated next to each other at an official banquet in his honor at the Hôtel de Paris, and friends started joking to Philippe, saying, "There goes your marriage! You've got some competition now!" But Philippe was completely undaunted and trusted in his mutual love with Caroline, realizing that it was no more than an official duty for her to entertain the Prince.

Shortly after the Grand Prix, Caroline and Grace were in Paris for fittings at Dior on the Avenue Montaigne and shopping for the trousseau. Now that there was no question of stopping the marriage, Grace decided to make the best of it and give Caroline all the support possible. For my own part, I was looking forward to the wedding, because now, with any luck, Philippe would be able to introduce a more contemporary flavor to the palace and to our medieval court.

Before Caroline and Grace went back to Monaco, Lynn Wyatt gave a big pre-wedding dinner party at Maxim's in Paris. Among the guests were King Fuad of Egypt and his wife, Princess Marie-Gabrielle of Savoy, Prince Michel of Bourbon-Parma, the Duke and Duchess of Cadiz, Philippe Niarchos, the Rothschilds, and many others of the international set. Uncle Rainier was conspicuous by his absence. He stayed in Monaco.

Now the preparations for the wedding itself began. The first problem was the invitations list. It began with fifty names but swelled to eight hundred. The list had to include all the members of the royal family including distant relatives, the royal families of the rest of Europe, the obligatory Monaco "elite," the royal couple's personal friends, Caroline and Philippe's friends, and the guests of Philippe's parents and stepmother.

Eight hundred were invited to the ball and three hundred to the wedding luncheon; few had an invitation to both. A major problem was who would be left out, as the ball was considered the most sought-after social event of the decade. One woman who was excluded was a socially prominent figure whom Grace had earlier seen smoking grass at a party. This omission proved awkward for Philippe and Caroline, as the woman was the sister of one of Philippe's closest friends, a man who would be present with his parents at the religious ceremony. Florence Gould, widow of the multimillionaire Jay Gould and queen of Cannes society, was invited to the luncheon but not, much to her chagrin, to the ball. Uncle Rainier refused to invite Philippe's mother's new husband, Monsieur Chassin. Princess Ghislaine of Monaco, my great grandfather's last wife, was refused permission to invite her son from a previous liaison with André Brullé, who had played a prominent role in French theater.

The invitation cards to the ball stipulated that guests had to be dressed in white tie and tails or full-dress uniforms. It was set for the 27th of June, 1978, at 10:00 P.M. The civil ceremony was to take place the following day at 5:00 P.M. in the throne room, where my uncle and aunt had celebrated their own marriage, and would be followed by a toast in champagne by the entire royal family on the balcony, with all the Monegasques gathered in the courtyard below. The religious ceremony would be the next day, the twenty-ninth, in the same courtyard, with an altar set up in the open air at the door to the chapel.

My uncle and aunt were anxious to avoid the chaos created by the *paparazzi* that had attended their own wedding. They restricted the number of reporters given credentials and controlled their movements. One British journalist was detained by the police when he questioned locals about their sentiments toward the wedding. To the infuriation of all the others, the only photographer allowed into the ceremony apart from the official palace cameraman was Grace's favorite, Howell Conant.

The press dug up once more the well-worn story of the witch who had condemned the Grimaldis to unhappy marriages.

Local shopkeepers were unofficially warned not to commercialize the event by selling wedding souvenirs.

I was told to be present at 9:30 P.M. on the twenty-seventh, when, just before the ball, there would be a gathering of the family and the crown heads of Europe in the private salon. It was made emphatically clear to me that I must not bring a date.

I drove up just after nine in my brown Ferrari. There was an immense crowd of *paparazzi* and journalists, outnumbering the guests three to one, waiting along with throngs of spectators held back by police cordons. The guards at the main gate of the palace were closely inspecting each invitation card. I was told by one of them that they were under orders to scrutinize everyone who entered, as it seemed that some ingenious Italian *paparazzi* had forged invitations. The guards had already caught one woman reporter trying to get in. He also told me that Cary Grant's and Gregory Peck's limousines had collided.

I made my way up the stairs to the salon, where the monarchs of Europe were gathered, along with my mother, my sisters, and Bernard Taubert-Natta. I saw the Count of Paris, the pretender to the French throne, King Constantine of Greece, King Umberto and Queen Marie José of Italy, the Count of Barcelona, King Fuad of Egypt, King Michael of Romania, and the Aga Khan. Prince Bertil of Sweden was deep in conversation with the Archduke Otto of Hapsburg, and the Grand Duke Vladimir of Russia was talking to Prince Gonzalo of Bourbon. Notable by his absence was Prince Charles, who had declined the invitation, saying that his engagements did not permit him to attend. Caroline's wedding ball was one of the rare occasions when all of these relics of lost empires found themselves in the same room.

When everybody was present, my uncle and aunt arrived with Philippe and Caroline. Caroline was wearing a diadem for the first time, and her hair had been done by Alexandre of Paris, who had been flown in for the occasion. Just as Grace and Uncle Rainier came down the foot of the staircase to join the guests and introduce their future son-in-law, my cousin Prince Egon von Furstenberg came sliding down the banister rail behind them. Grace and Rainier were so busy shaking hands they didn't notice. His highly original late entrance reminded me of the time I had seen Egon at Studio 54, where he had made an identical descent down the stairs from the washroom.

From the salon we proceeded up the grand staircase to the ballrooms, where I saw Gunther Sachs and his wife, Mirja, Jackie and Helen Stewart, Oscar and Lynn Wyatt, and Regine, who was at the palace for the first time. I also saw Cary and Barbara Grant, the Sinatras, Gregory Peck, Ava Gardner, David and Hjordis Niven, and the Niarchos family. Others there were Marc Bohan of Dior, Madame Artur Rubinstein, Maurice Druon and Edgar Fauré of the Académie Française, the French stage and screen star Marie Bell, the Rothschilds, Edmond, David, and Guy, and their wives, and the Duke and Duchess of Orleans.

The Duke of Huescar, the son of the Duchess of Alba, was wearing his black ceremonial uniform slashed by the blue cordon of Isabella II of Spain. A Scottish relative of ours was dressed in the family tartan and kilt.

Rainier opened the ball by dancing with Caroline and Albert with Grace. Then Philippe danced with Caroline, and Michel Junot with Philippe's mother. Just as the two families did not open the ball by dancing with each other, similarly, Philippe's parents had not been asked to join my aunt and uncle in receiving their guests. The ball began with a waltz, and then came other traditional dances. Only later was some contemporary music played.

As I sipped vintage champagne and greeted the guests, I

was pleased to see that quite a few mutual friends of Philippe's and mine from Regine's and Castel's were present: a surprising and agreeable departure from the usual palace guest lists. There was a look of amusement on their faces, as if they were saying to themselves, "My God! Philippe is actually going to get away with this!"

Grace danced with Philippe and then with me, putting on a cheerful face. Quite apart from her unease over the marriage, earlier that evening she had had a violent quarrel with Stephanie, who, at the last minute before the ball, had declared that she wouldn't wear a gown to it because "I'm wearing jeans nowadays!" Grace had consequently forbidden her to attend. As a result, Stephanie peeked in from time to time.

As I danced with Grace, I said to her that I had never seen Caroline look so happy and that I was sure everything would work out well. Grace said, "I only hope so. But I don't think it's going to last two years." She paused. "At least I'm happy to see you are no longer having that shocking affair with that Swiss woman. I do hope you will find somebody suitable and settle down soon." Grace knew that I liked Philippe, and she was considerate in not saying anything openly against him to me. However, as the dance ended and I moved away from Grace to the banquet table, I overheard my uncle in conversation with a guest who, while trying to make some small talk, asked Uncle Rainier, "What does your future son-in-law do, Your Highness?" He replied, "Anything!"

I went over to the buffet. The food was an unhappy contrast with the splendor of everything else. It was mediocre, and there wasn't enough of it to go around. The well-known author Roger Peyrefitte said, "The honor of being invited to the ball apparently exonerated the host from feeding his guests decently."

As the evening went on, longer and longer lines formed at one of the two bathrooms at the head of the grand staircase, where there stood a fully uniformed palace guard, whose face betrayed an increasing puzzlement as he saw the same people going back to the toilet again and again, staying in there longer and longer, while from inside came the combined sound of loud sniffs along with the tank flushing. As I at last got into the toilet after a long wait, I realized that the palace had suddenly jumped into the 1970s. There was enough cocaine spilled around the bathroom to keep the palace waltzing into the twenty-first century. It really was a white wedding!

Next day, the civil ceremony took place at 5:00 P.M. It lasted only twenty minutes. The president of the Council of State, Monsieur Louis Roman officiated. The civil witnesses for the bride were my cousin Albert and Grace's niece Grace Levine. The groom's witnesses were his sister, Madame Vouillon, and the Baron Michel Allard. Roman read during the ceremony the Princely Decree of 1882, which conveyed the status of the royal house, whereby every member of the family submits himself to the authority of the reigning prince, who will determine their duties and obligations.

By marrying Caroline, Philippe now entered the Monaco sovereign family, and this ordinance applied to him. The obligations spelled out for him did not sit well with his free-spirited nature, and, combined with Rainier's attitude toward him, all too clearly indicated the troubles that would lie ahead.

As we all gathered at the top of the double marble staircase after the ceremony to have a toast with the Monegasques gathered in the courtyard, I nudged Philippe, whispering to him, "Welcome to the club. As you just heard, you are now to submit yourself to your father-in-law's authority. You must be looking forward to it." Always humorous no matter what the circumstance, Philippe winked at me and said under his breath, "Like hell!" A minute later Rainier and Grace toasted the crowd and the newlyweds in champagne.

The religious ceremony took place the following day at noon before the chapel door in the same courtyard. Officiating was the Bishop of Toulon, Monsignor Gilles Barthe, who had presided at my uncle and aunt's wedding. He was assisted by the Bishop of Monaco, Monsignor Edmond Abele. This was the fifth religious marriage ceremony held in the palace. The first, in 1715, was that of the Princess Louise Hippolyte; then the Princess Florestine, sister of Charles III, in 1863; then Ghislaine to my great grandfather Louis II in 1946; and finally my two sisters in 1972 and 1974.

Caroline had the same witnesses as at the civil ceremony; Philippe now had the Count Alain de Montaigu and the lawyer Maître Hubert Michard-Pelissier, at whose apartment in Paris Philippe had first met Caroline. The children's choir of the Monaco cathedral sang the music, which Caroline herself had chosen and which included works by Fauré and Charpentier. Many of the royal figures were present, but the overall congregation was limited in number.

Rainier, in a black morning suit of tie and tails, wearing white gloves, led Caroline to the altar. She was all in white with a veil, carrying a bouquet of white flowers. Stephanie was also dressed in white, with yellow embroidery, and carried a bouquet as well as a sullen expression on her face. Grace had personally supervised the floral decorations of the courtyard and the chapel entrance in motifs of white and yellow. The staircase was completely lined with pink, yellow, and white flowers. Grace wore a yellow dress with a large matching hat. The pages, Junot's nephews, were in traditional white, and so were the flower girls. Caroline had the same trouble fitting the ring on her finger as Grace had had at her own wedding. Grace shed a couple of tears, and I could see that my uncle was extremely emotional.

During the ceremony a photographer flew over the palace courtyard in a hang glider. He took pictures from a camera strapped to his waist and screamed, *"Vive les mariés!"* He landed on the beach at Cap d'Ail and was surrounded at once by the Monaco police, who hauled him off to their headquarters and confiscated his films. *"Vive la democratie!"*

Following the ceremony Caroline and Philippe walked through the streets of the Rock, which were lined with cheering well-wishers standing behind the barriers, accompanied by Secret Service men. They returned to the palace in a white convertible Mercedes for a luncheon in the palace square, which had been cordoned off by the police. They cut the cake, which was made of chocolate covered in white and pink icing; on top of it was a small cage from which they released two doves. I could not help smiling at the irony: Philippe freeing the birds from their cage as he entered one at the palace.

The honeymoon destination was kept a secret. The same day at 5:30 P.M., Philippe and Caroline flew by helicopter to the Nice airport, where they changed to a private jet for Paris, where they spent the wedding night in a house that had been put at their disposal by friends. Philippe spent the following morning making last-minute arrangements for the apartment they would live in on the Avenue Bosquet, and that afternoon they boarded a commercial flight to Los Angeles and then Tahiti, traveling under the assumed name of Rollin. Despite every effort, the *paparazzi* were unable to locate them in Paris, and their departure went undetected, but by chance there happened to be a photographer on the plane, who took pictures of them sleeping. The pictures appeared in *Paris Match.*

When the couple got to Tahiti, they went to Mooréa, a neighboring island, where they stayed at the home of a friend, Dr. Jonville, known as the "Flying Doctor" because he flew from island to island, visiting patients such as Marlon Brando. Someone managed to track Philippe and Caroline down and took photos of Philippe jogging and of the couple strolling together on the "secret atoll." Uncle Rainier raged, accusing

Philippe of arranging for the photographs. In his customary manner, he let his suspicions filter through the grapevine.

Philippe had a very rough time as Caroline's husband. I could never understand why, once the marriage had taken place, Uncle Rainier didn't do everything possible for his daughter's sake to support the marriage and to make it last. Caroline was in love with Philippe, and surely her father should have respected that. However unhappy the situation made Grace, she at least handled herself with her usual taste and thoughtfulness. By contrast, my uncle did many things to privately and publicly humiliate Philippe, who told me later that he felt he was being knifed in the back at the palace.

My uncle compelled Philippe to refer to him as "*Monseigneur*," the equivalent of "Highness." Rainier also sent out word to all of the administrative departments of the principality to advise him the instant Philippe moved a finger to make a business deal. Philippe never did any business in the principality. Anywhere else, the son-in-law of the monarch would enjoy certain prerogatives and facilities in his adopted country. Yet if Junot so much as registered an automobile, or sought a line of credit, it was immediately reported to the palace.

There was one particularly unpleasant episode. It was at the WCT Tennis Championship, held at the Monte Carlo Country Club. Philippe, Caroline and various of their friends had attended some of the earlier rounds, occupying the royal box. On a later day, after lunch at the palace, Philippe suggested to Caroline that they again attend the matches. She said she wasn't interested in going this time, so he took off with some friends. When he arrived, the chief official of the tennis club appeared at the royal box and said that he was unable to open the door. He used the excuse that he couldn't find the keys. Philippe was furious. The obvious conclusion was that an order had come from my uncle, denying Philippe entry to the box if he was not accompanied by Caroline. It was an unnecessary and embarrassing thing to do.

I had known such petty demonstrations of his will and ill-favor to be typical of my uncle. But Philippe, a man of strong character who was accustomed to being straightforward with people with whom he had a problem, was frankly outraged by Rainier's behavior. When Philippe talked to me about this, all I could do was to share with him the example of my own situation with Rainier. Given our family's peculiar history, traditions, and sovereign laws, and the odd character of its royal chief, I had to admit there were no logical or rational guidelines that Philippe could follow in his own dealings with my uncle.

Caroline was caught in the middle. She was naturally loyal to her father, but she also loved her husband. This awkward position didn't help to make the marriage any easier. She refused to take sides and hoped that the problems between the two men would finally blow over. Unfortunately, she was mistaken.

Yet for all the frustrations and setbacks, Philippe's natural good humor pulled him through. I had a great deal of fun watching Philippe carrying off his obligations as an official member of the royal family. These consisted of acting, along with his bride, as host at a never-ending schedule of dull official or semiofficial occasions. Caroline had a great deal of experience in fielding every conceivable form of trivial conversation, but not Philippe. Nevertheless, he showed a remarkable talent and humor in dealing with these events. I watched him one night at a reception, talking to an ancient White Russian princess who was bombarding him with her reminiscences of the great ballet impresario Diaghilev and his protégé Nijinsky, both of whom she had known in the 1920s. Philippe cared little about ballet, but he managed to wing it, saying, with the appearance of knowledge and deep interest, something innocuous but reasonably convincing about Diaghilev's career. On another occasion Philippe made me laugh as I watched him try to look genuinely concerned during a conversation with a Monegasque minister about the various problems caused by the pollution levels of the Port of Monaco during the different seasons of the year. He was charming and courteous, never betraying the boredom he was surely enduring during these exchanges. He instead tried to have fun by being a masterful actor in the art of the masquerade, keeping a straight face as he would catch my eye. Palace receptions were becoming amusing.

Meanwhile, history was starting to repeat itself. Rainier seemed to develop feelings of resentment about the mass of favorable media attention Philippe was receiving, which was not unlike the feelings Rainier had exhibited toward my father during his days as an international tennis champion or toward me when I began to race. Philippe was becoming the darling of the French press, photographed boxing at a Paris gym, driving his Ferrari, always impeccably dressed, smiling and surrounded by celebrities. The fact notwithstanding that Rainier's principal achievement to date had been his marriage to Grace with all its attendant and continuing publicity, he hated sharing the limelight with anybody. It irked him to witness Philippe's growing popularity with the Monegasques and friendships won because of his open, free, and unpretentious nature. Philippe never played on the fact that he was the son-in-law of the Prince.

Maybe because of his frustrations, Uncle Rainier, in his own eyes at least, became a world authority on the international political scene. He would take himself very seriously, expressing his opinions on everything from international diplomacy to America's role in the world to the use of atomic weapons. He tended to forget that he was ruling over a mere 25,000 people, of whom only 800 voted, in a country smaller than Central Park. He seemed chagrined by the fact that Monaco had no international influence and that he played no prominent role in the world. He tried to rectify the situation by encouraging every possible international organization to hold its meetings there. He changed the legation in Paris to an embassy and upgraded other legations similarly. This caused a problem because Uncle Rainier didn't have enough people who were sufficiently qualified to be ambassadors, and he was forced into the embarrassing position of having the French ambassador to Belgium become the Monaco representative. He made sure that Monaco had a permanent observer at the United Nations, and even a delegate at the International Nuclear Commission! All these efforts to the contrary, Rainier must have known in his heart that his opinions on international affairs were insignificant, a recognition which would have only embittered him further. He would stride around the palace apostrophizing "shuttle diplomats" for their "incompetence," no doubt regretting the fact that he, Rainier, had not been asked to settle the Middle East problem. Indeed, one of his favorite themes was the "unquestionable advantages of monarchies." His theory was simple: not having to vote for a new leader at the end of each term, and thus avoiding the "ugly debates arising from conflicting opinions," the citizens of monarchies were assured of continual harmony and an absence of dissension! Yet while he strongly admired the Shah of Iran, who had also been at Le Rosey, and although he accepted invitations to visit Iran, and while Grace was friendly with the Shahbanou, it was widely rumored that when the Shah made discreet inquiries about acquiring a key property in Monaco that could serve as a residence-in-exile, his former schoolmate and friend replied no.

While Uncle Rainier contemplated dreams of glory, I had much more reachable objectives: to continue to have a good time. In the fall of 1978, on the Monte Carlo Beach, I met the warm and appealing Francesca. Like myself, she was very much a rebel in her own family; and a free-living girl after my own heart. I asked her out one evening, but she turned me down, saying that she had an appointment in Rome the following morning and was booked on an 8:00 P.M. flight out of Nice. There was no way I could let her go. I called around and found out that there was an airport across the Italian border at Genoa with a scheduled flight for Rome at 4:30 A.M. I could make it to Genoa in just over an hour if I drove at 120 mph. When I told her that, she laughed and accepted my invitation, making her reservation from Genoa instead.

We began the evening at the Hôtel de Paris, where we ran into Francesca's aunt and nephew. Her nephew said to her when I was temporarily out of the room, "You're crazy to go out with Christian de Massy. He's always having accidents." Francesca laughed when she told me later, but I did not.

We went on to Regine's, and at 2:00 A.M. I began driving Francesca in the Ferrari toward the Italian border. Her Gucci suitcase was too big for the trunk, and I didn't want to risk scratching the hood by tying it down with rope. So we put the case behind Francesca's seat, standing it on its side against the car roof, which forced her to sit forward with her legs uncomfortably squashed up against the glove compartment. As we came down the motorway, there was a violent thunderstorm. Driving conditions became immediately treacherous for a sports car like this, with its wide, low-profile tires. The road ahead was drenched. I drove through the first tunnel, braking to prepare for the wet surface ahead, and as I emerged into the blinding storm, the car hit a water-filled pothole and aquaplaned off the highway as though it were on ice. Before I could do anything, we hit a rail, bounded back to the right, and overturned, skidding along upside down at least 150 yards. My side of the roof caved in completely. Francesca's

remained intact thanks to the providential location of her suitcase propping up the roof. At last the Ferrari came to a halt.
We were trapped. I could smell gas leaking out of the tank:
the car could catch fire at any moment. I thought in that instant of my half-brother, Lionel, who had received third-
degree burns in his racing car at Le Mans in 1972.

My door was jammed. I tried to reach across Francesca, who
was stunned, to open hers, but it was impossible. I thought,
what a way to die. I blacked out, and when I came to, I miraculously found myself outside the car. Somehow I managed to
pull Francesca out of the other side. The rain was heavier than
ever. We began to stumble toward the tunnel, drenched in
blood. I glanced back for a moment and could see in the shine
of the moon reflecting through the rain the car shattered and
still emitting the sounds of Crusaders from the stereo cassette
player. I said, "Thank you, God! I owe you one!" And then I
had a strange thought. It occurred to me as we walked on that
if anyone who knew me were asked how they thought I would
die, they would have said exactly this: coming out of Regine's
in a fast car with a pretty girl. Having miraculously survived,
I wondered what the hell could be in store for me now.

I was brought back from my thoughts as we entered the
tunnel. Francesca said, "Christian. I think I should get to a
hospital." She showed me her arm. It was cut open all the way
to the elbow, exposing the bone and streaming blood. A few
minutes later a large truck came by. The driver had to slow
down as he saw the debris of the Ferrari straight ahead. We
flagged him down and showed him Francesca's wound. I asked
him to tell the next gas station of our crash, and then I asked
him for a cigarette. He told me, "When one has enough money
to drive a Ferrari, one should buy one's own cigarettes!" And
he sped off into the night.

A car appeared. Again we flagged down the driver. I asked
him to take Francesca to the local hospital. He replied, "No

way. She'll make a mess of my car with all that blood." He then relented a fraction. "But I'll have an ambulance called for you."

We waited in the tunnel, Francesca losing more blood as I did my best to bandage her arm. An ambulance finally came and took us to the Ventimiglia hospital. It was a primitive place, to say the least. A nurse poured a bottle of disinfectant straight into Francesca's wound. This was very painful for her. But Francesca never complained. She was the most courageous and good-humored girl I'd ever met.

I eventually got her to the Monaco hospital and saw her every day. Our first evening together had been a "crashtastrophe," but in the next two weeks we had something great going for each other. If only we had stayed together longer! But, unluckily, I would meet and marry someone else.

SEVENTEEN

THE FERRARI was totaled. Needless to say, the usual palace courtiers tried to claim that I was drunk at the time of the accident. I didn't bother to respond to them. I was too experienced a driver to willfully risk my own and Francesca's lives. Luckily the car was fully insured, and I immediately ordered another Ferrari, a 308 GTS. It was white, with black leather seating.

Until my new car arrived, I drove around in a rented Peugeot 504 sports convertible. Several months went by. Now it was spring and time for the World Tennis Championships, which rivaled the Grand Prix as one of our country's most exciting events. The country club where the matches took place overlooked the beach and the sea, just behind the tall cliffs of the Maritime Alps: it was one of the most beautiful tennis clubs in the world. One could take a table on the terrace overlooking the court and watch the game while one had lunch. I always had a table next to the railings and would enjoy afternoons with my crowd over glasses of white wine, seeing friends like Björn Borg playing their matches.

Like the Grand Prix, the tennis season attracted not only the European elite but also lots of the most beautiful girls from every part of the world. Regine's and the Hôtel de Paris were packed with them. On the morning of Friday, significantly April 13, 1979, I woke up with another one of my massive hangovers. I found that my blazer and white shirt were smeared in make-up. As usual, I went through my ritual of Tacconi's Alka-Seltzer, the pool, and the car check, but although I was now completely awake, I could remember nothing at all about the night before.

I called Paco and asked him what had taken place at Regine's. He said I had behaved "atrociously, darling," practically making love to a beautiful blonde right there on the dance floor. Knowing of his usual tendency to exaggerate, I did not take him seriously. Then, that morning, on my way to the country club, I wound up as usual at the Hôtel de Paris, where I ran into an acquaintance, who said that I had really overdone it the night before and had gotten completely out of hand with a beautiful girl. I told him I could not remember anything. Next, at the tennis club I ran into Penny Laubi, wife of the director of the Hôtel de Paris, who said to me with several tut-tut-tuts that she had seen me the night before almost lying on top of an exciting blonde at my banquette at Regine's. My mind was still completely blank. I was now very intrigued and wanted to see this girl again. Penny told me that she was part of the tennis crowd and she expected her to turn up at an SBM dinner that night hosted by Penny's husband at the rooftop Grill. John McEnroe, Vitas Gerulaitis, and Björn would all be there. If I promised to behave myself, she would be sure the girl was seated next to me.

I arrived at eight o'clock sharp at the bar, and when I got to the table, there was the empty place Penny had promised next to me. Quite late, a very tall blonde walked in. I still had no recollection of her. Although she was every bit as stunning as described, she wasn't my type. When I heard her ask for an extra chair for a friend, however, I looked over and saw a figure dressed in tight red leather jeans and white sneakers. The girl had a very sensual, sulky, angry face with cat's eyes and closely cropped golden-brown hair. She looked tough and aggressive, and had the most beautiful legs and ass I had seen. I was attracted at once. Most of my dates were the spoiled, finishing school–educated, genteel daughters of wealthy visitors to Monte Carlo. This girl, with her sullen look, was different. I told Penny I felt turned on by her, and she replied, "Oh, God, Christian, you're always creating new problems for us all!" Penny switched the placecards, and as a result the girl, who was a nineteen-year-old Scandinavian introduced to me as Michelle, was seated beside me.

We started to talk. I suggested to her that I choose her dinner from the menu, and she, indifferent one way or the other, poutingly agreed and then didn't eat a bite of what I had ordered. That night we went off to Regine's. During the course of the evening we met a friend of Junot's whom Caroline hated because of his constant use of amyl nitrate. When we got back to the Hôtel de Paris in the small hours, Vitas Gerulaitis and I played soccer around the lobby with the friend as the referee. Later that night the same friend crashed Junot's Ferrari going back to Caroline's house on the Rock, where he was staying.

I tried to persuade Michelle to come home with me, but she turned me down. I jokingly flagged down a patrol car and asked the policeman to "arrest" Michelle so she would have to come with me. This didn't work either, and she took off to the Hermitage. Before she went, I asked her to a dinner party that night at the apartment of Lord Michael Pearson, and we agreed to meet at the Hôtel de Paris bar at eight.

I couldn't get her out of my thoughts all day. That evening I got to the bar as arranged, but by 9:30 she still hadn't turned up. I thought maybe she had misunderstood me and gone directly to Michael's without me, but when I got to his place, there was no sign of her there either. It wasn't until 10:30, two and a half hours late, that she appeared. Immediately I led her by the arm and thrust her into the bathroom, where I kissed her for the next four hours.

By the time we were at Regine's, I was possessed. Like me, she had come from a broken home and had more or less had to take care of herself from the beginning. When we first made love, I saw that she had a scar that ran all the way from her throat to her solar plexus. It turned out that she had had two open-heart operations when she was four and sixteen, and it was perhaps the knowledge that her life hung in the balance that made her want to live it fully every moment. She had studied medicine in Milan and was thinking about becoming a model, but in fact she had no commitment to either—or any—career.

Michelle was even more unconventional than I. She didn't give a damn for anyone and was totally fearless. She did exactly what she wanted when she felt like it. She spoke her mind on every subject. She was direct and challenging. I would count the days between our meetings until I saw her again. She would spend most of the week in Milan, coming in by train on weekends. It was obvious to everyone I knew that I was in love.

She moved into my house that June. Having grown up without feeling any sense of love from my mother, and with an absent father, all my love had gone into my cars. But this time I had found a human being whom I cared for more than them, and more than myself. I began to think of the future. I had been partying non-stop for most of the last six years, and now felt I wanted to do something else and change my life style.

At that moment Bernard Combemale, the newly appointed American-educated head of the SBM, made a proposal to me. We had seen each other often at various social occasions, and he knew about my magazine venture and that I spoke five languages fluently and had contacts all over the world. He suggested that I join the organization. Inevitably I recalled my long-ago request to Uncle Rainier that I go to hotel school in Switzerland so that I might one day enter the SBM. Instead he had sent me to Africa. I knew very well that if I did join the SBM, I would be watched like a hawk by my uncle and his men, who would be looking for me to slip up so they could say, "I told you so." I liked the idea of rising to the challenge of proving them wrong, and now was ready to settle down and get serious. Combemale's plan was for me to become involved with the SBM offices abroad. I respected and liked Combemale, and the prospect of working for him by promoting my country, which I loved, in the most exciting cities in the world was very appealing.

I felt that Monaco needed to attract a younger crowd and that I could do much toward that goal. I began discussing my plans to go to New York with Michelle. I made it clear to her that I would have to keep regular business hours and that we couldn't possibly maintain the late-night existence we had been enjoying up to now. Manhattan would offer a great life, but I wanted to achieve something positive with my work, and I didn't want to give my uncle any reason to complain. I warned her that he would jump on me at the first opportunity. Michelle agreed to see it from that perspective and talked of attending Columbia University. I called Bernard and accepted the offer.

Only after many hesitations did my uncle agree to the arrangement. Could he have been concerned that if I did do well with the SBM, I might be in a position later to seek higher office in Monaco? Success at the job would show the Monegasques that I was capable of being more than just a playboy, chasing girls and driving fast cars. One would have thought that Rainier would have welcomed the opportunity. Respectability would pull me in to the mainstream of the royal family. Nonetheless, Combemale had to fight to secure his approval. One of the main arguments he used was that my foreign language fluency, contacts, and personality made me the ideal candidate for the position; that I would project a more contemporary image of what Monaco had to offer. For once my uncle was compelled to make a decision openly. If he decided against me without giving logical reasons for not appointing me, it would be known that it was his decision and his alone. And if he was unable to give logical reasons for his decision, it would simply confirm his negative attitude toward me from the beginning. For once, Uncle Rainier was against a wall. He approved.

Just before I left, Michelle and I took a final holiday in the Ferrari, driving through Spain and Portugal before visiting with my daughter in Biarritz. I then sold the car, and we began preparations for our journey.

I gave away two of my dogs, Cannabis and Nitrate, and decided that Cocaine and her son Nicotine would come with me. (Igor had died the year before.) Michelle went home to Norway to make her final preparations for the trip. One night I went to a party at Saint-Tropez with Adrian. When we drove back toward Monaco, Adrian was frightened by my speed along the winding road. He suddenly grabbed my arm and asked me to pull up to the roadside. I thought it was because he was panicking, but it wasn't. He took me by the shoulder and said, very meaningfully, "Christian, if you go to New York with that girl, we've lost you forever!" He went on, "I beg you to think again about taking her. She has a deadly habit that you cannot fight, and she will ruin you in every way." Much as I liked Adrian, I thought he was simply being dramatic. I knew what he meant, but I had "been around" quite a bit, and no girl had ever made me suffer. I couldn't conceive of that happening to me now. Blindly I pushed on into disaster.

Before our final departure, Michelle, now returned, wanted to bring about a reconciliation between me and my mother. Since she had a broken family of her own, she very much wanted me to mend my family relations, despite the fact that she knew all about the dissensions, rifts, and revenges that had plagued our history. She persuaded me to arrange a meeting with my mother, who had recently been laid up in the hospital after being bitten by one of her dogs. This was a curious irony: after hating dogs all her life, she had now assumed her own mother's role as a fanatic canine lover. We took Mother out to dinner in Monte Carlo. She and Michelle seemed to get on well with each other. And when Michelle left the room briefly, I told Mother I was very happy and that now I wanted to make something of myself.

There were other last-minute meetings. I gave lunch at my house for Philippe and Caroline and my good friends Alain and Katinka Boucheron. Caroline and Philippe had already started to have their quarrels and differences but seemed to be relaxed and enjoying themselves in the informal setting around my pool. Two nights before I left, my mother gave a farewell dinner at her house. Grace was out of town; my uncle and sisters came.

My mother's new house, which she had built behind Mereze, was furnished with plastic furniture replacing the beautiful antiques of her former home and contained scores of kennels as well as a full-time nurse for her dogs. At one stage, Uncle Rainier asked her plaintively for a real plate and cup, since Mother had become obsessed with the idea of being "egalitarian" and was serving off paper plates and plastic cups. I imagined that he had not heard about the party she had given a few months earlier for the Merv Griffin TV team, who were in Monaco covering a celebrity tennis tournament. They had been surprised to be served hamburgers and hot dogs on paper plates, rather than the lobster or sole they might normally have expected of the Prince's sister. This "democratic phase" of hers lasted till her next marriage.

During dinner, Uncle Rainier and I exchanged polite conversation. He avoided any reference to my new job and betrayed nothing to indicate that he had objected to it. I learned later, however, that shortly before the dinner took place, he told Bernard to reduce my salary by half. When the evening ended, he parted with an empty expression of good wishes to me in my New York future.

After farewell celebrations at both Regine's and the Hôtel de Paris, where I was touched when both staffs presented my table with champagne, Michelle and I at last took off. My indispensable valet, Tacconi, drove my two dobermans to the airport separately. Michelle carried her Shih Tzu with her.

We flew to New York, looking forward to the new experience that lay ahead. I was acutely aware that my every move would be reported to Rainier and that I mustn't blow this chance. Our offices were well located at Park Avenue and 59th Street; by a funny coincidence they were directly opposite Regine's. I began working hard from the beginning, established a good relationship with the other employees, and launched our plan to give Monaco a new image.

I got articles into *Town and Country*, arranged for Anne Klein and I. Magnin to present their fall collections at the Monte Carlo Casino, and, working with the Eileen Ford modeling agency, organized a Faces of 1980 competition, a beauty contest in which thirty models would be brought to Monaco, where a panel of judges would select the "new face of the eighties."

At the beginning, at least, everything seemed to be going well. I liked my job. Michelle and I had settled in. To many, including the journalists who photographed us dancing together in night spots, Michelle and I appeared to be among the happiest young couples in Manhattan. As the months went on, however, Adrian's predictions unluckily turned out to be correct.

I now realized that Michelle had a serious problem with cocaine. It became a nightmarish ordeal that went on round the clock. I had never realized, despite all my years of living in the fast lane, how insidious it could be or the toll the situation could exact on other lives. I had been no saint myself, but there is a certain limit and a way of doing things. I warned Michelle constantly that if she did not respect herself enough to mind making her excesses public knowledge, she could not be so egoistic as to jeopardize my future by giving Rainier the bullets to shoot me with. I began to feel miserable, and could barely get through the day.

In a desperate effort to help her, I sent Michelle home to Norway for a time, much as I hated the separation. Bernard lunched with me in Manhattan, saw my strain, and asked me what was wrong. He was as sympathetic as anyone in the world could have been, and I was grateful to him.

At Easter I went back to Monaco, where I met up with Michelle at the tennis tournament of 1980, which happened to coincide with the first anniversary of our meeting. At a party I gave in an Italian restaurant, at which Philippe, Caroline, McEnroe, Gerulaitis, and Borg were present, Junot drew me aside and told me he was having serious problems at the palace and with his marriage. Most of these concerned pictures of him in the paper with different girls, who, he told me, were no more than friends. I told him he also was giving Rainier the bullets to shoot him with. He told me that whatever he did would provoke Uncle Rainier to fury anyway. He was in a no-win situation, as I was. His feeling was that even if he went to bed every night after watching the ten o'clock news, Rainier would still complain, so why bother. He was going to live his own life regardless of the consequences.

Before he met Caroline, Philippe had believed that "staying single" was the natural condition for man and that marriage was simply a social convention. He had always said he would marry only if he met someone exceptional. He entered the marriage feeling it should be created freely by the people involved, while Caroline believed it took mutual determination and concessions to make marriage work. It was a case of disillusion leading to dissolution. After the marriage, Caroline had taken on many obligations for Monaco, notably the presidency of the Monegasque organizing committee for the International Year of the Child.

This was a new Caroline, one who now very much enjoyed being a princess. She started trying to resemble her mother. She criticized violence, permissiveness, sex, and nudity on television. She strongly disapproved of children watching too much TV. She started giving interviews on the role of the family, and very swiftly, in the purest tradition of female Grimaldis, turned coat and became an apostle of counter-revolution. Philippe had not been expecting his wife, the ex-rebel princess who had shared his life style and loved going out and having fun, to become "so old-fashioned." He, in turn, continued to like parties and the nightlife, and continued to see his old friends.

Philippe was frequently out of Paris on business trips. One of the first serious breaches between the couple followed, when pictures of him dancing with Agneta von Furstenberg at Xenon and Studio 54 in New York were published. Caroline had thought he was in Montreal on business. Having been so willing to cause a rift with her parents in order to marry him, she now felt she was being ridiculed by the pictures and stories about his escapades. Humiliated, her ego hurt, she went out to a club with an ex-boyfriend. From then on it went downhill, with Caroline either fighting him on his own ground, which was hardly a remedy, or consoling herself with her family. She tried to provoke Philippe's jealousy again at a WCT tennis tournament in Dallas by continuously phoning a famous Mexican tennis star. Grace was suffering a terrible ordeal, while Rainier seemed to revel in his fury at his son-in-law. Whenever they were together in Monaco, Philippe would get frozen silences from him. Finally Caroline's parents let her understand they would not object to a divorce. More altercations followed, and after a final showdown on the eve of the 1980 Grand Prix, Rainier and Grace let Caroline know enough was enough. They did not want her to make any further attempts toward reconciliation. Caroline was still in love and had felt marriage was supposed to be forever. She couldn't believe she had been mistaken and all this was actually taking place.

After the Red Cross Gala, on August 8, 1980, she issued a communiqué, which took Philippe by surprise, saying that the marriage was over and she would file for divorce. Philippe only learned about it from journalists awaiting his arrival at Istanbul's airport. Accompanying him happened to be a beautiful girl he identified as his secretary. Others present, however, recognized her as Giannina Facio, a Costa Rican diplomat's daughter.

Philippe didn't expect that Caroline would act with such finality. He had hoped she would eventually agree to go along with his casual idea of marriage. He truly loved her in his way and was very sad that the relationship was coming to an end.

As Philippe and Caroline's marriage came apart, so did her friendship for me. Among other reasons was her new attitude toward everything that was associated with the life style she reproached Junot—and me—for enjoying.

The civil divorce followed, but the Church of Rome, in spite of constant applications for an annulment, has still not recognized the dissolution. In the wake of the divorce, Junot went to Marbella, the Spanish resort, where he met the Princess von Hapsburg, daughter of the Archduke of Austria. He met the Archduke, who, Junot told me, was suspicious of him at first after all the bad press he had received, but after two days he turned out to be more royal and humane than Rainier, and Philippe got on much better with him than he had with his former father-in-law.

Grace had had her worst fears about the marriage confirmed. Yet even now that Caroline was out of it, her post-divorce days would give Grace cause for more worry. Grace was in Rome at the time of the divorce, with her lady-in-waiting, Virginia Gallico, making a documentary for the Vatican. On their flight back to Nice, Virginia picked up a copy of *Paris Match* and saw a photograph of Caroline, who was supposed to be going out with Robertino Rossellini, and the Argentinian tennis star Guillermo Vilas lying in each other's arms on a beach in Hawaii. Virginia tried to hide the magazine, hoping Grace wouldn't see it; however, Grace asked Virginia what she was reading, and Virginia had no alternative but to hand it to her. Grace was furious and gave Caroline hell over it. The affair collapsed shortly after, and Uncle Rainier, to avoid further scandal, insisted thereafter that my mother always be present at the tennis finals when Vilas was playing so that Caroline would not be embarrassed by having to present him with the winner's trophy.

While Junot and Caroline's marriage was coming to an end, Michelle and I returned to New York. Over the next year Michelle's problems unluckily continued and got worse, and their effect on me was disastrous. I had lost contact with all my old friends and was no longer going out to all the places I had frequented before. I was keeping to myself because of the bad time I was going through. I had lost most of my self-confidence, but unluckily I had not lost my stubbornness; looking back on it, I should have called it quits then and there, but I was determined not to turn my back on Michelle. Fortunately, not a word about the problem reached the papers, but it inevitably filtered back to my uncle, who now felt he was in possession of the rope to hang me with, which was what I was sure he had wanted from the beginning. My father, who was passing through Monaco, met with my uncle Louis de Polignac, president of the board of administrators of the SBM, who told him that Rainier wanted me to resign. I thought it over. The only thing on my mind was to help Michelle, which I could do better in Europe than in New York. I still had a good income from my office and my family allowance, and I could certainly manage. Living under the constant risk of public exposure, and knowing that if a scandal did occur Rainier would have the perfect pretext to shoot me down, was not very appealing. I turned in my resignation. It was accepted immediately.

Then everything really hit the fan. I learned that Mother, who had put my house in her name during the period of my divorce from Maria Marta on the pretext that I might lose it under division-of-property arrangements, had leased it without telling me for a mere five hundred dollars a month! She claimed that the house needed repairs and that the rental income would go toward that. Not wanting to give my uncle the pleasure of having a sword to hold over my head, I closed my office in Monaco. It was also my way of saying, to hell with you, I'll start up something new elsewhere. With no home or definite prospects, I asked Michelle to return to Norway temporarily while I tried to get things together.

I went to Houston and stayed with Stephen Wyatt while I tried to think things through. I woke up one morning on my way there to discover the whole left side of my face was paralyzed. A doctor told me it was brought on by nervous tension. Around the same time Philippe Junot had fallen prey to exactly the same form of palsy on the right side of his face. I was planning to go to Zurich where sometime before I had met an Arab investor who needed contacts worldwide and who had let me know that if I were to leave the SBM we could do business together.

I then heard from my sister Christine that my family allowance would be cut off by Mother if I returned to any part of Europe. So now I was penniless. I sold my car and flew to Switzerland. I had begun discussions with the Arab when I received more bad news.

EIGHTEEN

ICHELLE PHONED from Norway to say that after giving it much thought, she was convinced that our relationship was futile. She told me that in view of the palace's opposition, the difficulties created for us by my family, and the financial problems resulting from these that beset us, there was no hope for us and we should end it. I think in her heart she knew she had unwittingly caused all this disaster to happen.

I had lost everything for this girl, and it seemed now that I had done so for nothing. My Arab friend, who shared the traditional attitudes of his race, found it difficult to understand that a man could be destroyed by his love for a woman. It was clear from everything he said now that he was having serious second thoughts about our professional association. But I was still concerned about fixing up my relationship with Michelle. I once again called the indispensable Lionel Noghes, as well as my sister Christine, and told them I needed to see my mother. They came with Christine's young son Sebastien to the Nice airport and picked me up. Lionel said to me, "Your mother is waiting for you like Attila the Hun." When I walked into the living room of Mother's new house, my sister Betsy was also there. I could see from the look on Mother's face that Lionel's description was not an exaggeration.

Deep within me I understood that the final day of reckoning with her had come. I hadn't spoken to her since the farewell dinner two and a half years before. I told her that I had not come to ask for my house and money back. I wanted to explain to her that I had joined the SBM with the best intentions, but because of the circumstances the whole period had turned out to be the worst experience I had ever been through. I described to her what it was like to see someone you love slowly destroying herself. I said I had come to ask her only to send a letter to Michelle saying that my family didn't hold her responsible for my current problems, and that if the negative reports my mother had been getting ceased, then there would be no reason why she would not be accepted by the family. If Michelle felt that my family stood with her, I thought she would have some sense of hope. I was desperately trying to find anything I could to persuade her not to give up.

Mother refused me point-blank. I could hardly believe my ears. My attempt to gain her understanding and cooperation had been useless. Christine tried to intercede with her, but her reply was, "Over my dead body." I decided to leave and never see her again. As I left the house, I was staggered to hear Mother say to one of my sisters, "Maybe I have made him pay all these years for the hate I have for his father." This admission was the only partial satisfaction I got from the trip.

I returned to Zurich. My Arab friend proposed a one-year association. I would be based in Paris. He gave me an advance and told me I should find top-class accommodations. I rented a town house with a private garden and terrace, and hired a Portuguese valet and cook. I forced myself not to call Michelle.

Finally one evening Michelle had phoned from Oslo. She said that she was feeling better, and that she had heard that I seemed to have gotten my act together once more. She said she realized she still loved me and that maybe it was time for us to try again. She flew to Paris the following week. I had not felt such intense joy in a long time. I thought, at last, my life is on the right track again.

But months went by, and I received no money from my Arab business associate. I didn't want to press him because he had trusted me, and I did not want to seem overly concerned about what could be just an innocent example of Arab business practice. I decided to let it pass and went to the south of France and got a bank loan. By August 1982 I still hadn't received a payment from him. Michelle and I were in Saint-Tropez for the summer. Finally I went to see him at the house he possessed at Cannes. I told him that I believed we had an understanding and a business arrangement, but that I hadn't received any money from him, and that my overheads were crippling. He told me then and there that he had changed his mind after learning that I was together with Michelle again and that I was on my uncle's blacklist. I was back to square one. Fearing for Michelle's reaction when she heard the news of our having lost a second house and situation, and hoping it would contribute to giving her security and a sense of responsibility, I proposed that we get married. She was overjoyed and threw her arms around me. I thought that by being legally my wife she would settle down. I was in no position to marry her. I was destitute and in debt. But that was tomorrow's problem.

At that moment Jean-Claude Mimran, who was the owner, among other things, of the Lamborghini factory, and whom I had known in Monaco, offered me the use of his magnificent house in Saint-Tropez for the wedding reception. He was a rare example of a friend who stayed a friend even in difficult moments. He would be my best man. My friends Hans and Cardy Smith were at Gstaad at that time and drove to Mimran's for the marriage. So did Jose Trabal, who canceled a trip to New York and drove from Barcelona. I liked the idea of our being married a few miles down the road from Monaco: It was my way of saying to my mother and Rainier, "To hell with you." The Smiths lent me their white chauffeur-driven Rolls Royce as our marriage car; Michelle never looked more radiant, and the plans progressed. It was at that moment that I picked up the phone to call my aunt.

EPILOGUE

O N WEDNESDAY, September 15, four days after my wedding, I drove my motor bike into Saint-Tropez after breakfast as I always did to buy the morning papers. When I saw the headlines announcing the news of Grace's death, I went numb with disbelief. Only two days before I had been reassured by Christine that Grace's injuries were far from life-threatening. With memories of her starting to flood my brain, I rushed out of the newspaper store and picked up Michelle and drove immediately to Monte Carlo.

The principality seemed stunned by the death of its princess. We went to the Hôtel de Paris, ran through the lobby, and checked into a room. I then called the palace's new head of protocol and asked him what the procedure was at this stage. I asked him to convey my condolences to Uncle Rainier and said that I had just arrived at the hotel to attend the funeral, and asked, when should I come to the palace to pay my last respects? He told me that the family was distraught and my uncle was in seclusion, and that I should wait for further news. Two days went by, and on the seventeenth, the day before the funeral, I called the head of protocol again, saying I still had heard nothing. Had the arrangements been made? Should I meet the family in the royal pew or should I come to the palace first and proceed to the cathedral with them? He apologized for the delay in giving me a response and said he would ask Caroline, who was now taking care of all the arrangements in view of her father's grief-stricken condition. When he phoned me back, he told me bluntly, "There is no room for you or your wife in the cathedral for the Mass tomorrow!" I was stunned. This, following all the rest, including the boycott of my wedding, was the last straw. How could the palace refuse to let me come to Grace's funeral? How could they forbid me entry to God's house? Surely amidst such a tragedy Caroline and Rainier should have been able to put aside, even if only temporarily, family dissatisfactions and quarrels, and let us all be united to pay a last tribute to Grace, who had always sought to iron out the dissensions and bring peace to the family. I remembered how Mother had stopped me from attending my dear Nanny's funeral. And Nanny, next to Grace, was the finest human being who ever lived in the palace. Until now I had not fully realized the extent of the palace's capacity to be cruel and vengeful.

Mother had taken my house, stripped me of my family income, and done her best to ruin my wedding. Rainier had betrayed me, had sent me into exile, and had crushed my childhood dreams of a racing career. Now they were stopping me from going to Grace's funeral. My shock turned to anger, but I did not want to make a public row over this and appear like a Monegasque notable offended at not being invited to a social event. But I could never accept this. I called Christine, told her the news I had been given, and she was dumfounded. Caroline had apparently said to her, "One cannot say that Christian caused Grace many satisfactions lately." Could the decision have anything to do with my defying the famous 1882 decree by having married a few days earlier without first obtaining the sovereign prince's permission? In any case, I could not believe that the antics of my bachelor days could alone be reason for such a drastic decision.

On the day of the funeral, I drove alone up into the Maritime Alps. I knew that all of the local churches in Monaco and neighboring towns would have services. I wanted to pray in a place where I would be alone. I went all the way up to Notre Dame de Laghet. The church was filled with photographs of accidents, the victims saved, it was believed, by the intercession of the Virgin. There, far from the Riviera, I knelt and prayed for Grace's immortal soul.

I thought about Grace's death. She did not like driving and drove very seldom and slowly. Her children used to say that when Mom drove down from Roc Agel, they could reach Monaco by foot faster than she. But Grace also used to feel uncomfortable wearing a seat belt and did not use hers on the day of the crash. She was in perfect health, never smoked, drank very moderately, and in her fifties still looked beautiful. But there was a history of cardiovascular problems in her family. Her brother, Jack, would later die of heart failure. She had a stroke at the wheel, and I believed then and I believe now that Stephanie was not driving. Grace was far too respectful of the law to permit her daughter, who did not have a license, to break it. The hasty removal of the car from the scene of the accident and the way in which the palace press staff issued conflicting reports of what had happened probably sprang from the mistaken initial impression that Stephanie was at the wheel. But she was not.

I must give Uncle Rainier credit for his concern that the reputation of the car's British manufacturers not be damaged. After all the talk of the Rover being defective, he immediately bought another one to silence false rumors. The brakes had not failed.

Of my cousins, Grace's death hit Stephanie hardest. Not

only was she with Grace on that last catastrophic journey, but it may be that she unfairly blamed herself for not having been able to save her mother, though she did everything possible to slow down the car by pulling the hand brake and trying to take hold of the wheel. She was tied to Grace more than the other children, behaving like a little girl long after she was past the age. Rainier's lack of ability to communicate proved to be a further handicap to her. Later on, even though she had a small apartment in Rainier's Paris town house, days would go by when they did not see or speak to each other. Today Steph does not exactly project the classic image of the young, aristocratic family girl reassuring and gratifying her parents. Unlike Caroline, she does not enjoy being a princess. She is resolutely, aggressively modern, endowed with a futuristic allure and beauty. Dressed in leather or in her disco outfits, and with her short hair and sensual androgynous looks, she seems to step out of a space-age fairy tale.

A year ago she became one of the most sought-after and highly paid models in the world. But very soon Rainier put a stop to her career, and Steph came back to Monaco. But with her determination, she started up successfully again, first creating her own line of swimwear named "Pool Position," then releasing a hit record and video.

Caroline might physically have resembled the young Mamou more closely, but Steph has certainly inherited her grandmother's character and personality of independence. Totally defiant of convention and determined to do "her thing," she dares to try everything and mocks everything. At twenty-one she is a beautiful, rebellious princess, full of vitality and inventiveness, very openly and honestly outspoken, disliking the boring courtiers, having a thirst for adventure and a natural penchant for provocation. Not caring if she's being watched, she yawns openly when an official representation bores her, throws a bucket of ice on the head of a girl she thinks is looking too much at her date in a nightclub, and tells her brother to go to hell when he says it's time to leave the disco.

With her startling beauty, dressing more like Grace Jones than Lady Sarah Armstrong Jones and wanting to be free is not easy when one's name is Stephanie of Monaco and the world watches your every move. She is cool, and I hope that she gets all the happiness she deserves.

Albert continues to astonish me in how he resembles his mother in his correctness, his sense of balance, order, and dignity. He loves Stephanie, who adores him, and Rainier turns to him to intercede with her. He is a nice guy and will make a good sovereign. The only unavoidable problem he has is shaking off the self-interested leeches who go to any length to monopolize his friendship—which they turn around and use to their own benefit. This situation is handed down through generations because of the prime importance of the Prince's position in Monaco. But I hope he will be able to see through the majority of his jesters. Albert is also the first prince of Monaco to receive an education appropriate to his future role, and he is also the first one to be involved from an early age in meetings and tasks concerning the running of the principality. He is better prepared and qualified than his predecessors for his future duties.

Caroline took over Grace's role immediately after her death. From having invented what the press called "the modern princess look" and being the rebel who defied everyone by staying in discotheques until early hours and marrying Philippe Junot, she has completely made herself over, becoming now "*la grande dame.*" She is the first lady of Monaco and likes it. When Albert marries, however, or if Rainier remarries, Caroline will be in the same position as my mother, pushed out in favor of the new princess. She would therefore presumably like Albert to marry someone from her circle of friends. But for the time being, she is the most powerful person in

Monaco after her father. She has a lot of influence over him. Her character is stronger than Albert's; anyone seeing her Barbara Walters interview couldn't fail to notice her regal posture and air of authority. She is a very different person from the extroverted, cheerful young girl I knew.

My mother remarried in the mid-1980s—this time a ballet dancer!—John Gilpin, star of the Royal Festival Ballet in London and personal favorite of its director, Anton Dolin. It goes without saying that I was not invited to the wedding. But I felt compassion for Gilpin when I learned that within forty days of marrying my mother, he died of a heart attack. In a gesture of good will, I did attend the memorial service in London without being invited, but my mother and I remain unreconciled.

As for me, things went from bad to worse after Grace died. I realized that if Rainier could be so inhuman as to prohibit me from attending Grace's funeral, there seemed to be little sense in my trying to set up an office in Monaco again. Now that the word was out about my being totally at odds with my uncle, and with my father's example in mind, I knew that my business prospects in our tiny country could hardly be good.

My mother had seen to it that there were even fewer reasons for me to stay in Monaco by renting out my house. As a result, Michelle and I moved from city to city looking for an opportunity. I held no university degrees, no work permit or green card, and things were more than difficult. After losing my last financial resources in a car-importing business, I was totally exhausted and depressed by the twenty-four-hour job of trying to get between Michelle and her poison. Our relationship deteriorated into violent quarrels, paranoia, fixations; and her love sadly turned into hate. I was desperately trying to persuade myself that there could still be a happy outcome. I tried everything, but it just got worse. I thought I was in a nightmare. Blindly I tried to put off the inevitable, and during all that time, the only word from Monaco was, "Keep away."

Looking back on that fateful year of 1979, I had never asked anyone for a job: I had been asked to represent the SBM interests abroad and had accepted. At that time I had my house, a Ferrari, my dogs, and all the comforts of living in my country. I had expected that when I resigned, I could at least have gone back to my house. It could have been easier for Michelle if we were at Eze, far from the temptations easily available in the big cities.

Not being able to think, work, or concentrate on anything, I finally separated from Michelle on June 13, 1984. I was hoping that by going back to Oslo she would "clean out." I went to stay with friends in Munich, where I worked out four hours a day in a gym to be better able to clear the disillusions from my mind and better prepared to overcome my problems and face the future. Unluckily I kept on hearing that Michelle was far from cleaning out. After a few weeks I finally decided to act and fight for my family rights. I contacted a lawyer and went over my whole situation.

Among other things, he studied the official family's Civil List. Out of a total tax-free sum of 55,857,100 French francs (more or less $9 million) allotted to the sovereign family and for the upkeep of the palace, 27,400,000 FF (more or less $4.6 million) was cash given directly "for the Prince and the Prince's family." As "family" had traditionally included the siblings of the prince and their children—naturally my mother received her share—my lawyer saw no reason that I, as Rainier's only nephew, should not be entitled to mine. In fact, most Monegasques were convinced that I was receiving my allocation. But there was an amendment in the text that said the sum was to be "redistributed at the Prince's discretion"; a provision added during Rainier's rule. Again, he was in total command of his family.

Nevertheless, my lawyer wrote Rainier expressing his opinion about what he called "my rights by birth," stressing my haste to get Michelle out of Oslo for urgent medical attention. Rainier replied through his German lawyer in a short and severe letter, in three languages, that if I persisted in my demands he, *and my mother*, would attack me civilly and penally! At no point was a clear reason given as to the denial of my rights. Remembering Mother's endless refrain to Nanny of "no souvenirs" and the family's puzzling silence about the past and the mysteries surrounding it, after analyzing the vagueness and aggressiveness of the response, I started to wonder whether, after one more of her many "exploits" during my childhood, my mother could have, incredibly, renounced my family rights to appease her brother and regain lost favors for herself. With her calculating character, she was perfectly capable of this. If she had done so, it also might explain her hostility toward me, knowing that she could one day be legitimately reproached for having egoistically frustrated her child's future.

I was dumfounded by the possibility of my family being more Machiavellian than I had ever thought. At this point Norwegian journalist Knut Meiner phoned me and warned me Michelle was on the verge of getting into serious trouble. I flew to Oslo, but now realized that she was far different from the girl I had fallen in love with and that all was lost. Living hard had taken its toll. I tried to persuade her for a last time to "take a rest" and change her ways, but it was in vain.

I flew back to Monaco to file for divorce, not able to believe all that had happened to me and all I had lost in the last few years. I remembered Adrian's warnings and the Brazilian fortune teller's prophecies concerning a girl with cat's eyes.

Both had been correct. To be objective, I had to admit to myself that, in this instance, so had my family by objecting to the marriage. But it seemed to me that their objections were merely a pretext for their subsequent actions.

In the years since 1984, I've lived all over the world, an adventurer moving left and right. I've been back to Monaco a few times, where I have seen my sister, Christine, who has stayed close and faithful despite her very difficult position. I occasionally ran into Albert and Stephanie, and they were friendly. Caroline, who is remarried now, remained distant. I haven't seen my mother since the funeral mass for John Gilpin in London. I haven't seen Rainier since the farewell dinner, which may have been prophetic. I see my father as often as I can whenever I'm in the States.

I don't know where I'll be living, but I know it won't be Monaco. In May 1986 I was strongly advised to stay away for my own well-being after the palace learned of the upcoming publication of this book.

I haven't given up my dream of racing, which would of course be my best source of satisfaction—as my absence from Monaco is probably my family's. But as I think about my estrangement from them, I can't stop remembering what my mother said to my sisters when she tried to explain to them why she always wanted me away from Monaco. "He could one day cause trouble with the palace," she told them, "and this might reflect badly on me, causing me problems with Rainier." Let the last word of the story, however, be Grace's. She once said in an interview, beware "when you start slamming the door [on your children] . . . you have to leave that door open because when it's closed, it's finished."